POWER
and the PULPIT

The Center for Pastor Theologians Series

A diverse group of Christian intellectuals, both pastor theologians and academic theologians, addresses a myriad of complex and sometimes controversial issues to equip pastors and church leaders for the work of shepherding the church.

POWER
and the PULPIT

RECOVERING *a* THEOLOGY
of PREACHING

GERALD HIESTAND *and*
JOEL LAWRENCE, *editors*

CASCADE *Books* • Eugene, Oregon

POWER AND THE PULPIT
Recovering a Theology of Preaching

The Center for Pastor Theologians Series

Copyright © 2025 Wipf and Stock Publishers. All rights reserved. Except for brief quotations in critical publications or reviews, no part of this book may be reproduced in any manner without prior written permission from the publisher. Write: Permissions, Wipf and Stock Publishers, 199 W. 8th Ave., Suite 3, Eugene, OR 97401.

Cascade Books
An Imprint of Wipf and Stock Publishers
199 W. 8th Ave., Suite 3
Eugene, OR 97401

www.wipfandstock.com

PAPERBACK ISBN: 979-8-3852-4755-4
HARDCOVER ISBN: 979-8-3852-4756-1
EBOOK ISBN: 979-8-3852-4757-8

Cataloguing-in-Publication data:

Names: Hiestand, Gerald, 1974–, editor. | Lawrence, Joel, editor.

Title: Power and the pulpit : recovering a theology of preaching / edited by Gerald Hiestand and Joel Lawrence.

Description: Eugene, OR : Cascade Books, 2025 | Series: The Center for Pastor Theologians Series | Includes bibliographical references and index.

Identifiers: ISBN 979-8-3852-4755-4 (paperback) | ISBN 979-8-3852-4756-1 (hardcover) | ISBN 979-8-3852-4757-8 (ebook)

Subjects: LCSH: Pastoral theology. | Preaching.

Classification: BV4211.2 .P69 2025 (paperback) | BV4211.2 (ebook)

VERSION NUMBER 10/20/25

Scripture quotations marked (ESV) are from the ESV® Bible (The Holy Bible, English Standard Version®), © 2001 by Crossway, a publishing ministry of Good News Publishers. Used by permission. All rights reserved. The ESV text may not be quoted in any publication made available to the public by a Creative Commons license. The ESV may not be translated in whole or in part into any other language.

Scripture quotations marked (NASB) are taken from the (NASB®) New American Standard Bible®, Copyright © 1960, 1971, 1977, 1995, 2020 by The Lockman Foundation. Used by permission. All rights reserved. www.lockman.org.

Scripture quotations marked (NIV) are taken from the Holy Bible, New International Version®, NIV®. Copyright © 1973, 1978, 1984, 2011 by Biblica, Inc.™ Used by permission of Zondervan. All rights reserved worldwide. www.zondervan.com. The "NIV" and "New International Version" are trademarks registered in the United States Patent and Trademark Office by Biblica, Inc.™

Scripture quotations marked (NRSV) are taken from the New Revised Standard Version Bible, copyright © 1989 National Council of the Churches of Christ in the United States of America. Used by permission. All rights reserved worldwide.

Scripture quotations marked (BSB) are taken from The Berean Standard Bible. The Holy Bible, Berean Standard Bible, BSB is produced in cooperation with Bible Hub, Discovery Bible, OpenBible.com, and the Berean Bible Translation Committee. This text of God's Word has been dedicated to the public domain.

Scripture quotations marked (KJV) are from The Authorized (King James) Version. Rights in the Authorized Version in the United Kingdom are vested in the Crown. Reproduced by permission of the Crown's patentee, Cambridge University Press.

Scripture quotations marked (VOICE) are from The Voice Bible, © 2012 by Thomas Nelson, Inc. The Voice™ translation © 2012 Ecclesia Bible Society. All rights reserved. Used by permission.

To the Ecclesial Fellows of the Center for Pastor Theologians, who are pursuing God's calling to faithfully shepherd the church in these challenging days. Thank you for your commitment to the church, theology, and pastoral ministry.

Contents

Acknowledgments | ix
Introduction: Power and the Pulpit | xi
Contributors | xiii

Part One: The Centrality of the Pulpit

1   Why Preaching Still Matters | 3
    —Jeremy Treat

2   Recapturing Paul's Theology of Preaching | 25
    —Jason Meyer

3   Bring the Thunder! The Sources of Power According to Jesus's Teaching on Preaching | 32
    —Douglas Sean O'Donnell

4   The Ministry Is the Message: Union with Christ as a Theology for Gospel Proclamation | 52
    —Philip Ryken

5   The Answer: Revelation 5 | 69
    —Nicole Massie Martin

Part Two: The Humility of the Pulpit

6 Is Your Preaching Pain-Full? Adopting Paul's Theology of Homiletical Weakness | 79
   —Matthew D. Kim

7 From Bully Pulpits to Kata-Pulpits: Preaching with Well-Tempered Boldness in the Economy of Divine Communication | 93
   —Kevin J. Vanhoozer

8 The Pasteurization of the Pastorate: Preserving Pastoral Authority in the Wake of Pastoral Abuses | 111
   —Laurie Norris

9 "Treasures from an Earthen Pot": How the Pastor-Poet George Herbert Can Inform Our Theology and Practice of Preaching | 129
   —Stephen Witmer

Part Three: The Practice of the Pulpit

10 The Philanthropic Pulpit | 145
    —Ahmi Lee

11 The Purpose and Power of the Pulpit: P. T. Forsyth's Theological Wisdom for Evangelical Preaching | 160
    —Trygve D. Johnson

12 Incarnate, Embodied Power: Bodied Spiritual Practice as a Homiletical Resource | 178
    —Jaclyn P. Williams

13 Ambrose of Milan and Asia/Trans-Pacific Homiletics and Ecumenics: Reassessment of Mystagogical Preaching with *Kapwa* Theology and Their Implications for the Oikoumenē | 187
    —Neal D. Presa

14 We Are More Than Our Minds: Conforming Heart, Soul, Body, and Will to Love God and Neighbor Through Specific Statements of Application | 204
    —Eric Redmond

Subject Index | 217
Scripture Index | 219

Acknowledgments

As we have in each of these volumes, we want to express our gratitude to the contributors. The nature of preaching and the use (and, unfortunately, abuse) of the pulpit remains a critical conversation for evangelicalism, and we thank those who prepared thoughtful presentations and entered this conversation with a spirit of humility. We are grateful for women and men who have thought, and continue to think, deeply on this important issue.

In addition, we are grateful to the leadership team of the Center for Pastor Theologians (CPT), who devoted a great deal of time and energy to host the conference and who continue to work faithfully week in and week out to support the work of the CPT, all with the aim of seeing the church remain moored faithfully to the Scriptures.

In the same spirit, we are deeply grateful for the partnership of the CPT's five senior theological mentors: Scott Hafemann, Marc Cortez, Doug Sweeney, Vincent Bacote, Kevin Vanhoozer, and Peter Leithart. Their commitment to the CPT's mission, their contribution to the Fellowships, and their friendship and encouragement to the two of us have been an important catalyst for the CPT project and its commitment to growing the Pastor Theologian movement. These theological leaders are deeply devoted to the church, and we are grateful for their leadership and support of the CPT Fellows.

Calvary Memorial Church in Oak Park, Illinois, the location of the conference, has been, in so many ways, the spiritual home of the Center for

ACKNOWLEDGMENTS

Pastor Theologians. We continue to be deeply grateful for the many ways that Calvary invests in the mission of the CPT: hosting our various Fellowship gatherings, housing the CPT offices, and serving our organization in countless other ways. We are grateful for Gerald Hiestand, CPT co-founder and Senior Pastor of Calvary, for his leadership and advocacy of the CPT, as well as to the Calvary staff, elders, and congregation, who are such gracious hosts.

Lastly, we want to thank Seth Porch, the Publicity Coordinator of the CPT, for his work to make this volume a reality. Thanks, Seth, for your careful editing, your willingness to chase down authors, and your commitment to bringing this project to fruition.

Introduction

Power and the Pulpit

THROUGHOUT HISTORY, CHRISTIANS HAVE believed that the Living God takes up earthen vessels—mere human beings—to preach his word and build up his church. This miraculous reality is essential to our faith and to our understanding of God's mission in the world: our God is a speaking God who uses human words to speak his word.

The evangelical tradition places the sermon at the center of church life. We build buildings around pulpits and preachers. We champion gifted communicators. We celebrate effective homiletical techniques. But too often, these emphases are not the result of deep theological convictions but of the church's adoption of modern visions of communication and success. In our day, preaching is easily unmoored from its biblical, theological, and historical anchors. Too often, it has become a tool of celebrity. We have seen pulpits and preaching taken captive by political and pragmatic ideologies. The teaching office of the church has sometimes been manipulated to secure and maintain human power.

The condition of preaching in our time must compel us to ask: What is our theology of preaching? Is our vision of the sermon rooted in the miracle of God's word proclaimed or in the desire to entertain? Is our preaching a function of a theology of glory or a theology of the cross?

The Center for Pastor Theologians believes that if the church is to be a community of mature faith in our time, we must recapture the apostolic vision of preaching. This vision declares that preaching comes, not with wise and persuasive words, but with a demonstration of the Spirit's power, so that our faith might not rest on human wisdom but on God's power (1 Cor 2:4–5). The church must not trust in oratorical skill or the capacity to entertain but in the miracle of God's word, proclaimed to his people in a cruciform paradox of power and weakness.

A cruciform vision of preaching will move us beyond homiletical technique. It will challenge our confidence in our own capacities and call into question methods that have subtly shaped our vision of the sermon and elevated human power. As church leaders, we must remind ourselves again that we are, first and foremost, servants—both of God's word and of God's people.

In October 2023, the Center for Pastor Theologians hosted our eighth annual theology conference, "Power and the Pulpit: Recovering a Theology of Preaching." Drawing on our network of Pastor Theologians and academic theologians, we gathered together to reflect on the apostolic vision of preaching and how best to embody the New Testament's vision of preaching in an age that presses us to accept the opposite. The essays contained in this volume approach the topic of power and the pulpit from a variety of different angles: biblical, historical, and cultural. Reflecting on the theme of "power," we explored how the sermon is manipulated when it becomes a function of human power but is renewed when we truly grasp the Spirit's power in our weakness.

We commend this book to you as a means to reflect more deeply on a theology of preaching that must be recovered in the church today. We pray that God's Spirit will take up God's word in your life and ministry, as you take up the call of the cross in your ministry of the word.

Dr. Gerald Hiestand
Senior Pastor, Calvary Memorial Church, Oak Park, Illinois
Co-founder and Board Chair, Center for Pastor Theologians

Dr. Joel Lawrence
President, Center for Pastor Theologians

Contributors

Trygve D. Johnson (PhD, University of St. Andrews) is an ordained pastor in the Reformed Church in America. He teaches at the Eugene Peterson Center for Christian Imagination and is the author of *The Preacher As Liturgical Artist: Metaphor, Identity, and the Vicarious Humanity of Christ*. He is a member of the CPT's St. Anselm Fellowship.

Matthew D. Kim (PhD, University of Edinburgh) is professor of preaching and pastoral leadership and holds the George W. Truett Endowed Chair in Preaching and Evangelism at George W. Truett Theological Seminary, Baylor University. He is the author of *Preaching to People in Pain* and coauthor of *Preaching to a Divided Nation*. He is a member of the CPT's St. John Fellowship.

Ahmi Lee (PhD, Fuller Theological Seminary) is a preacher, author, and consultant for ministries and nonprofits and a member of the board of directors for Redeemer City to City. She is the author of *Preaching God's Grand Drama: A Biblical-Theological Approach*.

Nicole Massie Martin (DMin, Gordon-Conwell Theological Seminary) serves as the chief impact officer at *Christianity Today* and the executive director of Soulfire Ministries. She is the author of *Made to Lead: Empowering Women for Ministry* and *Leaning In, Letting Go: A Lenten Devotional*.

CONTRIBUTORS

Jason Meyer (PhD, Southern Baptist Theological Seminary) is the lead pastor at Urban Refuge Church in Minneapolis, Minnesota. He is the author of numerous books including *Preaching: A Biblical Theology*. He is a member of the CPT's St. John Fellowship.

Laurie Norris (PhD, Wheaton College) serves as professor of Bible and undergraduate dean of faculty at Moody Bible Institute in Chicago. She also coedited the *One Volume Seminary: A Complete Ministry Education from the Faculty of Moody Bible Institute and Moody Theological Seminary*. She is a member of the CPT's St. Augustine Fellowship.

Douglas Sean O'Donnell (PhD, University of Aberdeen) is the senior vice president of Bible editorial at Crossway. He has pastored several churches in the United States, served as a professor in Australia, and authored or edited over twenty books, including commentaries, Bible studies, children's books, and a Sunday school curriculum. He also wrote *The Pastor's Book* with R. Kent Hughes and *The Beauty and Power of Biblical Exposition* with Leland Ryken. He is a member of the CPT's St. John Fellowship.

Neal D. Presa (PhD, Drew University) is executive presbyter of the Presbytery of San Jose and associate professor of preaching and worship, vice president of student affairs and vocational outreach at New Brunswick Theological Seminary, and affiliate associate professor of preaching at Fuller Theological Seminary. He is a member of the CPT's St. Augustine Fellowship.

Eric Redmond (PhD, Capital Seminary and Graduate School) is professor of Bible at Moody Bible Institute and Moody Theological Seminary in Chicago, Illinois, and associate pastor of preaching and teaching at Calvary Memorial Church in Oak Park, Illinois. He is a fellow of Every Voice and a teaching fellow at the C. S. Lewis Institute. He is the general editor of *Say It! Celebrating Expository Preaching in the African American Tradition*. He is a member of the CPT's St. Augustine Fellowship.

Philip Ryken (PhD, University of Oxford) is the eighth president of Wheaton College. He has published more than fifty Bible commentaries and other books, including *The Message of Salvation*, *When Trouble Comes*, and *Beauty Is Your Destiny*.

Jeremy Treat (PhD, Wheaton College) is pastor for preaching and vision at Reality LA in Los Angeles, California, and adjunct professor of theology at Biola University. He is the author of *The Crucified King*, *Seek First* and *The Atonement: An Introduction*. He is a member of the CPT's St. John Fellowship.

CONTRIBUTORS

Kevin J. Vanhoozer (PhD, Cambridge University) is research professor of systematic theology at Trinity Evangelical Divinity School. He has also taught at the University of Edinburgh and the Wheaton College Graduate School. He is the author of *The Drama of Doctrine: A Canonical Linguistic Approach to Christian Theology* and *Pictures at a Theological Exhibition: Scenes of the Church's Worship, Witness, and Wisdom*.

Jaclyn P. Williams (PhD, University of Birmingham) serves as an Assistant Professor of the Practice of Preaching and Chaplaincy at Fuller Theological Seminary. She is an ordained American Baptist minister and a board-certified chaplain. She has contributed articles to numerous journals.

Stephen Witmer (PhD, University of Cambridge) is the lead pastor of Pepperell Christian Fellowship in Pepperell, Massachusetts. A council member of The Gospel Coalition and the co-founder of Small Town Summits, he has written *Eternity Changes Everything*, *A Big Gospel in Small Places*, and *The Preacher's Greek Companion to Hebrews*. He is a member of the CPT's St. Anselm Fellowship.

Part One

THE CENTRALITY OF THE PULPIT

1

Why Preaching Still Matters

JEREMY TREAT

INTRODUCTION

A LOT OF PEOPLE look down on preaching today. Some wonder if it will work with younger generations whose attention spans have been shaped by digital technology. Others fear that the rising distrust of religious institutions has eroded any credible foundation for pastors. Many question whether preaching is simply irrelevant and outdated in a post-Christian society. "Times have changed," they say, "and the church must adapt to stay relevant." Preaching, it seems, is not what it used to be.

I see the demise of preaching in my context in Los Angeles. I recently asked a fellow pastor in our city what he was preaching through. He responded by telling me that in place of sermons their congregation was doing origami workshops so that people could learn about the beauty of God in a hands-on way. The Methodist church down the street from us often shows movies in place of sermons. I have talked with more than one pastor who says monological preaching is authoritarian and so in place of sermons they have conversations. At the end of the day, a lot of people simply think preaching is no longer effective.

But if you think that modern people do not like preaching, just watch the Oscars. Every year in the sanctuary of the Dolby Theatre, filled with the celebrity saints of Hollywood, men and women stand at the Academy's pulpit and preach a gospel of self-fulfillment shaped by a vision of secular justice, inspiring the eschatological hope of humanity making the world a better place. I think of Joaquin Phoenix heralding an impassioned plea for veganism, or Leonardo DiCaprio reprimanding the world for global warming, or Spike Lee reminding his parishioners of the need to be on the right side of history. And, of course, there is the prince of preachers, Will Smith, who—moments after physically assaulting another man—talked about being "a vessel for love" and " an ambassador of . . . care, and concern."[1] And the congregation collectively expressed their "Amen!" with a standing ovation.

The question is not whether modern people like preaching or not. Rather, we must ask what is distinct about *Christian* preaching and whether it needs to be adapted in order to be effective in our society today.

I do not believe we need to do away with or reinvent preaching. I do believe that we need to revive and retrieve it from watered-down, entertainment-driven, avoid-offense-at-all-cost, consumeristic forms of preaching. We need preaching that is grounded in Scripture, socially aware, aimed at discipleship, sensitive to wounds, and centered on the good news of Jesus Christ. And we need to think carefully about how to preach in *this* new context—namely, in increasingly urban and diverse settings with churches that are reaching the next generations.

My task in this essay is rather straightforward: we need an apologetic for preaching in a post-Christian society. I want to show why preaching still matters.[2] But I do not expect you to take my word for it. I want to answer the question of whether preaching still matters by looking to God's word, and particularly to Paul's message in 2 Tim 4:1–5. What we will discover is nothing new or innovative but rather a reaffirmation of the basics. That is exactly what the church needs: not a new approach to preaching, but a fresh discovery in the midst of a new cultural context of the most foundational truths about preaching.[3]

---

1. Oscars, "Will Smith Wins," 5:13–5:15, 5:36–5:42.

2. I will not add anything theologically that you could not learn from great preachers like John Stott or Tony Evans. But those preachers came up in a different world and we cannot merely copy their methods to reach people today. Four weeks before he went to be with the Lord, I had the privilege of being part of a group that met with Tim Keller. In that conversation, Keller told us that the things he did throughout his ministry will not be sufficient for reaching the next generations. He challenged us to hold firm to the gospel *and* learn to contextualize in a changing world. Every generation must reaffirm foundational truths within the context of cultural and generational changes.

3. My context has forced me to wrestle with these changes. If the world is becoming increasingly diverse, urban, and digital, then Los Angeles is a glimpse into the future. Reality LA—the church that I am a part of and have the privilege of preaching to—is in the heart of the city, seeking the renewal of Los Angeles through the good news of Jesus. Like our city, our church is culturally diverse, with 116 nations represented in the congregation. We are young, filled primarily with Millennials and Gen Z. While the majority of our

Why Preaching Still Matters

One of the clearest places where Scripture answers the question of whether preaching still matters is in 2 Tim 4:1–5 (ESV). Paul writes,

> I charge you in the presence of God and of Christ Jesus, who is to judge the living and the dead, and by his appearing and his kingdom: preach the word; be ready in season and out of season; reprove, rebuke, and exhort, with complete patience and teaching. For the time is coming when people will not endure sound teaching, but having itching ears they will accumulate for themselves teachers to suit their own passions, and will turn away from listening to the truth and wander off into myths. As for you, always be sober-minded, endure suffering, do the work of an evangelist, fulfill your ministry.

Why does preaching still matter? Preaching matters because God commands it, the church needs it, and the world is already doing it.

God Commands It

The question of the place of preaching in the church today is not up to us to decide. This is not a conversation where we list out the pros and cons and then decide whether we should preach or not. No, God is clear: "Preach the word" (2 Tim 4:2). This is not an opinion or a pastoral suggestion. It is a command from God. Why does preaching still matter today? Because God says it does, regardless of the shifting winds of cultural norms.

It is important to feel the weight of Paul's command to Timothy. Context helps. Second Timothy 4 is the last chapter of the last book written by Paul in Scripture. How does Paul use his last words? To plead with the next generation about the importance of preaching. Read the charge once again in light of what comes before it: "I charge you in the presence of God and of Christ Jesus, who is to judge the living and the dead, and by his appearing and his kingdom: preach the word" (2 Tim 4:1–2). Do you feel the weight? Paul places us in the presence of God, before the judgement seat with eternity hanging in

---

congregation are creatives and professionals in their twenties and thirties, we also have many college students from USC, UCLA, and a variety of film and art schools. We are an urban church, not only in the sense that we are located in the heart of the city but also in that we have socioeconomic diversity. Our Community Meals ministry has created an environment on Sundays where it's not unusual to have an executive producer from NBC sitting next to someone who slept on the sidewalk the night before.

the balance, and all in such a dramatic way that emphasizes the sacred significance of this charge: "Preach the word."

Preach the Word

The command is not merely *to preach*, as if Paul cares only about the act of preaching and not the content. In other words, it would not meet Paul's standards if someone were to preach about themselves or tantalizing stories or a relevant topic. His exhortation is not simply *to preach*, but rather to preach *the word*.

I am deeply concerned about the state of preaching in our society today because I do not consistently hear pastors preaching *the word*. I recently went to a major American city and, since I rarely am able go to other churches, visited three churches in one Sunday. In those services I heard cultural exegesis, inspiring stories, and practical advice, but little of the Scriptures and nothing of the gospel. I was shocked. These were well-respected evangelical churches.

While this may seem obvious, it must be made explicit: we are called to preach *the word*. Preachers are not content creators. Preachers do not have to come up with something new every week. Preachers are called to exposit the word, proclaim the word, and apply the word. That is why the foundation of Christian preaching is exegesis. Preachers must "rightly [handle] the word of truth" (2 Tim 2:15) so that what is proclaimed is not merely the words of men but the word of God (1 Thess 2:13).

Exegeting Scripture, therefore, is the foundation for expository preaching. Charlie Dates defines expository preaching in this way: "Exposition seeks to expose, to uncover the meaning in the text. It actually believes that there is meaning in the biblical text. It does so through a serious search for the original context, people, and intent of the passage. Yet it does not stop there. Exposition seeks to build a homiletical premise for present-day application."[4] If we do not expose the meaning of the text, then we will impose our own desires upon it. This type of preaching does not proclaim the word but rather uses the word to proclaim personal preferences.

---

4. Dates, "African American Preaching," 16. Tim Keller defines expository preaching in the following way: "Expository preaching grounds the message in the text so that all the sermon's points are points in the text, and it majors in the text's major ideas. It aligns the interpretation of the text with the doctrinal truths of the rest of the Bible (being sensitive to systematic theology). And it always situates the passage within the Bible's narrative, showing how Christ is the final fulfillment of the text's theme (being sensitive to biblical theology)." Keller, *Preaching*, 32.

Whenever young or aspiring pastors ask me how to become a better preacher, they are almost always asking for techniques that will make their preaching more dynamic and effective. But my response to them is, "If you want to become a preacher, then first become a student of God's word." Rhetorical techniques—such as how to craft an introduction or use an illustration or vary your tone and pace—do not matter if you cannot interpret Scripture. In fact, someone who is gifted and trained in communication but is not grounded in God's word will likely do more harm than good. Preachers must stand on the word of God. Our hope is that the word which goes forth from the mouth of God will not return empty but will accomplish that which God purposes for it (Isa 55:11). The power of preaching is in the word.

Of course, when Paul wrote "preach *the word*," he was not referring to a leather-bound Bible with sixty-six books and maps in the back.[5] What did Paul mean by "the word"? Context is key. In the previous verses, Paul declares, "All Scripture is breathed out by God and is profitable for teaching" (2 Tim 3:16), and he speaks of the "sacred writings" which are able to make one "wise for salvation through faith in Christ Jesus" (2 Tim 3:15). When Paul says, "preach the word," he means "preach the God-breathed Scriptures which culminate in the good news of Jesus Christ."

To put it another way: preachers are called to preach the gospel according to the Scriptures. While the Bible is the inspired word of God, it is not an end in and of itself but rather is meant to point its readers to the Son of God (John 5:39). Therefore, whether preaching from Jonah or John, 2 Chronicles or 2 Corinthians, Ruth or Revelation, every sermon should ultimately be an exposition of Christ according to the Scriptures.[6]

A Biblical Theology of Preaching

The command to "preach the word" in 2 Tim 4:2 is not an outlier in the story of Scripture but a concise and clear command that represents a pattern throughout the Bible. A brief biblical theology of preaching will fill out the meaning of "preach the word."

In the beginning, we see the key principle that *God accomplishes his purposes through his word*. Genesis 1 presents God as a king who reigns through his word. He speaks ("let there be light") and it happens ("there was light")

---

5. All of the emphases in the Scripture quotations in this essay are mine.

6. In other words, because Scripture is gospel-centered, preaching Scripture should be gospel-centered. To learn more about how to interpret Christ in all the Scriptures, see Goldsworthy, *Gospel-Centered Hermeneutics*; and Greidanus, *Preaching Christ*.

(Gen 1:3). God is a speaking God (dare we say, a preaching God) who executes his will through his word.[7]

It comes as no surprise, then, that the serpent opposes God by questioning and twisting his word. "Did God actually say?" quips the serpent, both misquoting God and subtly sabotaging his character (Gen 3:1). After Adam and Eve give in to the serpent's temptation, however, God responds with a word of promise: the seed of a woman will crush the head of the serpent (Gen 3:15). Not only does God create through word, he will also save, heal, reconcile, judge, and rule through his word.

The rest of the Old Testament reveals more specifically that God's word comes in two forms: written and proclaimed. First, God accomplishes his purposes through his written word, from the Ten Commandments to the Torah and eventually the entire Hebrew Scriptures. And, secondly, God accomplishes his purposes through his proclaimed word—from the prophets of Israel to the poets of the Psalms—often proclaimed to the assembly of God's people (e.g., Exod 35:1). Occasionally, these two forms of God's word come together, with the proclaimed word expounding the written word. Nehemiah 8:8, for example, says, "They read from the book, from the Law of God, clearly, and they gave the sense, so that the people understood the reading."

In between the Old and New Testaments, the tradition developed in the synagogue where each week the Scriptures would be read, followed by a sermon that would explain and apply the Scripture for the people of God.[8]

Jesus stepped into this context and emerged as a preacher (certainly as more than a preacher, but nonetheless a preacher). Luke records that Jesus went to the synagogue, read the scroll of Isaiah, and then interpreted it as being fulfilled by his very presence (Luke 4:18–21). Jesus's ministry, of course, would be largely characterized by preaching (Matt 9:35) and he sent out his disciples to preach in the way that he had (Matt 10:5–7).

As the early church spread from city to city, it was clear that preaching was indispensable to God's mission. The apostle Paul says, "How then will they call on him in whom they have not believed? And how are they to believe in him of whom they have never heard? And how are they to hear without someone preaching?" (Rom 10:14). After Pentecost, the apostles prioritized preaching, saying, "It is not right that we should give up preaching the word of God to serve tables" (Acts 6:2). Then, as Paul and others went on missionary journeys, the spread of the church was equated with the spread of the word (Acts 6:7;

---

7. This characteristic sets God apart from the mute idols of the surrounding nations (Isa 44:6–8).

8. For an exploration of the theme of "assembly" in Scripture and its implication for the theology of preaching, see Ash, *Priority of Preaching*, 75–90.

13:49). And while the power is in the gospel itself (Rom 1:16), it is also clear that the *preaching* of the gospel is one of Jesus's primary instruments for building the church. That is why Paul does not merely say that the *cross* is the power of God but that the *message* of the cross is the power of God (1 Cor 1:18). It is clear in Scripture that all God's people have a "word ministry." Paul says to the whole church, "Let the word of Christ dwell in you richly, teaching and admonishing one another in all wisdom" (Col 3:16). All followers of Jesus are called to exhort and encourage one another with Scripture (Heb 3:13; 10:25). "Preaching," however, is not a generic term that refers to any type of teaching about God's word. It refers to a specific type of word ministry. In short, preaching is *a public proclamation of God's word by a commissioned leader.*[9]

When Paul says, "preach the word," therefore, he is tapping into a biblical pattern of God accomplishing his purposes through his word. And since the word is the content of preaching, and the word never goes out of season, the word must be preached "in season and out of season." Another way of talking about seasons is generations. Psalm 145:4 says, "One generation shall commend your works to another." How, then, can we preach the word from one generation to the next? More specifically, how can we effectively preach the word to the younger generations in the church today?

Preaching to the Next Generations

According to Jean Twenge, Gen Z is characterized by delayed adulthood (marriage, children, etc.), differing views on sexuality and gender, social consciousness, political polarization, anxiety and depression, digital dependence, and a

---

9. Claire Smith has demonstrated that three Greek verbs (*euangelizomai, katangello,* and *kerysso*)—usually translated as "preach" or "proclaim"—function as "semi-technical" terms for a particular type of gospel proclamation. Smith, *Pauline Communities*, 202. Building on her work, Jonathan Griffiths offers a deep study of each of these verbs and concludes, "These three verbs are rightly classified as 'semi-technical' because they appear frequently to refer to a particular concept: that of preaching. As used in the New Testament, the verbs typically refer to [1] the act of making a public proclamation, [2] the agent is generally a person of recognized authority; and [3] the substance of the proclamation is normally some aspect of Christ's person and work, the implications of the gospel, or some other truth from God's word." Griffiths, *Preaching in the New Testament*, 33. Griffiths also clarifies that "of these three semi-technical terms, *kerysso* is used with the highest degree of consistency in the New Testament to bear this meaning and has the narrowest semantic range, centred on the meaning to 'preach'" (33). Therefore, while everyone in the church has a word ministry, "preaching" is a particular type of word ministry: namely the *public proclamation of God's word by a commissioned leader.* According to Griffiths, "Nowhere does the New Testament call or instruct believers as a whole group to 'preach,' but it does call them to minister the word to one another" (49). This preaching of the word should be the catalyst and compass for the various types of word ministry throughout the church.

sharp decline in religious commitment.[10] Based on new research by Harvard's Cooperative Election Study, 49 percent of Gen Z claim to be atheist, agnostic, or have no religion in particular.[11] Ryan Burge concludes, "Generation Z is the least religious generation in American history. And they are becoming less religiously identified as each year passes."[12] But while Gen Z has legitimate reasons to disassociate from religion, they are still spiritually hungry and searching. The Barna Research Group refers to Gen Z as "the open generation" and reports that 77 percent of American teens want to learn more about Jesus.[13]

How can Gen Z be reached? First of all, we must "preach the word." While there are obstacles to overcome and adaptations that need to be made, faith still comes through hearing, and hearing through the word of God. The question is not "What do the younger generations want?" but rather "What do they need?" Gen Z needs to hear the gospel proclaimed according to the Scriptures. And yet, the word must be preached in a way that can be understood and applied by these generations. How, then, should we preach the word to younger generations? I propose three ways.

Contextualize the Message, Don't Change It

The typical approach to reaching the next generation is to say, "The times have changed, and if we're going to reach the next generation, we have to change with the times." This approach, however, often leads not merely to adapting the message but losing the heart of the message and then having nothing distinct to offer. Rather than adapting the message, we need to contextualize the message. Adapting the message is telling people what they want to hear. Contextualizing the message is telling people what they need to hear in a way that they can understand.

Be Culturally Sensitive, Don't Let Culture Set the Agenda

Growing up in a society where people are more aware (through social media) of the problems in the world, many young people are turned off by churches that seem to ignore the pain and injustice across the globe. However, seeking to reach younger generations by addressing cultural events (whether the latest racial incident, political controversy, or global tragedy) often allows culture to

10. Twenge, *Generations*, 502.
11. Burge, "Gen Z and Religion."
12. Burge, "Gen Z and Religion."
13. Barna, "Gen Z Teens."

set the agenda for the church. I propose, however, that the expository preaching of the word of God sets the agenda, while being sensitive to how cultural events are impacting our congregations. Pastors certainly need to shepherd the church through difficult situations and God's people need God's perspective on cultural issues. But it is possible to be responsive without being reactionary while keeping the church's focus on making disciples of Jesus through proclamation of the gospel.

Preach to the Unchurched in Church

To reach younger generations, we must acknowledge that they will have much lower levels of biblical literacy. Only 22 percent of Americans read the Bible daily,[14] and that number is certainly lower for Gen Z. Furthermore, people do not approach Christianity with a blank slate but rather with associations and misconceptions. My neighbors in Los Angeles assume that Christians are narrow-minded, bigoted, self-righteous, anti-gay, anti-science, Trumpers. With our country becoming less Christian (in terms of formal self-identification), our preaching will need to be sensitive to and anticipate common critiques and questions about Christianity. And yet, doing so will reach beyond the unchurched. Every believer still has the "old self" warring within them and is being shaped (often unknowingly) by the surrounding secular culture. Therefore, apologetic preaching will not only reach the unchurched but will also strengthen the church and equip God's people for the task of witnessing to Christ in a society that does not recognize his rule.

The Church Needs It

So why does preaching still matter? First, because God commands it. But as we keep reading in 2 Tim 4, we will also see that preaching still matters because the church needs it. In other words, it is not that God wants us to do something that we do not need, as if we preach the word to keep God happy. Rather, God commands the word to be preached because the church needs it.

That is why, after Paul charges Timothy to "preach the word . . . in season and out of season," he unpacks the nature of preaching when he says, "Reprove, rebuke, and exhort, with complete patience and teaching" (2 Tim 4:2). These descriptors are not meant to be exhaustive; they represent the variety of needs in the congregation. To the church in Thessalonica, Paul says to "admonish the idle, encourage the fainthearted, help the weak" (1 Thess 5:14). There are a

---

14. Braddy, "Discipling."

variety of ailments in the church, and the preacher's job is to show how God's word offers the holistic remedy to real-life problems.

Preaching, therefore, is not merely declaring the truths of Scripture in a vacuum. Paul is referring to believers in the local church. And not only is that clear in 2 Tim 4:2, but the broader context reveals that this is a letter written to a local church with elders and deacons. Based on this, I want to draw out two key implications for preaching regarding its context and its essence.

The Context for Preaching

Individualism, consumerism, and the digital revolution have transformed the way people think of preaching. Expressive individualism makes the sermon another resource to help me be "the best version of myself." Consumerism creates a marketplace of sermons where each is a product to be used for the spiritual customer's benefit. The digital revolution enables people to consume hundreds of sermons without ever stepping foot in a church building. In short, the sermon has been detached from the local church and turned into another consumer good for personal transformation.

And yet, in Scripture, the primary context for preaching is the local church.[15] We can see this by comparing a sermon to a TED Talk. What is the difference? A preacher is not merely a speaker who shows up for an event but an elder/overseer who meets the character qualifications of 1 Tim 3 and is committed to caring for the congregation throughout the week. A sermon is not a talk filled with opinions and ideas but an authoritative exposition and application of God's word. The congregation is not a crowd to be entertained but an assembly of the redeemed who have come together to hear from the Lord. The purpose of preaching is not to spread ideas but to make disciples. In sum, preaching is not a TED Talk used for spiritual purposes by a collection of individuals. It is the proclamation of God's word to God's people in God's ways.[16] In the context of the local church, then, what is preaching?

---

15. "Hebrews (especially chs 3–4 and 12) and 2 Corinthians (especially ch 3) reflect the expectation that preaching should take place within the context of the Christian assembly." Griffiths, *Preaching*, 121.

16. What, then, about preaching in the book of Acts that largely happens outside of Sunday gatherings? First, we must recognize that the book of Acts occupies a unique place in redemptive history and therefore is not entirely prescriptive for the nature of the church today. Second, it must be recognized that the book of Acts is largely the story of *planting* churches, not necessarily the ongoing organization of churches. That said, in many ways Acts shows that the planting of churches is centered on the preaching of the word, and for that reason, the preaching in Acts *does* have an ecclesial context—church planting.

The Essence of Preaching

What *is* preaching? There are many ways to answer this question. Augustine says that preaching teaches the mind, delights the heart, and moves the will toward loving God and neighbor.[17] John Stott defines preaching as building a bridge between the world of the text and the world of the hearers today.[18] Rather than attempting a theoretical definition myself, I want to simply offer four words that get to the essence of preaching.

Proclamation

Preaching is first and foremost proclamation. Preachers are not content creators. We are heralds who have been given a message to deliver. And that message is an announcement of grace. It is not good advice about what we should do for God; it is good news about what God has done for us in Christ.

Proclamation is one of my favorite parts of preaching. Each Sunday, I get to look at my congregation, filled with people who are struggling with sin and weary from life, and remind them, "Your greatest problem has already been solved" and "Your relationship with God doesn't depend on your religious performance but on his unchanging grace." I get to proclaim their identity over them: "Because of the gospel, you are forgiven, set free, washed clean, made whole, adopted into a family, and participants in a glorious mission."

Shepherding

Mark 6:34 says that Jesus had compassion on the crowd "because they were like sheep without a shepherd." So what did Jesus do? He shepherded them through preaching. So it should be with preachers today. The flock needs to hear the voice of the Shepherd, and one of the primary ways that happens is through the preaching of the word.

The ecclesial context of preaching has completely changed the way I understand what I am doing when I am preaching. I am not merely giving a talk or sharing ideas. When I preach, I am shepherding through the word. The people I preach to are all struggling with something. They are grieving loss, confused with God's plan, frustrated with their lives, in need of provision,

---

17. Augustine, *De Doctrina Christiana*, 4.12.74.
18. Stott, *Between Two Worlds*, 101–2.

tired of being single, battling mental illness, and so on. My job as a preacher is to shepherd them through the preaching of the word.[19]

When I speak at a conference, therefore, I am not technically "preaching" in the truest sense of the word. I do not know the people I am speaking to, nor am I responsible for their souls. But when I preach at Reality LA, I am looking out at the congregation and seeing a couple who just had a miscarriage, a woman who is anxious about taking the bar exam, a young man who is experiencing gender dysphoria and wondering where God is in the midst of it. And as I prepare and preach my sermon, I know that my job is to bring the truth of God's word to bear on their real-life situations—to shepherd them through the word.

What Christians need is not a celebrity preacher who entertains them but a local shepherd who knows them. We need preachers who are pastors and have a reputation of being above reproach, sexually pure, sober-minded, gentle, and hospitable (1 Tim 3:1–6). We need preachers whose character outpaces their gifting. We need preachers who love people more than they love platforms and who reflect God's shepherd heart for the church.

Teaching

Preaching is more than teaching, but it is not less. A key part of a preacher's job is to teach the meaning of Scripture so that it can then be applied to people's lives. Teaching, however, is not an end itself; it serves the purpose of proclamation, shepherding, and discipleship. For example, the preacher who plans to *proclaim* the good news that Jesus is the Messiah must *teach* what it means to be the Messiah and the promises of Scripture attached to this title. The preacher who wants to *shepherd* hurting people with the truth that God is their refuge must *teach* them what a refuge is and why it was such a powerful image in the Old Testament world. The key to understanding biblical teaching is that while it necessarily includes learning new ideas, the goal is never merely information but rather transformation.

Discipleship

The type of "teaching" that Scripture refers to takes place not in the classroom but on the road of discipleship. The goal is not to learn information to pass tests but to learn how to follow Jesus in all of life. In fact, Jesus made

---

19. Two of the primary tasks of elders are shepherding and teaching (so it is no surprise that these would overlap).

clear in the Great Commission that teaching is a key part of making disciples (Matt 28:18–20). Preaching must be aimed at discipleship. Paul qualifies his command to "preach the word" in 2 Tim 4:2 by saying it must be done with "complete patience and teaching." Preaching is a work that is most effective when seen as a formative practice that shapes people's hearts and minds over time. In other words, while people overestimate how much of an impact preaching can have in one week, they underestimate how much the weekly preaching of the word can form people over the span of years.

Preaching to a Digital, Disembodied, and Individualized Society

How does the context and essence of preaching impact the way that we preach in our world today? Preaching is being transformed by the digital revolution and gradually being uprooted from the context of the local church. Artificial intelligence will only accelerate this movement. Many churches have leaned into this trajectory (e.g., video preaching at multi-site churches) and many are doubling down with more recent advancements (e.g., multiverse churches and AI preaching tools).[20]

My concern is that while churches are attempting to leverage technology to reach more people, they are not thinking through the implications of how the medium shapes the message. While churches should use technology and innovate to make disciples, I propose that when it comes to preaching, rather than attempting to one-up the world in its race to digital maximization, the church should subvert the digital trajectory and offer preaching in the context of embodied, enmeshed communities.

In a post-Christian digital society, we need preaching that happens in person, in community, over time. Our congregants can find excellent preaching online whenever they want. What they cannot find online is a pastor who knows their story, a community that is committed to doing life together, and a shared mission in a particular place. There is an overabundance of information, inspiration, and entertainment in our society today. The church should not try to compete in those areas. But there is a lack of (and a deep hunger for) connection, care, and wisdom. These the church can offer through in-person preaching in an embodied community.

---

20. The impact of technology on preaching is not new. The printing press allowed sermons to be published. The microphone allowed bigger crowds to hear sermons. The automobile brought listeners from different contexts to hear preaching. The internet enabled the mass dissemination of preaching. Video technology allowed preachers to preach virtually at multiple campuses. Social media enables preachers to go viral. Technology has always been and will always be an important shaping factor for preaching.

PART ONE: THE CENTRALITY OF THE PULPIT

The World Is Already Doing It

Why does preaching still matter today? Because God commands it, the church needs it, and the world is already doing it. Paul writes, "For the time is coming when people will not endure sound teaching, but having itching ears they will accumulate for themselves teachers to suit their own passions, and will turn away from listening to the truth and wander off into myths" (2 Tim 4:3–4).

Finding What You Want to Hear

If the church does not preach truth, then people will look elsewhere. And when they do, there will be plenty of options. This is more applicable than ever in the information and digital age because it is easier than any time in world history to find teachers who will say what you want to hear and justify what you want to believe. Want to believe that real Christians vote as Republicans or Democrats? An abundance of shows, podcasts, books, and "experts" are available to confirm your bias on either side. Tired of holding the tension between loving all people *and* believing that homosexual practice is a sin? There are educated, influential teachers who can relieve that pressure for you and guide you into a new way of being Christian. In fact, it is not enough to say that it is easier to *find* teachers who will say what you want them to say. The algorithms of social media and internet search engines have made them come to you. Whether through TikTok or Google, Facebook or YouTube, you are constantly being fed information tailored for you and designed to make you more extreme, more polarized, and less empathetic toward anyone who disagrees with you.

The world is "already preaching" in two ways. First, there are secular narratives and ideologies being preached by the world *out there* to non-Christians. But we cannot stop there. The world has crept into the church. And so, second, "the world" is preaching *in the church* through Christians who have been influenced by the ways of the world. Our task, then, is to understand the world's preaching and respond to it with a reinvigorated understanding of Christian preaching. But first, we have to understand secular narratives and ideologies.

The World Preaches Secular Narratives and Ideologies

Earlier I mentioned the "preaching" that takes place every year at the Academy Awards. But it does not happen only there. Heralds preach competing gospels of political salvation at the Republican and Democratic national conventions.

Influencers preach the good news of self-fulfillment through social media channels. YouTubers declare remedies to the world's ills. Podcasts are filled with prophets declaring truths that you must know. TED Talks offer the wisdom of the age in abundance. But what is the message that is being preached in our society? We can think of it in terms of narratives and ideologies, or "myths" and "teachings" as Paul refers to them.

Narratives bring meaning and coherence to life, telling us where we are, who we are, and how to live. And while there are many narratives swirling in our society, the reigning cultural narrative preached today is the narrative of the sovereign self where the authority is individual desire, the process is discovering and expressing my identity, and the goal is personal happiness. We hear this narrative coming through in day-to-day life with phrases like "no one can tell me who I am" because I just have to "be true to myself."

Not only is the world proclaiming secular narratives, it is also preaching secular ideologies.[21] Some of the strongest ideologies being preached in our society are political ideologies, whether a conservative vision of nationalism or a progressive vision of diversity, equity, and inclusion.[22] But what is happening in politics is similar to what is happening in sexuality and gender. It is not just that much of the Western world happens to disagree with Christianity about sexuality and gender, as if they were isolated and arbitrary topics. Rather, there are ideologies that have been developing for hundreds of years behind these secular beliefs.[23] To effectively preach the Christian message in this context, we must see how the changes in our society are ideologically driven.

For example, Pride Month is an illustration of how the preaching of a secular narrative with ideologies is making disciples and advancing its mission further into society. While Pride Month began like many American holidays, it has come to represent somewhat of a civic religion. Where I live in Los Angeles, Pride Month has become an all-encompassing celebration of secular values, whether it is my grocery store reminding me that "trans women are women," the public library waving the Pride flag, or Christians in the workplace being pressured to partake in office activities that would not be allowed in any other circumstance. The preaching of these narratives and ideologies results in a type of civil religion. Its gospel is "be true to yourself." Its values are inclusivity, tolerance, and self-expression. Its creed is "love is love." Its saints are celebrities. Its discipleship is being written into school curriculums. And

---

21. By ideology, I simply mean a system of ideas and ideals, often with strong implications for the public sphere.

22. Koyzis, *Political Visions and Illusions*.

23. Trueman, *Rise and Triumph*.

its evangelism is happening in stores and business all around. The world is preaching, and numbers are being added to its congregation day by day.

The Secular Gospel Has Crept into the Church

There are many people outside the church proclaiming untrue messages, but God consistently warns his people the most about false teachers within the church. And while there are simply teachers who misinterpret Scripture and therefore lead people astray, I want to focus on the ways that teachers within the church are led astray because they are unknowingly shaped by the world. People in our country who identify as Christians have deeply been shaped by the narratives and ideologies of the world.

A recent study called "The State of Theology" has revealed the following:

- 53 percent of evangelicals believe that "the Bible, like all sacred writings, contains helpful accounts of ancient myths but is not literally true"
- 56 percent of evangelicals believe that "God accepts the worship of all religions, including Christianity, Judaism, and Islam"
- 43 percent of evangelicals believe that "Jesus was a great teacher, but he was not God"
- 38 percent of evangelicals believe that "religious belief is a matter of personal opinion; it is not about objective truth"
- 37 percent of evangelicals believe that "gender identity is a matter of choice"[24]

My greatest concern, however, is not that many Christians are off on a doctrine here or there, but rather they have been unknowingly co-opted by a cultural narrative and are simply appealing to God's power for our society's secularized purposes. In other words, many people in the church are living by the narrative of expressive individualism and pursuing a secular vision of justice while maintaining a veneer of Christianity spirituality, simply slapping Jesus onto it.

Preaching Truth in the Public Sphere

While the Christian response to secular narratives and ideologies is multifaceted, a recovery of preaching must be at the core. We are never merely preaching to the choir. Preaching is the *public* declaration of the good news of

---

24. "State of Theology."

Jesus Christ according to the Scriptures (even if the audience primarily consists of the congregation). We are proclaiming the truth of God's word into a marketplace of ideas, narratives, ideologies, and creeds.

To combat the cultural narratives that are being preached in our society, we cannot merely explain the details of texts or preach systems of theology. We need to proclaim a more compelling narrative. And Christians have one. Our church gathers on Sunday on Sunset Boulevard and our next-door neighbor is Netflix. I like to remind people that, even though Netflix is next door, "We've got the best story in town." We may not always tell it as well, and we certainly do not have the production level. But we truly do have the best story. As preachers, we have to remind the church that the story we live by is not the story of building our own kingdoms and making a name for ourselves. We live by the story of God's kingdom, where we find purpose in witnessing to his reign and living for the glory of his name. That is the story that will tell us why we are here, who we are, and how to live.

To counter the ideologies in our society, we must preach sound doctrine. And to do this, we have to reclaim the theological nature of preaching. Theology is not reserved for ivory towers or academic conferences. Rather, theology's natural habitat is the church. In other words, theology is expressed best not in textbooks or debates but in prayer, praise, and preaching. That does not rule out the need for academic theologians and scholarly engagement. But it does mean that academic theology and Christian scholarship ultimately exist to serve the church. When a preacher preaches theologically, he is not borrowing from the sphere of the academy in such a way that takes something theoretical and makes it personal and practical. Theology, rightly understood, *is* personal and practical. As Martin Lloyd-Jones says, "Preaching is theology coming through a man who is on fire."[25] And while theology should be taught in many forms and contexts within the church, the pulpit is the epicenter for the formation of a theological community. As Kevin Vanhoozer says, "The sermon is the best weapon in the pastor's arsenal for taking every thought, and our imaginations, captive to Christ, which is why preaching may be the quintessential theological act."[26]

Preaching in a Multicultural Context

But if we are called to preach *the* truth of God's word and *the* narrative of Scripture, then how can we do that to a variety of different cultures? This will be

---

25. Lloyd-Jones, *Preaching and Preachers*, 97.
26. Quoted in Lee, *Preaching God's Grand Drama*, i.

key for preachers in the present-day because our contexts are becoming much more culturally diverse. The United States as a whole is rapidly growing in racial diversity. In 1980, 80 percent of the US population was white. By 2020, it was only 60 percent.[27] And, for the first time, more than half of the nation's population under age sixteen are people of color from a variety of different cultural backgrounds.

Preachers, therefore, must learn to preach in ways that are sensitive to and appropriately contextualized to various cultures. But this is not merely something that we *have* to do because the world is changing. It is something that we *get* to do because it represents the heart of God. The ultimate vision of Scripture is the eternal kingdom of God made up of every tribe, tongue, people, and nation (Rev 5:9). And we get to experience a foretaste of that now in the church.

Multiculturalism is important for *preaching* because the Bible is a multicultural book written for a multicultural people on a multicultural mission. This has important implications for preaching.

Multicultural Book

Written in three languages, by forty authors, on three continents, over fifteen hundred years, and in countless contexts, the Bible truly is a multicultural book. Even to exposit Scripture well, we have to be sensitive to different cultural contexts, whether of Babylon, Athens, Jerusalem, or Rome. If we do not appreciate the different cultures of Scripture, then we will be tempted to read our own cultural assumptions into the text. For example, as a white preacher (who has lived in a culture that is individualistic and appeals to guilt more than shame) I have to be aware of my blind spots as I read Scripture, lest, for example, I take something that is meant for the community and apply it merely to the individual. We have to exposit the text in its original cultural context and only then build a bridge to our own cultural contexts.[28]

---

27. Frey, "Nation Is Diversifying."

28. These contexts vary, and so the style of expository preaching will vary in ways that meet the needs of the local context whether it be a black, Korean, white, multi-ethnic church, etc. As Eric Redmond says, "The consensus about biblical, expository preaching is that the author's idea in the text is primary. . . . However, the communication does not require a particular mode of verbal delivery. Expository preaching concerns only the *content* of a message with respect to the words of Scripture." Redmond, "African American and Exposition," 26.

Multicultural People

From the very beginning, God's plan was to redeem a people of all nations. He promised this to Abram in Gen 12:1–3 and reaffirmed it to Israel in Isa 49:6. The thread of bringing Jews and gentiles together runs throughout the entire New Testament. Paul clearly contextualized his preaching based on his audience. To the Greeks he quoted the Greeks (Acts 17:28) and with the Jews he reasoned from the Scriptures (Acts 17:2). Likewise, we must know the makeup of our congregations and preach in such a way that applies the truths of Scripture accordingly.

For example, I recently preached through 2 Corinthians and talked about embracing weakness as a way of experiencing God's strength. But I talked with several Asian-Americans in our church who found this concept especially difficult because "embracing weakness" for them does not just mean being vulnerable as an individual but also potentially bringing shame on their family for being perceived as weak by the world. It created a great conversation about honor and shame in Scripture and how we can learn from one another's cultures in such a way that helps us be more faithful to Christ.

Multicultural Mission

The church's mission is multicultural at its core, with Jesus commanding the church to make disciples "of all nations" (Matt 28:19). The Jerusalem Council in Acts 15 was largely about how the gospel is to be translated to different cultures. Paul's confrontation of Peter in Gal 2 is about how the gospel impacts ethnic differences. Andrew Walls has demonstrated that the history of Christian mission is the transmission of the gospel into new cultures, languages, and concepts.[29] And much of this transmission has happened, and will continue to happen, through preaching.

Preachers can learn cultural agility by listening to and learning from those of different cultural backgrounds. Listening to other cultures reveals our own cultural assumptions and can correct our culturally-conditioned reading of Scripture. There is much to learn from the black church about cultivating joy and hope amid oppression. There is much to learn from the Asian-American church of how Jesus bears our shame and gives us his honor. There is much to learn from the Latino church about how God's people are family. There is much to learn from the Eastern European church about embracing our unity

---

29. Walls, *Missionary Movement*.

in Christ amidst unthinkable political division. There is much to learn from the Middle Eastern church about remaining steadfast through persecution.[30]

Fulfill Your Ministry

The last verse of this passage provides a fitting conclusion. Paul says, "As for you, always be sober-minded, endure suffering, do the work of an evangelist, fulfill your ministry" (2 Tim 4:5). We need preachers who are godly, faithful, and hold fast until the end.

One such man is a small-town pastor in Indiana. Pastor Joe baptized my wife when she was in college and faithfully preached the word to my in-laws for decades. I first met with Pastor Joe when he was seventy years old. He had pastored for five decades and had a file cabinet with five thousand sermons in it (that's two sermons a week for fifty years). When I sat down with Pastor Joe, I said, "I want to finish well like you. How'd you do it?" Pastor Joe replied, "A lot of young pastors focus on the breadth of their ministry—how many people they can reach and how big their church can be." He then paused, looked me in the eye, and said, "You focus on the depth of your relationship with Jesus and let him determine the breadth of your ministry." This is the vision for preaching we need—preaching that is the overflow of an intimate relationship with the Lord and a life transformed by the gospel.

Conclusion

Preaching still matters because God commands it, the church needs it, and the world is already doing it. I began this essay by saying that if you do not think modern people like preaching, then just watch the Oscars. I will close with a story.

Our church meets right down the street from the Dolby Theatre where the Oscars are hosted. Several years ago, we rented the Dolby Theatre for our Easter service. On that Easter Sunday, I stood on the stage in the same place where Joaquin Phoenix, Leonardo DiCaprio, and Spike Lee stood, and I preached the gospel at the top of my lungs. Of course, the message I preached was different than what you typically hear from that stage. It was not one of worldly impressiveness. Rather, I proclaimed a gospel of a king who came as a servant, pursued the outcasts and pariahs of society, gave his life for his

---

30. One way I communicate this to our church is by quoting Majority World theologians in my sermons, which reminds our congregation that we are a part of a global movement and provides different perspectives than mine, of which they get a lot.

enemies, and then emerged triumphant from the tomb, beginning a movement that had about as much potential as a mustard seed.

After the sermon we did baptisms, right there on the stage of the Dolby Theatre. Many people were baptized, but there was one that I will never forget. A woman came forward in her wheelchair, paralyzed from the waist down. As she was picked up out of her wheelchair and lowered into the waters of baptism, all I could think was how different are the values of the kingdom. Power is made perfect in weakness. The last shall be first. Blessed are the poor in spirit. Christ's death is what brings us life. As this woman rose up out of the water, symbolizing that she was washed of her sins and raised to new life in Christ, the congregation erupted in praise, giving glory to God, our savior and king.

There is power in the gospel, and preaching is one of God's ordained ways for the gospel to go forth to all cultures, including our post-Christian society.

Bibliography

Ash, Christopher. *The Priority of Preaching*. Rev. ed. Fearn Ross-shire, UK: Christian Focus, 2009.

Augustine. *De Doctrina Christiana*. Translated by R. P. H. Green. Oxford: Clarendon, 1995.

Barna Group. "Over Half of Gen Z Teens Feel Motivated to Learn More About Jesus." February 1, 2023. https://www.barna.com/research/teens-and-jesus/.

Braddy, Ken. "Discipling in an Age of Biblical Illiteracy." Lifeway Research, July 10, 2017. https://research.lifeway.com/2017/07/10/discipling-in-an-age-of-biblical-illiteracy/.

Burge, Ryan P. "Gen Z and Religion in 2022." Religion in Public, April 3, 2023. https://religioninpublic.blog/2023/04/03/gen-z-and-religion-in-2022/.

Dates, Charlie. "The Treasure and Potential of African American Preaching." In *Say It!: Celebrating Expository Preaching in the African American Tradition*, edited by Eric Redmond, 13–20. Chicago: Moody, 2020.

Frey, William H. "The Nation Is Diversifying Even Faster Than Predicted, According to New Census Data." Brookings, July 1, 2020. https://www.brookings.edu/articles/new-census-data-shows-the-nation-is-diversifying-even-faster-than-predicted/.

Goldsworthy, Graeme. *Gospel-Centered Hermeneutics: Foundations and Principles of Evangelical Biblical Interpretation*. Downers Grove, IL: IVP Academic, 2006.

Greidanus, Sidney. *Preaching Christ from the Old Testament: A Contemporary Hermeneutical Method*. Grand Rapids: Eerdmans, 1999.

Griffiths, Jonathan. *Preaching in the New Testament: An Exegetical and Biblical-Theological Study*. New Studies in Biblical Theology. Downers Grove: IVP Academic, 2017.

Keller, Timothy. *Preaching: Communicating Faith in an Age of Skepticism*. New York: Penguin, 2016.

Koyzis, David T. *Political Visions and Illusions: A Survey and Christian Critique of Contemporary Ideologies*. 2nd ed. Downers Grove: IVP Academic, 2019.

PART ONE: THE CENTRALITY OF THE PULPIT

Lee, Ahmi. *Preaching God's Grand Drama: A Biblical-Theological Approach.* Grand Rapids: Baker Academic, 2019.

Lloyd-Jones, Martin. *Preaching and Preachers.* Grand Rapids: Zondervan, 1971.

Oscars. "Will Smith Wins Best Actor for 'King Richard.'" May 3, 2022. YouTube, 8:07. https://www.youtube.com/watch?v=7CX7jmZvytA.

Redmond, Eric. "The Joining of the African American and Exposition." In *Say It!: Celebrating Expository Preaching in the African American Tradition,* edited by Eric Redmond, 21–38. Chicago: Moody, 2020.

Smith, Claire C. *Pauline Communities as "Scholastic Communities."* Tübingen: Mohr Siebeck, 2012.

"The State of Theology." 2022. https://thestateoftheology.com.

Stott, John R. W. *Between Two Worlds: The Art of Preaching in the Twentieth Century.* Grand Rapids: Eerdmans, 1982.

Treat, Jeremy. *The Crucified King: Atonement and Kingdom in Biblical and Systematic Theology.* Grand Rapids: Zondervan, 2014.

Trueman, Carl. *The Rise and Triumph of the Modern Self: Cultural Amnesia, Expressive Individualism, and the Road to Sexual Revolution.* Wheaton, IL: Crossway, 2020.

Twenge, Jean M. *Generations: The Real Differences Between Gen Z, Millennials, Gen X, Boomers, and Silents—and What They Mean for America's Future.* New York: Atria, 2023.

Walls, Andrew. *The Missionary Movement in Christian History: Studies in the Transmission of Faith.* Maryknoll, NY: Orbis, 1996.

2

Recapturing Paul's Theology of Preaching

JASON MEYER

INTRODUCTION

PASTORAL MINISTRY SUFFERS FROM a plague of uncertainty when it comes to preaching. There are endless debates about who can preach, how to preach, and whether preaching should be a priority at all. The real problem with trying to answer these questions is that they are nearly impossible to answer if we do not start with clarity concerning what preaching is.

One popular preaching cliché is that a mist in the pulpit creates a fog in the pews. This homiletical proverb states that if a preacher is unclear in their own mind, then that lack of clarity will grow exponentially in the minds of the hearers. The same principle is true, not only concerning a lack of clarity *in* preaching but a lack of clarity *about* preaching. If the one who is called to preach does not know what preaching is, then the preaching landscape will resemble the book of Judges where everyone does what is right in their own eyes.

A lack of clarity about what preaching also creates a scenario in which everyone is a judge. The hearers of sermons will feel duly deputized to serve as the judges of sermons. The people will end up judging the preacher's performance based on their own personal likes and dislikes. But how can they evaluate preaching if no one knows what it is? We will address this plague of uncertainty by attempting to recapture the apostle Paul's theology of preaching in 1 Cor 2:1–5 (ESV).

PART ONE: THE CENTRALITY OF THE PULPIT

Context and Background

Paul opens with a reference to the report from Chloe's people that the Corinthians have splintered into various factions (1:10–11). He then shares a summary of the report: "What I mean is that each one of you says, 'I follow Paul,' or 'I follow Apollos,' or 'I follow Cephas,' or 'I follow Christ'" (1 Cor 1:12).

Paul responds to this report with a litany of rhetorical questions in verse 13:

- Is Christ divided?
- Was Paul crucified for you?
- Were you baptized in the name of Paul?

The apostle expresses relief over the sparse number of people that appear on the baptism section of his resume because he does not want anyone to fall into the trap of believing that those whom he baptized were somehow baptized in the name of Paul (vv. 14–16).

Paul does not want anyone to construct an identity forged in allegiance to their favorite minister. Followers of Christ do not identify with their favorite follower of Christ (i.e., Paul, Apollos, Cephas). The Lord of the church certainly did not create a leadership competition that elevates the leader with the most followers. The Corinthians suffer from category confusion. Paul, Apollos, and Cephas are being put in the wrong category. They were not crucified for anyone. And although those leaders baptize, they emphatically do not baptize in their own name or create followers for themselves. The follower of Christ finds their identity in Christ alone.

Now we come to Paul's special focus. He says that Christ did not send him to baptize but to preach the gospel (1 Cor 1:17). He could have stopped there and the sentence would be complete. His calling is to preach the gospel. But his point is much more specific. Paul wants to put the spotlight on how *not* to preach. He does not preach "with words of eloquent wisdom" (v. 17). Why? Preaching with words of eloquent wisdom creates an appalling scenario in which the cross loses its power (v. 17).

The apostle refuses to add eloquence to the cross because eloquent words of wisdom will actually empty the cross of its power (1 Cor 1:17). But this text raises a crucial question. Why do eloquent words of wisdom empty the cross of its power rather than add to its power? Answer: the cross itself is a direct assault upon worldly wisdom. The cross is on a seek-and-destroy mission with the world's system that places pride in achievement, power, and privilege. God has designed salvation in such a way that tears down pride and all forms of human boasting.

1 Corinthians 2:1–5

Paul then takes the framework constructed in chapter one and applies it in chapter two. He has already stated that eloquent wisdom will empty the cross of its power. Therefore, power in preaching does not come from *how* he preaches (i.e., eloquence), but from *what* he preaches (i.e., the cross). Now he directly identifies another source of power for preaching. Listen to verses 1–5 and look for the contrast he constructs between eloquent words of wisdom and divine power.

> And I, when I came to you, brothers, did not come proclaiming to you the testimony of God with lofty speech or wisdom. For I decided to know nothing among you except Jesus Christ and him crucified. And I was with you in weakness and in fear and much trembling, and my speech and my message were not in plausible words of wisdom, but in demonstration of the Spirit and of power, so that your faith might not rest in the wisdom of men but in the power of God. (1 Cor 2:1–5)

What gives preaching its power? Paul answers with a negation first and then an affirmation. The source of power does not come from how well we speak. The source of power comes from the double divine power of (1) the cross of Christ proclaimed in concert with (2) the work of the Spirit.

We can all agree that eloquent speech is a poor substitute for the powerful combination of the cross and the Spirit. But why not just affirm the superpower of combining all three? Why not add the power of eloquence to the power of the cross and the Spirit? We have already stated that eloquence will empty the cross of its power. But there is a deeper connection to make between the cross and the Spirit. The weakness of the cross and the power of the Spirit create a cruciform connection to Christ's death and resurrection.

Two Paradigms: Cruciform vs. Perform

Paul's paradigm for preaching is thoroughly cruciform. Preaching the weakness of the cross in the power of the Spirit puts on display the death and resurrection of Christ. Daniel Patte states that "Paul sees God at work in situations which are Christ-like, that is, in situations which include both a cross-like experience and a resurrection-like experience."[1] Preaching is a demonstration of our lack of power, eloquence, and knowledge. Paul did not seek to wow the Corinthians with his knowledge or eloquence. He resolved to preach

---

1. Patte, *Preaching Paul*, 25. See also Knowles, *We Preach Not Ourselves*, 17–25.

Christ and him crucified. That is why Paul emphasizes his weakness. "I was with you in weakness and in fear and much trembling" (1 Cor 2:3). Paul is not talking about weakness and fear in terms of stage fright but as the embodied enactment of cruciform preaching. His own weakness in preaching displays the weakness of the cross. He preaches the cross in cross-like weakness.

But there is also a powerful resurrection-like experience through the power of the Holy Spirit. This demonstration of power through the Spirit creates "faith" (1 Cor 2:5) and "full conviction" (1 Thess 1:5) so that the faith of Paul's hearers is something that comes about through the power of God, not the power of eloquence (1 Cor 2:5).

By way of contrast, a worldly approach to preaching fits a performance paradigm that stands in stark opposition to a cruciform paradigm. A performance mentality in preaching centers on the speaker's ability to manufacture the desired response. The response of the people is the result of the preacher's performance. If he does his job well, then they will respond well. Duane Litfin provides a table to summarize the fundamental difference between Paul and the orators of his day in 1 Cor 2:1–5.[2]

Speaker	Audience	Orator's Efforts	Results
Greco-Roman Rhetorician	Given dependent	Independent variable	Given dependent
Paul	A given	A constant	Dependent variable

The rhetoricians of Paul's day look at the message as the independent variable. They start with the response they want to create, and then they craft the message to reach that result.

Paul's approach is exactly the opposite. The message is precisely the thing that cannot change. It is a precious stewardship that must be heralded faithfully. Paul chooses to preach the message faithfully and puts his trust in God's Spirit to produce the results. Litfin's assessment is worth quoting in full.

> Paul's determination to hold his preaching constant threw the variability in the equation to the end. Hence for Paul the results became the equation's *dependent variable*, a factor which could scarcely even be addressed until after the fact. Each time Paul preached the Gospel he perceived himself to be introducing the *Constant*, the message of Christ crucified, but it was the Spirit who would use this message to distinguish between οἱ ἀπολλύμενοι [those being destroyed] and οἱ κλητοί [the called]. The former would find the

---

2. Litfin, *St. Paul's Theology*, 205.

> simply proclaimed Gospel foolish, or even offensive, but the latter would come to view it, through the supernatural force of the Spirit's conviction, as the truth of their own salvation. In this way Paul's unchanging message of the cross carried the stench of death to the one, but became a fragrance of life to the other, depending strictly upon the work of the Spirit. Paul could not know beforehand which listeners were which, of course; it was only afterwards as he observed and assessed the consequences of the preaching that he could reach any conclusions. (1 Thess. 1:4–5; 2:13)[3]

Paul does not want the response of the people to be the result of his eloquence, but to be the result of the Spirit's power. Preaching the cross with eloquent wisdom would empty the cross of its power and cater to human pride. Preaching in proud reliance on eloquence to produce the results would destroy the cross and resurrection paradigm of human weakness and divine power.

This essay has presented a contrast between a perform model and a cruciform model. Paul's paradigm for preaching follows the cruciform model that combines human weakness and divine power to display the cross and resurrection of Christ. Now the question before us is what role eloquence plays within the cruciform model.

Redeeming Eloquence in a Cruciform Model of Preaching

Eloquence is not evil in and of itself. The contrast Paul constructs is not between speaking that is good and speaking that is bad—or else he would be saying that bad speaking is good and good speaking is bad. Paul would never say "aim to speak as poorly as possible because if people actually respond, it will be a miracle and then we will know beyond a shadow of a doubt that it had to be the Lord." We have to come to grips with the fact that the Bible itself speaks with great literary excellence. God's word is full of literary devices that set it apart from sophomoric or ordinary literature. You do not have to look very far to see acrostics and alliteration, metaphor and meter, repetition and rhyme, satire and simile. Surely God does not want his preachers to eviscerate this literary creativity with boring, half-baked sermons.

It is this very point that helps us preachers take our stewardship seriously. We do not need to give the Bible a makeover; we give it a voice. We are servants of the word. We trust that the word will not return empty when preached in the cruciform paradox of human weakness and divine power. This paradigm frees the preacher from performance anxiety. If the power is

---

3. Litfin, *St. Paul's Theology*, 249–50.

not from us, then the pressure is not on us to perform. Great truths create great preachers, not the other way around. The power is not found in how we preach, but what we preach. The gospel is the power of God for salvation (Rom 1:16; 1 Cor 1:18).

This approach also sets the preacher free from the temptation to manipulate. If the response of an audience is dependent upon the speaker's ability to move an audience, then preaching invariably veers towards manipulation. Paul's aim is not to be clever, but to be clear. His resolve to know nothing except Christ and him crucified (1 Cor 2:3) represents an ambition to make Christ *clear*. Paul does not want to cancel this aim by being *clever*. What is the difference? One preacher wants clear speech so that *what* he preaches will be clearly recognized; the other uses clever speech so that *how* he preaches will be clearly recognized. Paul wants his preaching to point to Christ, not himself. The ambition of his preaching is to preach Christ clearly so that Christ is clearly seen.

What is wrong with clever speech? Clever speech implies that one makes the truth *real* by how one says it. The speaker trusts in his ability to shape words that will move audiences. Clear speech implies trust in the Spirit to make the truth real. Paul contrasts his communication calculus with the one that orators utilize:

Orator: concept + clever communication = conviction

Paul: word of God + clear communication + Spirit's work = conviction

It is not wrong to use homiletical techniques and preaching strategies; it is just wrong to trust them. We trust the supernatural combination of the word and the Spirit, brought together in the cruciform paradox of power and weakness.

Conclusion

These truths take me back to the beginning of my call to ministry in college. This whole discussion is not academic and abstract, but profoundly personal. A great transformation took place in my life after my call to preach. There were fountains of compassion for people that came out of nowhere. There was a boldness to speak about Jesus. Everyone could see a difference. People started to notice. A group of my friends said, "You are called to ministry, huh? Would you like to preach for our Campus Crusade gathering?" I said, "Um, yeah, I guess."

I was really nervous because I did not have any training. I did not know how to preach! But I had something burning that felt like a fire shut up in my bones, so I figured I needed to say it. In my reading through the Bible, I was up to the book of James, where I read that "faith without works is dead"

(Jas 2:26 NASB). I thought, "Wow . . . I have seen that a lot of that kind of 'faith' growing up—people that profess to be Christians but their lives do not show it—there are no spiritual signs of life." I was so earnest on the one hand and so clueless on the other. "Lord, how do I say this? How do I get this point across that just as the body without the soul is dead, so faith without works is dead?" I knew that a sermon should have illustrations. While I was preaching I could not think of a way to illustrate that truth by telling a story, so I just laid down on the ground and pretended to be dead. I did that for one whole minute. Do you know how long one minute is when you are speaking? Then I suddenly got up and said, "How many people thought I was dead?" They all looked at me with skeptical looks. I said, "OK, you knew I was playing dead, but I sure didn't look alive, did I? But now there are no doubts. You hear my voice, you see my energy and my gestures and hand movements and whatever. There is no doubt that I am alive." Then I said, "James is asking, which one are you? Do you claim to be a Christian and yet there are no spiritual signs of life for anyone to see? Can people actually see that you are a Christian?"

I finished and prayed. I looked at my watch. Five minutes. The whole message was five minutes (one minute of which I was on the ground pretending to be dead). But here is the crazy thing—God used it. People were convicted and helped. They told me how much God used it in their lives. I was dumbfounded. "Are you kidding? That was terrible. It felt like a failure. I couldn't even preach for five minutes. How does anyone preach for thirty minutes?" But I remember seeing the response. Later that night I got alone with God and said to him, "If you can use *that*, then I guess you really can use anything—even me." I realized that full surrender is true freedom. It is so freeing to stop telling God what I could not do and what he could not possibly do through me.

In the same way, I conclude this essay with a question for all preachers. Do we believe in cruciform preaching as the power of God for salvation? Do we think the power resides in our performance or in his power? If the power for preaching truly comes from divine power, then we should approach preaching the way Spurgeon did as he ascended the pulpit steps. Let us join him in repeating this phrase under our breath with every step we take: "I believe in the Holy Spirit."

Bibliography

Knowles, Michael P. *We Preach Not Ourselves: Paul on Proclamation*. Grand Rapids: Brazos, 2008.
Litfin, Duane. *St. Paul's Theology of Proclamation: 1 Corinthians 1–4 and Greco-Roman Rhetoric*. Cambridge: Cambridge University Press, 1994.
Patte, Daniel. *Preaching Paul*. Philadelphia: Fortress, 1984.

3

Bring the Thunder!

The Sources of Power According to Jesus's Teaching on Preaching

DOUGLAS SEAN O'DONNELL

INTRODUCTION

IT IS COMMON IN preacher's parlance to talk about bringing the thunder, that is, to preach with power. Perhaps the idiom comes from James and John, who were called the "Sons of Thunder" (Mark 3:17, ESV) and who asked Jesus, "Lord, do you want us to tell fire to come down from heaven and consume" the Samaritans who "did not receive" you (Luke 9:53, 54)? More likely it comes from the connection between thunder and the voice of God. When the Ten Commandments are given to Moses on Mount Sinai, we read that "God answered him in thunder" (Exod 19:19) and that "all the people saw the thunder and the flashes of lightning" and they "were afraid and trembled" (20:18). The book of Job makes clear this connection as well. "Keep listening," says Elihu, "to the thunder of his voice" (Job 37:2). Moreover, it makes clear that the idiom is one for power: Job speaks of "the thunder of his [God's] power" (26:14); and "the Lord spoke to Job out of the whirlwind," saying of himself, "Have you an arm like God, and can you thunder with a voice like his?" (40:6, 9).

This book is called *Power and the Pulpit: Recovering a Theology of Preaching* and our goal is to articulate a robust theology of preaching, specifically helping the church understand and apply Paul's vision of preaching in

1 Cor 2:1–5, where Paul speaks of "the power of God" in the proclamation of the gospel coming not through "lofty speech or [human] wisdom" but from the presence of "the Spirit" and the message of Christ crucified ("I decided to know nothing among you except Jesus Christ and him crucified"). Of course, Paul's theology of preaching has as its ultimate source the life and teachings of Jesus. So, in this chapter, what I set out to do is answer the question, "Where, according to Jesus, does the power for effective preaching come from?" I arrive at my answer to that major question by asking and answering another question: "Where in the Gospels and Acts is the language of power, especially the word δύναμις (along with an eye on ἐξουσία), used in relation to preaching?"

Expectedly, δύναμις is used in the Gospels for Jesus's miracles, sometimes translated "miraculous powers" (Matt 14:2) or "mighty works" (13:54).[1] Luke 5:17 records, "And the power of the Lord was with him to heal." Moreover, Jesus equates the resurrection from the dead to "the power of God" (Luke 22:69) and his second coming ("the powers of the heavens will be shaken" and then "the Son of Man" will come "in a cloud with power and great glory" (Luke 21:26, 27); "you will see the Son of Man seated at the right hand of Power" (Matt 26:64) and the coming kingdom ("the kingdom of God") will "come with power" (Mark 9:1).

Perhaps unexpectedly, the language of power is found often in relationship to effective preaching. It is specifically used in four ways, and we can think of these as the four sources for effective preaching, both then and now. First, power and preaching are linked to God's commissioning of people to preach. Second, power and preaching are linked to the work of the Holy Spirit. Third, power and preaching are linked to prayer. Fourth, power and preaching are linked to the preaching of Christ crucified.

1. Commissioned: "He Gave Them Power"

First, power and preaching are linked when God—the Father, Son, and Spirit—commissions or sends someone or a group of people to preach. In John's Gospel, Jesus is often described as "the one who was sent."[2] Moreover, "the Father who sent" Jesus (John 5:37) gave him his mission and message: "My

---

1. In the miracle of the bleeding woman, Mark uses the language "power had gone out from" Jesus (Mark 5:30; cf. "power came out of him and healed them all [the crowd]," Luke 6:19). When Jesus healed a man with an unclean demon, the people in the synagogue in Capernaum said, "What is this word? For with authority and power he commands the unclean spirits, and they come out!" (Luke 4:36).

2. For a list of the twenty-six references, see Köstenberger, *Theology of John's Gospel*, 134.

teaching is not mine, but his who sent me" (John 7:16; cf. 8:29; 10:36). Similar "sent" language is also employed in Matthew, Mark, and Luke. For example, in the parable of the wicked tenants, Jesus speaks of his Father (the "master") who "sent his son to them" (Matt 21:37; cf. Mark 12:6). Moreover, all three evangelists use Jesus's line "him who sent me" (Matt 10:40; Mark 9:37; Luke 9:48; 10:16); Jesus speaks of being "sent . . . to the lost sheep of the house of Israel" (Matt 15:24); of being "sent for" the "purpose" of preaching the "good news of the kingdom" (Luke 4:43) and, quoting Isaiah, he declares that "The Spirit of the Lord is upon me, because he has anointed me to proclaim good news to the poor. He has sent me to proclaim liberty to the captives" (Luke 4:18).

When Jesus commissions the twelve to preach to the Jews throughout Israel, his commission begins with the words, "Behold, I am sending you" (Matt 10:16). In Luke's version of the same event the language directly connects power and preaching: "And he *called* the twelve together and *gave them power and authority* [δύναμιν καὶ ἐξουσίαν][3] over all demons and to cure diseases, and he *sent* them out to *proclaim* the kingdom of God and to heal" (Luke 9:1–2).[4] This same connection is made in the Great Commission, where it is only because of Jesus's God-granted power ("All authority in heaven and on earth has been given to me") and presence ("And behold, I am with you always"), that the eleven are empowered to "go . . . and make disciples of all nations" (Matt 28:18–20). In Acts, Jesus through the Holy Spirit ("the Spirit of Jesus," 16:7) directs and commissions evangelists (Paul and Barnabas were "sent out by the *Holy Spirit*," 13:4).

Our Pattern

This pattern of sending—the Father sent Jesus, the Father and Son sent the Spirit, the Son and Spirit sent the apostles—should be the church's pattern for power in preaching. In practical terms, those who proclaim the gospel must

---

3. "Luke adds 'power and' to Mark's 'authority.' The immediate link here will be 8:46 ['But Jesus said, "Someone touched me, for I perceive that power has gone out from me."'] . . . but there may also be an anticipation of post-resurrection empowering (cf. Acts 1:8). The Twelve will be carriers of Jesus' own power." Nolland, *Luke 1–9:20*, 426. Moreover, as Joseph A. Fitzmyer points out, "The Greek words *dynamis* and *exousia* have already been used by Luke to describe Jesus' own status, his power (4:14, 36; 5:17; 6:19; 8:46) and authority (4:32, 36; 5:24). . . . Jesus is thus granting the Twelve a share in the dominion that he enjoyed as God's special emissary." Fitzmyer, *Gospel According to Luke*, 753. Following C. F. Evans, I take "the transference of Jesus's power" that is communicated with the phrase δύναμιν καὶ ἐξουσίαν as "a Lukan hendiadys" (see Luke 4:36; cf. Acts 2:43; 3:6; 4:7; 5:12; 10:38) that is, a singular idea expressed with two synonymous, interchangeable words. Evans, *Saint Luke*, 395.

4. All of the emphases in the Scripture quotations in this essay are mine.

be called by God and confirmed by his church. In my faith tradition (Presbyterianism), as in most faith traditions within the Christian church, one's inward calling is confirmed by the outward affirmation of the church through ordination—the laying on of hands (Acts 13:3). It is then that the ordained preacher is sent out like Paul and Barnabas were ("being sent on their way by the church," Acts 15:3; cf. 15:22; 13:3), under the authority and affirmation of God and his people, to preach the good news. God's power comes through that human process. Of course, the church recognizes the prior work of the Spirit to sanctify and empower the ones whom she ordains and commissions. God's empowering work is recognizable even to the crowds, who recognize the authority of Jesus's teaching (Matt 7:28–29; cf. 9:8; Mark 1:27); and in Acts 6:3 the church recognizes those in whom the Spirit was already at work (they appoint "seven men of good repute, full of the Spirit and of wisdom").

2. The Holy Spirit: "Power from on High"

Second, power and preaching are linked to the work of the Holy Spirit. In the second post-resurrection appearance in John, Jesus stood among his disciples and said to them, "Peace be with you. As the Father has sent me, even so I am sending you." After he said that, "he breathed on them and said to them, 'Receive the Holy Spirit'" (John 20:21–22). That reception plus sending equals empowering, a pattern found in the Gospels and throughout Acts.

Just as Jesus was Spirit-empowered to accomplish every aspect of his mission (e.g., "God anointed Jesus of Nazareth with the Holy Spirit and with power," Acts 10:38; cf. Matt 12:28; Luke 3:21–22; 4:1, 14; 5:17), notably preaching ("I will put my Spirit upon him, and he will proclaim justice to the Gentiles," Matt 12:18), so Jesus empowers his church to preach effectively through the gift of the Holy Spirit. Put differently, power for preaching both for Jesus and his church comes through the Spirit's anointing.

There are many examples of this. The most prominent are found at the end of Luke and the beginning of Acts. In Luke 24, Jesus "opened their minds to understand the Scriptures" (Luke 24:45; cf. 24:32), that is, "everything written about [him] in the Law of Moses and the Prophets and the Psalms" (v. 44), namely "that the Christ should suffer and on the third day rise from the dead" (v. 46). Then he commissioned them, as "witnesses of these things" (v. 48), to preach "to all nations" those truths alongside the "repentance for the forgiveness of sins . . . in his name" (v. 47). However, before they start their mission that would begin "from Jerusalem" (v. 47) and move "to the end of the earth" (Acts 1:8), they are to wait for the promise of power. Jesus puts it this way in Luke 24:49: "And behold, I am sending the promise of my Father upon you.

But stay in the city until you are clothed with power from on high." That power we know from earlier in Luke, in Gabriel's annunciation to Mary, is the Holy Spirit: "And the angel answered her, 'The *Holy Spirit* will come upon you, and *the power of the Most High* will overshadow you'" (Luke 1:35).

Throughout Acts the connection between the coming of the Holy Spirit and the power for preaching is absolutely clear. Acts 1:4–8 reads,

> And while staying with them [Jesus] ordered them not to depart from Jerusalem, but to wait for the promise of the Father, which, he said, "you heard from me; for John baptized with water, but you will be baptized with the Holy Spirit not many days from now." So when they had come together, they asked him, "Lord, will you at this time restore the kingdom to Israel?" He said to them, "It is not for you to know times or seasons that the Father has fixed by his own authority. But [back to the point I was making!] you will receive *power* when *the Holy Spirit* has come upon you, and [then!] you will be my witnesses in Jerusalem and in all Judea and Samaria, and to the end of the earth."

Like Jesus, John the Baptist promised the baptism of the Holy Spirit to the church through the person of Jesus (Matt 3:11; Mark 1:8; Luke 3:16; John 1:33). That happened on Pentecost. As foretold in Joel 2 ("I will pour out my *Spirit*, and they shall *prophecy*," Acts 2:18; "the Holy Spirit, he has poured out," Acts 2:33),[5] the twelve "were all filled with the *Spirit* and [so then they] began to *speak* in other tongues *as the Spirit gave* them utterance" (Acts 2:4).

Spirit-Empowered Preaching in Acts

There are seven direct connections in Acts between the power of the Holy Spirit and preaching.[6]

---

5. "It was revealed to them that they were serving not themselves but you, in the things that have now been announced to you through those who *preached* the good news to you *by the Holy Spirit* sent from heaven, things into which angels long to look" (1 Pet 1:12).

6. To clarify, what I am doing here is equating the presence of the "Spirit" to "power" and then showing how the Spirit effectually empowers preaching throughout Acts. I justify this move because Luke links "power" and the "Spirit" in Luke 4:14 ("And Jesus returned in the power of the Spirit to Galilee"), but also because Paul links the two terms in his epistles. He uses the same phrase "the power of the Spirit" in Rom 15:19 in relation to the "power of signs and wonders" and the fulfillment of "the ministry of the gospel of Christ." He writes in Eph 3:7 of being "made a minister according to the gift of God's grace, which was given [him] by the working of [God's] power," power which comes "through his Spirit," as he clarifies the specific source in verse 16. Moreover, he writes in 1 Thess 1:5 that the gospel came to the church in Thessalonica "not only in word, but also in power and in the Holy Spirit and with full conviction."

The first direct connection between the Spirit and preaching is what occurred in Acts 2, covered above.

Second, in Acts 4, after Peter and John have been arrested and brought before Annas the high priest and other members of the high-priestly family, we read, "They inquired, 'By what *power* or by what name did you do this [heal a lame beggar]?' Then Peter *filled with the Spirit* [that's the power!], *said* to them" (vv. 7–8) and off he goes again with another sermon on Jesus—crucified and raised, and the only "name under heaven given among men by which we must be saved" (v. 12).

Third, in that same chapter, after Peter and John are released, the church in Jerusalem gathered and prayed, and after they prayed Luke records that "they were all *filled with the Holy Spirit* and continued to *speak the word of God* with boldness" (v. 31). Then he states, "And with *great power* the apostles were giving their *testimony* to the resurrection of the Lord Jesus" (v. 33). In Acts 5:32, after the apostles "have filled Jerusalem with [their] teaching" about Jesus, Luke uses these interesting lines about the mutual ministry between the apostles and the Spirit, "And we are *witnesses* to these things, and so is *the Holy Spirit*."

Fourth, when the church decides to add deacons to assist the apostles' ministry of "prayer and . . . the word" (Acts 6:4), they select "seven men of good repute, full of the Spirit and of wisdom" (6:3). Those men surely performed deaconate duties, but they also preached! Through them and others "the word of God continued to increase, and the number of disciples multiplied greatly in Jerusalem" (6:7). Stephen, who is described both at his selection and the end of his life as being "full of the Holy Spirit" (6:5; 7:55), is also portrayed as a powerful preacher ("But they could not withstand the wisdom and the *Spirit* with which he was *speaking*," 6:10). Philip is described in a similar manner. After the church was "scattered" due to persecution, they "went about preaching the word" (8:4), including Philip who "went down to the city of Samaria and proclaimed to them the Christ" (8:5).[7]

---

7. Another example is the Ethiopian eunuch (Acts 8:26–40). The narrative is bookended with God's guidance of Philip: at the start an angel directs him to "go toward the south to the road that goes down from Jerusalem to Gaza" (v. 26) so that he might encounter "an Ethiopian, a eunuch, a court official of Candace, queen of the Ethiopians" (v. 27); at the end, the Holy Spirit takes Philip directly to his next mission ("the Spirit of the Lord carried Philip away" and "Philip found himself at Azotus," vv. 39, 40). Before that miraculous trek, the Spirit commissions him to approach the eunuch ("the Spirit said to Philip, 'Go over and join this chariot,'" v. 29); and Philip, as God's appointed and sent guide, guides him from Isa 53 to "the good news about Jesus" (v. 35). The message is received, the man is "baptized," and "the eunuch . . . went on his way rejoicing" (vv. 36–39). See O'Donnell, "Him Who Calls."

Fifth, the power of the Spirit is prevalent in Paul's preaching ministry. For example, after he and Barnabas were "sent out by the *Holy Spirit*" (13:4), and when "they arrived at Salamis, they *proclaimed* the word of God" (13:5). Later when they encountered Elymas the magician, who sought to turn the proconsul (Sergius Paulus, a man who "sought to hear the word of God," 13:7) "away from the faith" (13:8), Paul rebuked him: "Paul, *filled with the Holy Spirit . . . said*" (13:9, 10a). Even in short sermons to wicked sorcerers the power of the Spirit is necessary! Paul also blinded Elymas ("behold, *the hand of the Lord* is upon you, and you will be blind and unable to see the sun for a time," 13:11) and that show of power, along with the power of preaching, led Sergius Paulus to faith. "Then the proconsul believed, when he saw what had occurred, for he was astonished at the *teaching* [not merely the miracle!] of the Lord" (13:12).

Another example of the Spirit's role in Paul's preaching ministry, perhaps the clearest example of the necessary connection between the two, is the Macedonian call, recorded in Acts 16:6-10, where "the Spirit of Jesus" (16:7) forbids Paul, Silas, and Timothy to speak in one region; then, blocks their attempt to take it to another; and finally, through a vision ("Come over to Macedonia and help us," 16:9), directs their paths elsewhere. "And when Paul had seen the vision, immediately we sought to go on into Macedonia, concluding that God had called us to preach the gospel to them" (16:10). When Paul and Timothy arrive in Philippi, "the leading city of the district of Macedonia" (16:12), Lydia—a woman from Asia (Thyatira)—becomes the first convert to Christ in Europe. Her conversion is described in the short sentence, "*The Lord opened* her heart to pay attention to what was *said* by Paul" (16:14).[8]

Sixth, the power of the Spirit is given to help God's preachers know what to say. We see that clearly throughout Acts where the apostles and deacons give impromptu sermons in a variety of situations. This promise was given by Jesus. He promised a "Helper" to help them speak. In the Upper Room Discourse, Jesus announces this three times:

> The Helper, the Holy Spirit, whom the Father will send in my name, *he will teach you* all things and bring to your remembrance all that I have said to you. (John 14:26)

---

8. This leading of the Spirit characterizes Paul's ministry. Paul "resolved in the Spirit" where to preach ("I must . . . see Rome," 19:21), and "the ministry" of the word "that [he] received from the Lord Jesus, to testify to the gospel of the grace of God" (20:24) was guided (e.g., "constrained by the Spirit," 20:22; "the Holy Spirit testifies to me in every city that imprisonment and afflictions await me," 20:23) and sustained ("the Lord stood by him and said, 'Take courage, for as you have testified to the facts about me in Jerusalem, so you must testify also in Rome,'" 23:11) by the Spirit.

> When the Helper comes, whom I will send to you from the Father, the Spirit of truth, who proceeds from the Father, *he will bear witness* about me. And *you also will bear witness*. (John 15:26–27)

> When the Spirit of truth comes, he will guide you into all the truth, for he will not speak on his own authority, but whatever he hears he will speak, and *he will declare to you* the things that are to come. He will glorify me, for *he will take what is mine and declare it to you*. (John 16:13–14)

Similar claims are recorded in the Synoptics:

> Behold, *I am sending you out* as sheep in the midst of wolves . . . When they deliver you over, do not be anxious how you are to speak or what you are to say, for what you are to say will be given to you in that hour. For it is not you who speak, but *the Spirit of your Father speaking through you*. (Matt 10:16, 19–20)

> *I will give you a mouth and wisdom*, which none of your adversaries will be able to withstand or contradict. (Luke 21:15)

> When they bring you to trial and deliver you over, do not be anxious beforehand what you are to say, but say whatever is given you in that hour, for *it is not you who speak, but the Holy Spirit*. (Mark 13:11)

While an emphasis is placed on the Spirit speaking through the preacher, all these passages point to the trinitarian work behind effective preaching. Jesus includes himself and his Father ("*I* will give you a mouth," Luke 21:15; "The Spirit *of your Father* speaking through you," Matt 10:20). We see the same patterns in the verses from John. We need our triune God's power to preach effectively!

The seventh connection between God's power and human preaching is the work of the Spirit on the hearers.[9] In Acts, the language of the baptism of the Holy Spirit is used when the Spirit comes upon the preacher, but it is also used when the Spirit comes upon the listener. The necessity of a Spirit-baptism is true for preacher and hearer alike. John uses the language of "born of the Spirit" (John 3:6; cf. 3:5), namely, that "the Spirit" would be received by "those who believed in" Jesus (7:39) after his death, resurrection, and ascension. "It is the Spirit," Jesus declares, "who gives life; the flesh is no help at all" (6:63).

Luke explicitly uses the language of Spirit-baptism to describe the same phenomena. Take, the conversion of Cornelius which Luke describes in Acts 10. As Peter was proclaiming the gospel, "the Holy Spirit fell on all who heard

---

9. "If there is going to be any lasting spiritual fruit in our preparing and preaching of biblical sermons, it will only come as a direct result of the Spirit's illumination of the human heart." Crotts, *Illuminated Preaching*, 8.

the word," or put differently, "the gift of the Holy Spirit was poured out even on the Gentiles" (Acts 10:44, 45). Then, as Peter retells the story in Acts 11 about how "the Gentiles also had received the word of God" (11:1), he reports,

> As I began to speak, the Holy Spirit fell on them just as on us at the beginning. And I remembered the word of the Lord, how he said, "John baptized with water, but you will be *baptized with the Holy Spirit.*" If then God gave the same gift to them as he gave to us when we believed in the Lord Jesus Christ, who was I that I could stand in God's way? When they heard these things they fell silent. And they glorified God, saying, "Then to the Gentiles also God has granted repentance that leads to life." (Acts 11:15–18)

Know and Ask

As those called by God to preach today, we must remember that we depend on the work of the Holy Spirit to effectively communicate the gospel. We can summarize what we must remember with the words *know* and *ask*.

First, we are to *know*, in the sense of acknowledge and appreciate, how God-dependent we are in our calling. Do we believe that we must abide in Christ and that "apart from" him we "can do nothing" (John 15:5)? Do we acknowledge that we were made ministers "according to the gift of God's grace, which was given [to us] by the working of his power" (Eph. 3:7), power that comes "through his Spirit" (Eph 3:16), and is "at work within us" (Eph 3:20)? Do we truly believe that God alone grants "repentance that leads to life" (Acts 11:18),[10] that he alone opens ears and hearts "to pay attention to" and receive the gospel (Acts 16:14)?

Second, we should *ask*. Like Jesus's first followers we should ask, "Lord, teach us to pray" (Luke 11:1), praying daily the prayer our Lord taught us to pray—that his name in our preaching would be hallowed, that his kingdom would soon rule over all the earth, that he would provide for our every physical and spiritual need (bread, the forgiveness of sins, the power to overcome the temptations of the evil one)—and we should ask directly for "God's best gift," the Holy Spirit,[11] he who is most necessary for our Christian walk and our Christian pulpit ministry, in confidence that God will indeed answer that prayer (see Luke 11:9–13).

---

10. Gaventa, *Acts of the Apostles*, 173, argues that the phrase "God has granted repentance that leads to life" (11:18) means that "God gives the Gentiles not simply the possibility of repentance, but repentance itself."

11. "God's best gift to those who pray is the Holy Spirit." Garland, *Luke*, 471.

We should also pray, "Lord, give me 'the power of the Holy Spirit'" (Rom 15:13; cf. 15:19). "Fill me, Spirit. Strengthen me. Renew me. Keep me. Empower me to preach." Why not pray the following lines from this classic Puritan prayer?

> O Lord God, I pray not so much for graces as for the Spirit himself, because I feel his absence, and act by my own spirit in everything. Give me not weak desires but the power of his presence, . . . Am I mistaken in feeling I am empty of the Spirit because I do not sense his presence within when all the time I am most empty and could be more full by faith in Christ? Was the fullness of the Spirit in the apostles chiefly a power, giving the subsistence outside themselves in Christ, in whom was their life and joy? Teach me to find and know fullness of the Spirit only in Jesus.[12]

3. Prayer: "Pray to the Lord of the Harvest"

Our praying for the Spirit leads us to the third point of this argument: namely, power and preaching are linked to prayer. One of the images George Herbert uses to describe prayer in his (aptly named) poem "Prayer" is "reversed thunder." Through prayer we fire up petitions to heaven like a thunderbolt.[13] In the Gospels and Acts it is clear that prayer is the surge behind the storm.

There is an interesting and important pattern to Jesus's preaching ministry: Jesus prays, then acts; or, said differently, he powers up before he works out. Jesus prayed before he selected the twelve (Luke 6:12–13), he prayed before his passion at Gethsemane (22:41), and he prayed simply to commune with his Father (Matt 14:23; Mark 6:46). Before setting out for his expanded preaching ministry throughout Galilee, he took time to pray (Mark 1:35–39).[14] This pattern of withdrawing to pray before ministry (whether preaching, healing, or defeating demonic forces) was, according to Luke 5:16, Jesus's holy habit.

The apostles, as recorded in Acts, follow this same pattern. After Peter and John are released, the church in Jerusalem gathered and prayed for strength to continue preaching the word with boldness (Acts 4:29). What happens next? "And when they had prayed, the place in which they were gathered together was shaken, and they were all *filled with the Holy Spirit* and continued

---

12. Adapted from Bennet, *Valley of Vision*, 52–53.
13. Herbert, "Prayer," in Ryken, *Soul in Paraphrase*, 88–89. For further explication on the poem, see Ryken, *Devotional Poetry*, 54–55.
14. Mark 1:15 records Jesus's first words, a summary of his preaching: "The time is fulfilled, and the kingdom of God is at hand; repent and believe in the gospel." However, Mark 1:14 tells us that Jesus didn't begin to preach until "after John was arrested."

to *speak the word of God* with boldness" (Acts 4:31). The church also prayed whenever they gathered (Acts 2:42), when needs arose (Acts 12:5, 12), and when commissioning people to preach (Acts 13:3; cf. Acts 6:6). They did this because they believed that prayer has "great power [ἰσχύει]" (Jas 5:16), and, as Paul phrased it, because they knew they bowed their "knees before the Father" and that he grants his children "to be strengthened with power [δυνάμει]" (Eph 3:14, 16).

Pray Always

This pattern in the Gospels and Acts is both descriptive and prescriptive. We should pray "always . . . and not lose heart" (Luke 18:1). And what do we pray for? We "pray that [we] may not enter into temptation" (Luke 22:40, 46). We pray for our forgiveness and others (Mark 11:25). We pray that we "may have strength" to endure trials (Luke 21:36). We pray for such things with confidence that we will be heard if we pray according to God's will (Mark 11:24; cf. John 16:23–24). We "pray" specifically and "earnestly for the Lord of the harvest to send out laborers into the harvest" (Luke 10:1–2). *And* we pray before we preach.

The longer I have been in ministry the more prayerful I have become before sermons and as I prepare sermons. (The irony of gospel ministry is the more experienced we become, the more we need God's help!) Let me share, and commend to you, four current practices.

The first is what I call *Spirit-filled Sitzfleisch*, or the "prayerful art of sermonizing." Here is my summary:

> *Sitzfleisch* is a German word comprised of the words *sitzen* (to sit) and *fleisch* (flesh). To preach God's Word well it takes "sitting flesh," that is, the ability to stay glued to a chair . . . in order to see what God's Word says. I add the adjective "Spirit-filled" before *Sitzfleisch* to emphasize that the art of observation of the holy canon requires the illumination of the Holy Spirit.[15]

Reflecting on that same theme elsewhere, I write,

> We are used to hearing the phrase "Spirit-filled preaching," which emphasizes the Spirit spontaneously assisting the preacher in the act of preaching. I take no issue with Spirit-filled preaching so long as it is properly defined and acted out. Let us "give room" for the Spirit in the pulpit. But let us also "give room" for the Spirit in the study. Why not ask the Spirit to give you the desire to sit and study?

---

15. O'Donnell, "Spirit-Filled *Sitzfleisch*," 208.

Why not ask the Spirit to open your eyes to see the text's truths, implications, and applications? Why not ask the Spirit to inspire you to study the text in community—with other pastors, interns, commentators? Why not ask the Spirit to broaden your mind with the reading of the best books of poetry, novels, and theology? Why not ask the Spirit to make you a pastor-scholar, someone who lives and works by the discipline of Spirit-filled *sitzfleisch*?[16]

My sermon preparation always begins with Spirit-filled *Sitzfleisch*. That is, I sit with the text opened on Monday morning so I might stand with it opened on Sunday morning.[17]

Second, beyond Spirit-filled *Sitzfleisch*, I rely heavily and prayerfully on God's providence. This relates mostly to illustrations, but it can also include exegesis. Regarding exegesis, I have my eyes and ears open to learning from others—through a seemingly random conversation with a friend, coworker, or my wife—about the text. Regarding illustrations, throughout the week I prayerfully believe, and so often come across, the perfect sermon illustrations. For example, my wife and I were watching episodes of some home makeover program, and when I came to preach on Eccl 2:1–11, which describes King Solomon's luxuries, overindulgences, and emptiness, I titled the sermon "The Hollow House of Hedonism" and walked the congregation through four rooms (that really needed some spiritual renovation), especially the treasury and bedroom. Even as I write this chapter, a DMin student I supervise from Westminster Theological Seminary in Philadelphia submitted a chapter which included a section on Charles Spurgeon's dependence on the Holy Spirit when he preached. Spurgeon, my student providentially reported, repeated this phrase each time he walked to the pulpit: "I believe in the Holy Spirit. I believe in the Holy Spirit. I believe in the Holy Spirit."

The third practice is to take my sermon manuscript the morning of the sermon, place my hands on each page, and pray through the sermon. I pray for big picture items, like "May this sermon edify and encourage your people," and I pray for little things, like "Help me pronounce this word correctly on the first try." I also have specific people in mind for certain sections. For example, I recently preached on Job's suicidal soliloquy (Job 3) and I prayed for those who were depressed, those who had lost a loved one to suicide, and that what I said would be exegetically and emotionally acceptable and helpful. Because I am a manuscript preacher, I often talk about "having the sermon in my head" so I

---

16. O'Donnell, "As One Approved," 9.

17. As Alyce McKenzie and Owen Lynch humorously put it, "The Holy Spirit is available for consultation at times other than Saturday night." McKenzie and Lynch, *Humor Us!*, 41.

can better communicate orally and visually ("Eyes up!"). I also aim to "have the sermon in my heart," as I hope to have a heart for those to whom I preach.

The fourth practice is to pray a prayer of illumination the moment before I preach. In a prayer of illumination, we ask the Holy Spirit to help us to faithfully (and powerfully!) explain, illustrate, and apply the Spirit-inspired Scriptures. George Herbert is an excellent example of this. He prayed,

> O, make your Word a swift Word,
> passing from the ear to the heart,
> from the heart to the lip and conversation;
> that, as the rain returns not empty,
> so neither may your Word,
> but accomplish that for which it is given. Amen.[18]

In similar fashion, John Stott prayed before each sermon,

> Heavenly Father, I bow in your presence. May your Word be my rule, your Spirit my teacher, and your greater glory my supreme concern, I ask through Jesus Christ my Lord. Amen.[19]

Finally, here is the 1889 prayer of Orrin Stone, the African-American preacher from Charleston, South Carolina, titled "A Prayer of Power." It begins,

> O Lord, give thy servant this Sunday morning the eye of an eagle that he may see sin from afar. Put his hands to the gospel pulpit; glue his ears to the gospel telephone and connect him with thy glory in the skies. . . . Fill him full of the dynamite of your awful power [and] set him on fire with the Spirit of your Holy Ghost.[20]

4. Christ Crucified: The Power of the Cross

Fourth, power and preaching are linked to preaching Christ crucified. What did Jesus preach? What did the apostles after him preach? What then should we preach? I will first summarize the content of their sermons in one sentence and will proceed to break that sentence down, explaining and applying it line by line.

The summary of what Jesus and the apostles preached (and therefore what we, too, should preach) is: *Christ crucified from the Hebrew Scriptures*. Since the focus here is on the cross, I will save the aspect of "crucified" till the end.

---

18. Quoted in Gibson, *Be Thou My Vision*, 189.

19. Adapted from the prayer that John Stott prayed before preaching, as noted in Bartholomew, *Excellent Preaching*, 68.

20. Quoted in Washington, *Conversations with God*, 34–35.

Christ Preached Christ

First, Christ preached Christ. I am not saying that he did not teach ethics. He certainly did. However, the center and culmination of his preaching was himself. The Sermon on the Mount is one place we can clearly see this.

We begin at the end. After the sermon, Matthew adds the crowds' response, namely, that they "were astonished at his teaching, for he was teaching them as one who had authority, and not as their scribes" (Matt 7:28–29). Not only did Jesus *not* cite various rabbis to support his claims and instructions ("You have heard that it was said. . . . But *I* say to you," Matt 5:21–22), he also made audaciously authoritative claims about himself. "Do not think," Jesus says, "that I have come to abolish the Law or the Prophets; I have not come to abolish them but to fulfill them" (Matt 5:17). In fact, he begins and ends his sermon with perhaps the highest marks of authority. He starts with the Beatitudes where he determines who qualifies to enter the kingdom of heaven, including this final beatitude: "Blessed are you when others revile you and persecute you and utter all kinds of evil against you falsely *on my account*. Rejoice and be glad, for your reward is great in heaven" (Matt 5:11–12a; cf. 24:9). And he concludes the sermon with a plethora of penetrating first-person personal pronouns:

> Not everyone who says to *me*, "Lord, Lord," will enter the kingdom of heaven, but the one who does the will of *my* Father who is in heaven. On that day many will say to *me*, "Lord, Lord, did we not prophesy in *your name*, and cast out demons in *your name*, and do many mighty works in *your name*?" And then will *I* declare to them, "*I* never knew you; depart from *me*, you workers of lawlessness." Everyone then who hears these words of *mine* and does them will be like a wise man who built his house on the rock. And the rain fell, and the floods came, and the winds blew and beat on that house, but it did not fall, because it had been founded on the rock. And everyone who hears these words of *mine* and does not do them will be like a foolish man who built his house on the sand. And the rain fell, and the floods came, and the winds blew and beat against that house, and it fell, and great was the fall of it. (Matt 7:21–27)

End of sermon. Christ preached Christ. (And with some authority!)

PART ONE: THE CENTRALITY OF THE PULPIT

Christ Preached from the Hebrew Scriptures

Second, Christ preached Christ from the Hebrew Scriptures. We see this clearly in two of his sermons in Luke. In Luke 4, after he overcame Satan's temptations by the sword and shield of the Spirit-inspired Scriptures, "Jesus returned in the power of the Spirit to Galilee" and he went throughout the region teaching "in their synagogues" (Luke 4:14–15). What did he preach? His sermon in Nazareth gives us a glimpse. Luke begins, "And as was his custom, he went to the synagogue on the Sabbath day, and he stood up to read" (Luke 4:16). Then, after the scroll of Isaiah was handed to him, he opened it, read Isa 61:1–2, adding a phrase from Isa 58:6 ("to set at liberty those who are oppressed"), and proceeded with some shock and awe: "Today," he claimed, "this Scripture has been fulfilled in your hearing" (Luke 4:21). He preached Christ (himself) from the Hebrew Scriptures. He put himself at the center of the promises of God's written revelation. And his sermon, like some of ours, did not go over so well. His hometown reception waned. They wanted to throw him off a cliff.

The same thing happens in a more informal setting at the end of Luke. After rising from the dead, Jesus came upon two of his doubting disciples on the road to Emmaus incident. Hearing their sorrowful report, he responded, "Was it not necessary that the Christ should suffer these things and enter into his glory?" (Luke 24:26). He proceeded to give the world's greatest, and perhaps longest, lesson on biblical theology: "And beginning with Moses and all the Prophets, he interpreted to them in all the Scriptures the things concerning *himself*" (Luke 24:27). Later he opened the minds of the rest of his disciples "to understand the Scriptures," showing them that it was written "that the Christ should suffer and on the third day rise from the dead, and that repentance for the forgiveness of sins should be proclaimed in his name to all nations" (Luke 24:46–47a).

What Jesus taught in Luke is precisely how the apostles explained the gospel. In almost every sermon in Acts, the apostles preach Christ from the Hebrew Scriptures. For example, when Paul and Silas entered Thessalonica, they entered the synagogue and "on three Sabbath days [Paul] reasoned with them from the Scriptures, explaining and proving that it was necessary for the Christ to suffer and to rise from the dead, and saying, 'This Jesus, whom I proclaim to you, is the Christ'" (Acts 17:2–3). Paul's great summaries of the gospel in Rom 1:1–7 and 1 Cor 15:1–7 (Christ died, was buried, and "was raised on the third day *in accordance with the Scriptures*," v. 4) emphasize the same connection between Christ and the Scriptures.

It is a sad irony that too many attend Bible churches (a church that has "Bible" in the name) and receive no Bible on a Sunday morning—no songs from the Bible, no readings from the Bible, no sermon from the Bible, and no benediction from the Bible. But if there is no Bible, there will be no power of the Spirit. We must know and believe that there is a connection between the gospel and preaching Christ from the Old Testament and between "the power of God" and "the Scriptures" (Matt 22:29). And we should repent if we are not tapping into this power every time we gather to worship!

Christ Crucified

So, to return to my definition of the content of what Jesus preached, we conclude with my reflections of the one word we haven't covered: Christ preached Christ *crucified* from the Hebrew Scriptures.

I am aware that Jesus gave a number of commands and spoke on a number of topics. I am also aware that when the apostles preached the gospel in Acts they included "the lordship of Jesus; the ministry of John the Baptist; the life of Jesus in Galilee; his power, miracles, healings, and exorcisms; the death of Jesus by crucifixion; his resurrection; his appearances to the believers in full bodily form after his death; the command to preach forgiveness of sins through faith in Christ; and the assertion that the Old Testament prophecies pointed to all these things." Or, more simply, "God's offer of salvation; the life, death, and resurrection of Jesus; and the call to faith in light of coming judgment."[21] However, I offer four reasons for the preaching of the centrality of the cross.

First, all four Gospels move toward the cross as the literary climax and emphasize the cross as the theological center. For example, John the Baptist's first words about Jesus in the Gospel of John are "Behold, the Lamb of God [the sacrificed Passover Lamb], who takes away the sin of the world!" (John 1:29, cf. 1:36). Jesus repeatedly summarizes his mission by centering on the cross: "I lay down my life for the sheep" (John 10:15; cf. John 10:11, 17–18); "as Moses lifted up the serpent in the wilderness, so must the Son of Man be lifted up, that whoever believes in him may have eternal life" (John 3:14–15); "Now is my soul troubled. And what shall I say? 'Father, save me from this hour'? But for this purpose I have come to this hour" (John 12:27; cf. John 17:1); "For even the Son of Man came not to be served but to serve, and to give his life as a ransom for many" (Mark 10:45).

Second, in Jesus's passion predictions his sufferings are central ("the Son of Man will be delivered up to be crucified," Matt 26:2). Furthermore, his death is featured in his resurrection appearances: "you seek Jesus who was crucified"

---

21. O'Donnell, *Daily Liturgical Devotional*. See Acts 2:14–36; 3:17–26; 4:8–12; 5:29–32; 7:2–53; 10:34–43; 13:16–41.

(Matt 28:5; Mark 16:6), not Jesus who has been raised. The same emphasis of "the cross" at "the centre of our system"[22] is found in many of the sermons on Acts,[23] most pointedly in Philip's sermon on Isa 53 to the Ethiopian eunuch in Acts 8:32–35.

Third, the sacrament of the Lord's Supper that Jesus established centers on his crucifixion. At the Jewish Passover, Jesus connects the Passover to his coming sufferings. "I have earnestly desired to eat this Passover with you," he says, "before I suffer" (Luke 22:15). The meal points to his death on the cross—the sacrifice of his body in the breaking of bread and the shedding of his blood in the cup of the new covenant. This event is what the new covenant community is to repeatedly celebrate in remembrance of him (Luke 22:19b; cf. 1 Cor 11:24–25). In Matthew no lamb is named,[24] perhaps to emphasize what Paul would write in 1 Cor 5:7, "For Christ, our Passover lamb, has been sacrificed" (cf. 1 Pet 1:19) and later in 1 Cor 11:26, "For as often as you eat this bread and drink the cup, you proclaim the Lord's death until he comes." We proclaim his death! What a strange, but beautiful, proclamation. And throughout eternity we will feast at "the marriage supper of the Lamb" (Rev 19:9).[25]

Fourth, the evangelists emphasize the theological centrality of the cross not only through Jesus's statements but also through the rich theology depicted in their passion narratives.[26] Regarding the rich theology depicted in the passion narratives, Matthew's unique crucifixion account especially relates to the theme of power.[27] Matthew does not explain to us in propositional language his doctrine of the atonement. He does not write, as Paul does, "Christ died for our sins" (1 Cor 15:3), or as John does, "He is the propitiation for our sins" (1 John 2:2a). Rather, Matthew *shows us* his "crucifixion theology" through Jesus's last two cries from the cross—"My God, my God, why have you forsaken me?'" (Matt 27:46); "And Jesus cried out again with a loud voice and yielded up his spirit" (Matt 27:50)—and God's supernatural signs before and after Jesus's death.

---

22. Charles Spurgeon, quoted in Tidball, *Message of the Cross*, 22.

23. See Acts 2:23, 35; 3:13–15, 18; 5:30–31; 7:52; 10:39–40, 47; 13:27–31; 26:23.

24. Compare Exod 12:1–28 where it is mentioned six times.

25. Jesus is labeled "Lamb" twenty-nine times in Revelation, and the specific details of his death are occasionally attached to the title ("the Lamb who was slain," Rev 5:12; 13:8; cf. 5:6; believers are "made . . . white in the blood of the Lamb," Rev 7:14; and the saints "conquer [Satan] by the blood of the Lamb," Rev 12:11).

26. I could add Paul's summary of his message in 1 Cor 2:1: "For I decided to know nothing among you except Jesus Christ and him crucified." A few verses earlier he also writes, "We preach Christ crucified . . . the power of God" (1 Cor 1:23–24).

27. Some of this section is adapted from O'Donnell, *Matthew*, chap. 86.

After Jesus gives up "the spirit," the Spirit of God gets to work on the world. Heaven showers down its signs of vindication and victory. The justification of God outshouts the voice of scorn and confusion. The Father has not abandoned his righteous suffering Son, and he throws an earth-shaking, tomb-breaking, curtain-tearing ceremony to celebrate!

> *And*[28] behold, *the curtain of the temple was torn in two, from top to bottom. And the earth shook, and the rocks were split. And the tombs were opened. And many bodies of the saints who had fallen asleep were raised, and coming out of the tombs after his resurrection they went into the holy city and appeared to many.* (Matt 27:51–53)

The first post-crucifixion supernatural sign is the rending of the temple's veil, an event that teaches, as Dale Brunner puts it, "two truths about the temple: (1) judgment ('it is all over!') and (2) salvation ('it is all open!')."[29]

The second supernatural sign is the earthquake. God gives us an eye-opening earthly *inclusio* right before and after Jesus's death. Before Jesus dies the earth turns black. After Jesus dies the earth shakes. The earth is telling earthlings that something *seismic* is happening. The sun hides its face and the earth shakes its feet to teach us to see and hear that a new earthly era has dawned in the death of Christ.

The crescendo of the cataclysmic signs, however, is not the ground shaking or rocks breaking. Rather, it is the tombs opening and real resurrected human beings (not disembodied souls!) walking about Jerusalem. This is the third supernatural sign.[30]

The final sign is the climax, and that climax continues into verse 53: "*And* coming out of the tombs after his resurrection they went into the holy city and appeared to many." Note that the actual event happens after Jesus's resurrection, not after his death. Yet Matthew places it here to open our eyes to the *resurrection power* of Jesus's death. Matthew's post-crucifixion scene is more spectacular than Ezekiel's rising and marching bones. The holy ones in the holy city after the holiest event in the whole of history is wholly awesome! Matthew believes in the resurrection of the body and he cannot even wait till Easter to tell us about it. So, "not only is Jesus' death strong enough to split the veil of the Holy of Holies and so cancel *sin*; it is also strong enough to open tombs and so cancel *death*. Sin and death are humanity's two greatest

---

28. "The series of καὶ conjunctions closely connects the events of verses 51–53 with Jesus's death." Quarles, *Matthew*, 342.
29. Bruner, *Churchbook, Matthew*, 757.
30. Davies and Allison, *Critical and Exegetical Commentary*, 3:628.

problems, and Jesus' death conquers both."[31] After all Jesus's sufferings—physical (the scourging, the crown of thorns, the weight of his own body on the cross, the thirst, the loss of blood), mental (the mockeries and desertion of his followers), and spiritual (the felt "desertion" of the Father)—Jesus dies victorious. Christ conquers the world (the darkness and the earthquake). Christ conquers sin (the torn veil). Christ conquers death (the resurrected bodies). That is the power of the cross of Christ to Matthew, and that is to be the power of the cross of Christ to us.

In Rom 1:16, Paul writes, "For I am not ashamed of the gospel, for it is the power [δύναμις] of God for salvation to everyone who believes." In 1 Cor 1:24 he calls the preaching of the cross of Christ "the power [δύναμιν] of God." Do we believe that? You can go into a Bible church and never hear a Bible reading; you can go to an evangelical church with a cross at center stage and atop the steeple and never hear a sermon on the cross of Christ. But that is where the power is! Woe to us if we do not preach Christ and him crucified.

Conclusion

"Where, according to Jesus, does the power for effective preaching come from?" That is the foundational question I set out to answer. I arrived at my answer to that question by asking another question: "Where in the Gospels and Acts is the language of power, especially the word δύναμις (along with an eye on ἐξουσία) used in relation to preaching?" The language of power is found often in relationship to effective preaching in four ways: first, power and preaching are linked to God's commissioning people to preach; second, power and preaching are linked to the work of the Holy Spirit; third, power and preaching are linked to prayer; and fourth, power and preaching are linked to the preaching of Christ crucified. If our preaching is to be more effective, we must tap into these four sources of power—for the good of the church and the glory of God.

Bibliography

Bartholomew, Craig. *Excellent Preaching: Proclaiming the Gospels in Its Context and Ours.* Bellingham, WA: Lexham, 2015.

Bennet, Arthur, ed. *The Valley of Vision: A Collection of Puritan Prayers and Devotions.* Edinburgh: Banner of Truth Trust, 2006.

Bruner, Frederick Dale. *The Churchbook, Matthew 13–28.* Vol. 2 of *Matthew: A Commentary.* Rev. and expanded ed. Grand Rapids: Eerdmans, 2007.

---

31. Bruner, *Churchbook, Matthew*, 760.

Crotts, Jeffrey. *Illuminated Preaching: The Holy Spirit's Vital Role in Unveiling His Word, the Bible*. Leominster, UK: Day One, 2010.

Davies, W. D., and Dale C. Allison Jr. *A Critical and Exegetical Commentary on the Gospel According to Saint Matthew*. International Critical Commentary. Edinburgh: T&T Clark, 1991.

Evans, C. F. *Saint Luke*. TPI New Testament Commentaries. London: SCM, 1990.

Fitzmyer, Joseph A. *The Gospel According to Luke I–IX: A New Translation with Introduction and Commentary*. Anchor Bible 25. New York: Doubleday, 1970.

Garland, David E. *Luke*. Zondervan Exegetical Commentary on the New Testament. Grand Rapids: Zondervan, 2011.

Gaventa, B. R. *Acts of the Apostles*. Abingdon New Testament Commentaries. Nashville: Abingdon, 2003.

Gibson, Jonathan. *Be Thou My Vision: A Liturgy for Daily Worship*. Wheaton, IL: Crossway, 2021.

Köstenberger, Andreas. *A Theology of John's Gospel and Letters: The Word, the Christ, the Son of God*. Grand Rapids: Zondervan, 2009.

McKenzie, Alyce M., and Owen Hanley Lynch. *Humor Us! Preaching and the Power of the Comic Spirit*. Louisville: Westminster John Knox, 2023.

Nolland, John. *Luke 1–9:20*, Word Biblical Commentary 35A. Nashville: Nelson, 2000.

O'Donnell, Douglas Sean. "As One Approved: Passing the Preacher's Test." In *Interpretation and Application*, edited by Craig Brian Larson, 3–14. Peabody, MA: Hendrickson, 2012.

———. *Daily Liturgical Devotional: 40 Days of Worship and Prayer*. Wheaton, IL: Crossway, 2024.

———. "Him Who Calls: Efficacious Grace in the Synoptic Gospels and Acts." In *Thine Eye Diffused a Quickening Ray: Efficacious Grace in Historical, Biblical, Theological, and Pastoral Perspective*, edited by Jonathan Gibson and David Gibson. Wheaton, IL: Crossway, forthcoming.

———. *Matthew: All Authority in Heaven and on Earth*. Preaching the Word. Edited by R. Kent Hughes. Wheaton, IL: Crossway, 2013.

———. "Spirit-Filled *Sitzfleisch*: The Prayerful Art of Sermonizing." In *Unashamed Workmen: How Expositors Prepare and Preach*, edited by Rhett Dodson, 207–15. Fearn Ross-Shire: Christian Focus, 2014.

Quarles, Charles L. *Matthew*. B&H Exegetical Guide to the Greek New Testament. Nashville: B&H Academic, 2017.

Ryken, Leland. *The Devotional Poetry of Donne, Herbert, and Milton*. Christian Guides to the Classics. Wheaton, IL: Crossway, 2014.

———. *The Soul in Paraphrase: A Treasury of Classical Devotional Poems*. Wheaton, IL: Crossway, 2018.

Tidball, Derek. *The Message of the Cross*. The Bible Speaks Today. Downers Grove, IL: InterVarsity, 2001.

Washington, James Melvin, ed. *Conversations with God: Two Centuries of Prayers by African Americans*. New York: HarperCollins, 1994.

4

The Ministry Is the Message

Union with Christ as a Theology for Gospel Proclamation

Philip Ryken

Introduction

Whether fairly or not, seminary offerings in practical theology have been criticized for not being especially practical. But there are also reasons to have the opposite concern, namely, that such coursework is insufficiently theological—that it fails to delineate from Scripture the doctrinal dimensions of gospel ministry. Although Thomas Oden tried to rectify this problem in the 1980s, he also lamented that "no systematic, scripturally grounded pastoral theology" had been "written for an English-speaking ecumenical audience" in the twentieth century.[1] Although the situation has improved somewhat in recent decades, there remains a need to think more deeply about pastoral theology, especially when it comes to preaching.

The Co-Inherence of Christian Doctrine

It is hard to think of very many important doctrines that do not have fairly direct bearing on the proclamation of the gospel. Maybe this is because of the

---

1. Oden, *Pastoral Theology*, 9.

interconnections between biblical doctrines—what we might call the co-inherence of Christian theology, in which everything relates to everything else.

By way of analogy, think of doctrine as a massive, transparent diamond. It has many facets, of course, casting many illuminating rays of light. But the analogy becomes more penetrating if by seeing through any particular facet of Christian theology we may gain perspective into all the other facets. Any one doctrine has interior connections with all the other doctrines. Light illuminates light in multivalent splendor within the diamond of doctrine. Perhaps there are exceptions to this claim. But could it be that the unity and beauty of Christian thought is the way everything connects to everything everywhere all at once, whether directly or more distantly?

If this claim is correct, then every cardinal doctrine of the Christian faith has some relevance for a theology of preaching. Several of these theological connections are explained elsewhere in this volume. Connect gospel proclamation to the Trinity, as Kevin Vanhoozer has done, and "the preacher's role in the triune economy of communication" becomes evident. The purpose of the Father is for the good news of the Son to be declared in the power of the Holy Spirit. Or consider the incarnation. What are the implications of the unity of divinity and humanity in the incarnate Word for understanding what it means for mere human beings to bear a divine message? Perhaps it is mysteriously essential in every sermon for the congregation to be aware of the preacher's human limitations so that the sermon's efficacy is recognizably divine.

Or, to take another example, look more closely through the lens of the threefold office of Christ—his divine anointing as prophet, priest, and king—to see how this biblical-theological structure illuminates our homiletical theology, in which the preacher carries out regal, prophetical, and sacerdotal functions. The preaching of the word of God is a royal proclamation of the kingdom of God, a prophetic declaration of the once and coming Messiah, and a priestly ministration of divine consolation.

Next, connect preaching to the multi-faceted doctrine of God. View it as a manifestation of his mercy, a display of his power, a gift of his goodness, and so on. Follow Ahmi Lee and see preaching as a labor of self-giving love, like the minister in one of Marilynne Robinson's novels, who stood in the pulpit "straight and strong, parsing the broken heart of humankind and praising the loving heart of Christ."[2] The point here is not simply that these divine attributes are important to include in the gospel message; rather, preaching itself *is* a living enactment of the divine character—God's mercy, power, righteousness, and love.

---

2. Robinson, *Home*, 50.

Or what about beauty, which sometimes gets slighted or neglected in the doctrine of God? Consider the proclamation of the gospel as a display of the beauty of the Savior and of salvation in him—what Hans Urs von Balthasar calls "a beauty crowned with thorns and crucified."[3] If Isaiah considered even the feet of those who proclaim good news to be beautiful, then what magnificent splendors might be beheld in their saving message? And what happens when preaching gets connected more closely to aesthetical theology?

Then, finally, theologize about preaching according to its internal connections with the *ordo salutis*. Think of preaching as calling to salvation in Christ, as means of regeneration, as declaration of justifying righteousness, as instrument of sanctifying holiness, as revelation of future glorification in the coming kingdom of God (as Nicole Massie Martin has done). Think of preaching *as* certification of the adoption by which believers become the children of God—whether as young scoundrels or self-righteous older siblings, to use the categories of Jesus's parable about the two lost sons in Luke 15.

Turn the gemstone of Christian thought this way and that—looking through the facet of preaching—and see endless possibilities, inviting further doctrinal exploration into the multiple dimensions of homiletical theology. Perhaps this book can point us toward a grander project, in which we view preaching theologically from the vantage point of *every* locus in Christian theology. Some of these *loci* are closely tied to gospel proclamation, while others may appear more distant, but all bear some relation to a proper doctrine of preaching and thus have their place in a fully biblical homiletical theology.

Here is another closely related and thrilling thought: if every doctrine has a place in homiletical theology, then any sermon on any passage can be something even more than an opportunity to proclaim Jesus Christ freshly. Any sermon on any passage can also afford unique ways to understand preaching itself. Preachers study the text to see who God is, how Jesus saves, who God's people are called to become, and *what preaching is*, as the Holy Spirit empowers a sermon to enact the truths that it proclaims. Here, then, is another question to ask about every gospel message: what do the doctrines in this text mean for what the Spirit does when we preach them?

Union with Christ in Biblical Theology

As a test case, this chapter uses a homiletical oculus to take a closer look into and through the doctrine of union with Christ. Consider the believer's personal and ministerial union with the crucified, risen Christ, according to

---

3. Balthasar, quoted in Schneider, "Why Does Creation Groan?," 44.

which his crucifixion and resurrection serve as the *method for* as well as the *message in* the proclamation of the gospel. Stated another way, the ministry is also the message.

Simply put, the doctrine of union with Christ teaches that when we trust in Jesus, the Holy Spirit so closely unites us to Christ's death and resurrection that everything that is his becomes ours. This doctrine can and should be central to a theology of preaching with its starting and ending point in Paul's holy ambition to "know [Christ] and the power of his resurrection, and [to] share his sufferings, becoming like him in his death, that by any means possible I may attain the resurrection from the dead" (Phil 3:10–11 ESV). Stated more simply, like everything else in gospel ministry, preaching is dying and rising with Jesus.[4]

Given the consistent priority that the New Testament places on being "in Christ"—the phrase appears more than one hundred and sixty times, especially in the writings of Paul (e.g., Eph 1:3; Phil 3:9; 2 Cor 5:17)—the doctrine of union with Christ properly occupies a primary place in systematic theology. To give perhaps the most notable example, union with Christ serves as one of the organizing principles for Calvin's *Institutes*. "We must understand," wrote the Geneva Reformer, "that as long as Christ remains outside of us, and we are separated from him, all that he has suffered and done for the salvation of the human race remains useless and of no value for us. . . . All that he possesses is nothing to us until we grow into one body with him."[5] Earlier, Calvin had beautifully explained the implications of our union with Christ.

> We see that our whole salvation and all its parts are comprehended in Christ (Acts 4:12). . . . If we seek salvation, we are taught by the very name of Jesus that it is "of him" (1 Cor 1:13). If we seek any other gifts of the Spirit, they will be found in his anointing. If we seek strength, it lies in his dominion; if purity, in his conception; if gentleness, it appears in his birth. . . . If we seek redemption, it lies in his passion; if acquittal, in his condemnation; if remission of the curse, in his cross (Gal 3:13); if satisfaction, in his sacrifice; if purification, in his blood; if reconciliation, in his descent into hell; if mortification of the flesh, in his tomb; if newness of life, in his resurrection; if immortality, in the same; if inheritance of the Heavenly Kingdom, in his entrance into heaven; if protection, if security, if abundant supply of all blessings, in his Kingdom; if untroubled expectation of judgment, in the power given to him to

---

4. The following material is adapted (with both omissions and expansions) from chapters I contributed to *The Practical Calvinist* (edited by Peter Lillback) and *Theology for Ministry* (edited by William R. Edwards, et al.).

5. Calvin, *Institutes*, 3.1.3.

judge. In short, since rich store of every kind of good abounds in him, let us drink our fill from this fountain and from no other.[6]

At every point, Calvin connects the believer to Christ in ways that position every Christian's spiritual journey in the context of the wider narrative of redemption. Sinclair Ferguson stands in the same theological and pastoral tradition when he writes,

> If we are united to Christ, then we are united to him at all points of his activity on our behalf. We share in his death (we were baptized into his death), in his resurrection (we are resurrected with Christ), in his ascension (we have been raised with him), in his heavenly session (we sit with him in heavenly places, so that our life is hidden with Christ in God), and we will share in his promised return (when Christ, who is our life, appears, we also will appear with him in glory).... Rather than view Christians first and foremost in the microcosmic context of their own progress, the Reformed doctrine first of all sets them in the macrocosm of God's activity in redemptive history.[7]

THE SUFFERING AND THE GLORY

When Calvin and later Reformational theologians described the work of Christ, they often made a distinction between humiliation and exaltation.

Humiliation is the work of Christ in suffering and dying for sin. It includes everything that Christ endured in his earthly travails, starting from the moment he came into this world. The Son of God left behind the glories of heaven. He became a human being, was born in a stable, and endured all kinds of indignities at the hands of fallen humanity. Then at the end of it all he died the godforsaken death of the cross.

Exaltation is the work of Christ in conquering sin and death through his resurrection and ascension. After the cross came the crown. God raised Jesus from the dead, lifted him up to heaven, and exalted him to the highest place, where he gave him the name above every name.

These two aspects of Christ's work are both clearly in view in Phil 2 and 3, as they are in Rom 5 and 6 and Col 2 and 3. To know Christ is to share in his crucifixion/humiliation and resurrection/exaltation. In Phil 2, the apostle traces the trajectory of the grand parabola of redemption that swept from equality with God down to the obedience of the cross, then back up to the

---

6. Calvin, *Institutes*, 2.16.19.
7. Ferguson, "Reformed View," 58–59.

highest place in the cosmos. In chapter 3, as Paul contemplates what Christ had done, he seems to say, "Now *that's* the Jesus that I want to know: the crucified and risen Christ, who went from glory to glory by way of Calvary."

In one sense, this is a surprising declaration, for if anyone knew Christ already, it had to be Paul of Tarsus. The man had known Christ for decades, ever since he met him on the road to Damascus (Acts 9). In fact, he had just testified to the "surpassing worth of knowing Christ Jesus my Lord" (Phil 3:8). But knowing Christ only made Paul want to know him all the more. So he declared, emphatically, "I want to know Christ."

This is usually taken as a general comment on the Christian life. But what the apostle says about being conformed to the cross and the empty tomb should also be considered from the specific vantage point of gospel ministry. It was in his preaching—more than anywhere else—that Paul prayed for God to satisfy his desire to be humiliated and exalted with Christ.

Union with Christ in suffering and glory became Paul's primary paradigm for pastoral theology. His message was also his methodology. Whenever the apostle speaks about his sufferings as a preacher, invariably he puts them in the context of Christ's resurrection glory. And whenever he preaches the Christ of the empty tomb, he proclaims the crucifixion in the context of his own ministerial sacrifice. Paul really was "*always* carrying in the body the death of Jesus" (2 Cor 4:10; cf. 1 Cor 15:31).[8] We see his paradigm in the simple exhortation he gave Timothy: "Remember Jesus Christ, risen from the dead, the offspring of David, as preached in my gospel, for which I am suffering" (2 Tim 2:8–9). Paul was preaching what he practiced. Pastors do not simply proclaim the gospel; they live it.

Becoming Like Jesus in His Death

Following the pattern of Christ's own ministry, in which the cross came before the crown, means beginning with suffering. Preaching is not a matter of life and death, but a matter of death, then life: "We suffer with him in order that we may also be glorified with him" (Rom 8:17; cf. 1 Pet 4:13). Gospel ministry is cruciform. As Stu Weber has written, "The pastor who is most Christlike is not the one who is most gloriously fulfilled in every moment of ministry, but the one whose ministry has in it unbelievable elements of crucifixion."[9]

The biblical history of gospel proclamation is primarily a story of suffering. Few if any biblical preachers were successful by any worldly standard, and

---

8. All of the emphases in the Scripture quotations in this essay are mine.
9. Goetz, "Tour of Duty," 30.

for every success there seem to be dozens of failures. For every preacher who turned the nation back to God, many others were mocked and persecuted, some so severely that they were tempted to leave the ministry or even to despair of life itself. God said, "I will send them prophets and apostles, some of whom they will kill and persecute" (Luke 11:49). Readers of this verse look in vain for a third category, but there are only two: the persecuted and the dead.

Consider the Old Testament prophets whose call narratives make for such inspiring reading. Sadly, what most of them were called to do was to suffer. Samuel heard God's voice in the night, yet the message he received made his ears tingle with fear: judgment on Eli, his father in the faith (1 Sam 3:11–14). Jeremiah was assured that God would always be with him, but at the same time he was informed that the entire nation—the people, the priests, and the politicians—would fight against him (Jer 1:17–19). The story of Isaiah's call is the most inspiring of all, with its thrilling response, "Here am I! Send me" (Isa 6:8). But what was Isaiah sent to do? God said, "Go, and say to this people: 'Keep on hearing, but do not understand; keep on seeing, but do not perceive.' Make the heart of this people dull, and their ears heavy, and blind their eyes; lest they see with their eyes, and hear with their ears, and understand with their hearts, and turn and be healed" (Isa 6:9–10). From the outset, Isaiah's preaching ministry was doomed to fail, for its purpose was not to help people come to faith but to confirm their unbelief.

Most prophets faced rebellion from the people of God. People grumbled about Moses's leadership style from the beginning of his ministry. By the time he was ready to lead them to the promised land, they refused to go! Other prophets suffered persecution, like Elijah, who in many ways was the most successful prophet in the Old Testament. Elijah called fire down from heaven and destroyed the prophets of Baal (1 Kgs 18:38–40). But the next day he was so afraid that he ran for his life. His discouragement led to such dark depression that he begged God to take his life (1 Kgs 19:3–4). Or consider Jeremiah. The "Weeping Prophet" was tormented by false prophets (Jer 14:14), mocked, beaten, imprisoned, and left to die (Jer 20:1–20; 38:6). When Jeremiah interceded for God's people, his prayers went unanswered (Jer 15:1). At the end of his life, he saw the city he loved destroyed, while the people he loved suffered and died in the streets (Jer 14:17–18; Lam 1–5). Little wonder that he cursed the day that he was born (Jer 20:14–18).

Even this brief survey shows how thoroughly the Old Testament prophets anticipated the agonies of the Christ. This explains why Jesus could prove the necessity of his humiliation from what they suffered. "Was it not necessary that the Christ should suffer these things and enter his glory?" he asked his disciples. "And beginning with Moses and all the Prophets, he interpreted to them in all the Scriptures the things concerning himself" (Luke 24:26-27; cf. 1 Pet 1:11).

On various occasions Jesus was accused of insanity, illegitimacy, and blasphemy. He was unlawfully arrested, unfairly accused, unjustly convicted, and unmercifully beaten. But he endured his greatest sufferings on the cross, where he died a Godforsaken death. Thus, his crucifixion became the apotheosis of the humiliation suffered by his prophets (see Luke 11:47-51; Acts 7:52-53).

Remarkably, at the time of his death Jesus had virtually nothing to show for his preaching ministry. At the end he had only eleven disciples, and even they abandoned him. His public ministry, therefore, turned out to be no more successful than Isaiah's. People were forever hearing Jesus, but never understanding him; forever seeing his miracles, but not perceiving his message (Matt 13:13-15; cf. Isa 6:9-10). Jesus suffered greatly for this. We find the lament of this Suffering Servant previously recorded in the book of Isaiah: "[God] said to me, 'You are my servant, Israel, in whom I will be glorified.' But I said, 'I have labored in vain; I have spent my strength for nothing and vanity'" (Isa 49:3-4). At the time of his death, the preaching ministry of Jesus Christ could hardly be judged anything except a failure. The main thing it accomplished was getting him killed!

And what of Christ's followers? What happened to them? According to the best historical records, nearly every one of his original disciples died a violent death. The first martyr was Stephen, who preached only one great sermon before being stoned (Acts 7). These gospel preachers suffered all these things because they were united to Jesus Christ in his sufferings and death.

The one who endured the most excruciating torment was Paul. When the apostle first came to Christ, God showed him how much he would suffer for the sake of the gospel (Acts 9:16). And suffer he did. Paul faced trouble, hardship, and distress. He was frequently imprisoned and often on the run—in danger by land and by sea. He was whipped, beaten, stoned, and left for dead (2 Cor 6:4-10; 11:23-27). "To the present hour we hunger and thirst," he wrote, "we are poorly dressed and buffeted and homeless.... We have become and are still, like the scum of the world, the refuse of all things" (1 Cor 4:11, 13).

What this means is that Paul's prayers were answered! He did indeed become like Christ in his death—specifically, in the context of his proclamation of the gospel.

PART ONE: THE CENTRALITY OF THE PULPIT

Sharing in Christ's Sufferings

What contribution does this litany of misery make to homiletical theology? Daniel A. Payne—America's first African American college president—wrote,

> To set aside figures and speak plainly, the ministers of Christ should ever have their souls filled with the love of their Master, so that like Him they may endure hunger and thirst, poverty and toils, reproaches and insults, persecution and death. In a word, they must have that love and that degree of it that never shrinks from the cross, giving to their souls the endurance of the ox, the meekness of the lamb, the courage of the lion, the innocence of the dove, the swiftness of the eagle, and the omnipotence of Him whose victory was greatest when He suffered most![10]

Bishop Payne was not exaggerating, but properly insisting that any authentic theology of preaching must be adequate to face the extreme hardship that many ministers still suffer today in many parts of the world. Pastor Corey Jackson from Trinity Park Church in Cary, North Carolina, recently set things in proper global perspective when he said,

> I've learned that when I suffer as a pastor, it is both normal and essential. Chinese pastors are not surprised by suffering. When they signed up for ministry, they signed up to suffer. I didn't do that! I signed up for seminary because I love to study theology, I wanted to use my gifts, I felt a sense of calling to the ministry, and maybe I'd have some fun, too. . . . There are a lot of reasons. But I did not necessarily wed my call to the ministry to a call to suffering. But the last two and a half years have shown me that the call to suffer is not just a call to the global church or the international missionary. It's a call for every pastor. My Chinese brothers and sisters are teaching me that suffering is not something to be afraid of, but rather it is something that is essential for the growth of the church, even here in the United States.[11]

Furthermore, any ministry that is united to Christ will face unfair criticisms, unfounded rumors, and unjust accusations. It is simply a fact: "We share abundantly in Christ's sufferings" (2 Cor 1:5; cf. 2 Tim 3:12). Preaching ministry could not be in union with Christ unless it entailed difficulty, discouragement, and sometimes death.

---

10. Quoted in Anyabwile, *Faithful Preacher*, 93.
11. Corey Jackson, quoted in Nation and Gordon, "Imaginations Awakened."

Nevertheless, many ministers are surprised by suffering. Unmet expectations are one of the main reasons why some preachers get discouraged and may even leave the ministry altogether.[12] Has there been a failure to grasp the implications of pastoral ministry in union with Christ? The words of Thomas à Kempis are striking for their contemporary relevance.

> Jesus today has many who love his heavenly kingdom, but few who carry his cross; many who yearn for comfort, few who long for distress. Plenty of people he finds to share his banquet, few to share his fast. Everyone desires to take part in his rejoicing, but few are willing to suffer anything for his sake. There are many that follow Jesus as far as the breaking of bread, few as far as drinking the cup of suffering; many that revere his miracles, few that follow him in the indignity of the cross.[13]

According to Paul, such trials of pastoral ministry are not only to be expected, but also to be embraced. "I *want* to know Christ," he said in Phil 3:10, which necessarily included wanting to share in his Savior's sufferings.

Why Paul Wanted a Crucified Ministry

As Paul reflected on the role of suffering in gospel ministry, he expressed manifest joy in suffering for the cause of Christ. "Now I rejoice in my sufferings for your sake," he wrote in Col 1:24. Or to the Corinthians, "I am content with weaknesses, insults, hardships, persecutions, and calamities" (2 Cor 12:10). Paul really did *want* to know Christ by sharing in his sufferings!

There were at least two reasons for Paul's readiness to share in Christ's sufferings. One was his belief that his hardships were necessary for the evangelization of the lost. The world could not understand the message of the cross unless those who preached it were themselves marked by its suffering and shame. This is the meaning—at least in part—of Paul's enigmatic claim, "In my flesh I am filling up what is lacking in Christ's afflictions" (Col 1:24). What is still lacking is the communication of the gospel by a suffering church. The unsaved people of the world cannot see Jesus hanging on the cross, but they can see a community that shares in his sufferings and thus confirms the truth of his passion. The sufferings of the apostles—and, by implication, of the church and its ministers today—were public exhibitions of Christ and his cross, and this was the very heart of the apostle's strategy for making known the crucified Christ (see 2 Cor 4:11, 15).

---

12. Lane, "So Many Pastors."
13. Thomas à Kempis, *Imitation of Christ*, 76–77.

Another reason for Paul's passion to know Christ in his sufferings is that such fellowship affords a deep, personal knowledge of Christ. As George Whitefield once observed, "Ministers never write or preach so well as when under the cross; the Spirit of Christ and of glory then rests upon them."[14] This is one of the promised blessings of gospel ministry. During seasons of hardship and difficulty, a minister experiences the closest possible identification with Christ. Lutheran bishop Lajos Ordass eloquently testified to this intimacy after spending six years in prison for protesting the Communist oppression of churches and Christian schools in his native Hungary.

> They placed me in solitary confinement. It was a tiny cell, perhaps six feet by eight feet with no windows and sound-proofed. They hoped to break down my resistance by isolating me from all sensory perceptions. They thought I was alone. They were wrong. The risen Christ was present in that room. And in communion with Him, I was able to prevail.[15]

All of this helps to explain why Paul wanted so very badly for the humiliation of Christ to be worked out in his own life and ministry. What he desired was not the sufferings themselves, but the fellowship of sharing them with Christ. He reasoned that since he was a minister of the gospel, difficulties were bound to come, and that when they came, it would be much better to experience them in union with Christ and thus to receive them as one of God's gifts: "For it has been granted to you that for the sake of Christ you should not only believe in him but also suffer for his sake" (Phil 1:29).

This does not mean that suffering needs to be sought out. It will come in all the sorrows a shepherd shares with the flock and in all the burdens a shepherd bears on their behalf. In the meantime, the kind of spiritual intimacy that Paul sought in union with Christ may come inwardly from dying to self. To preach the gospel in the biblical way, a preacher must first be able to say, "I have been crucified with Christ. It is no longer I who live, but Christ who lives in me" (Gal 2:20). It takes a crucified preacher to preach a crucified Christ. Ministers must therefore die to self in all its grotesque forms: self-indulgence, self-promotion, self-love. They must be dead to pride, dead to financial gain, dead to recognition and approval.

The notable Scottish minister William Still gave his spiritual autobiography the memorable title *Dying to Live*. Still wrote about a form of union with Christ that every preacher needs to experience to be fully effective and maximally fruitful in ministry.

---

14. Whitefield, *Works*, 4:306.
15. Lajos Ordass, quoted in Dunnam, *Exodus*, 272–73.

> The deaths one dies before [preaching] can be of long duration—it can be hours and days before we minister, before the resurrection experience of anointed preaching.... From the moment that you stand there dead in Christ and dead to everything you are and have and ever shall be and have, every breath you breathe thereafter, every thought you think, every word you say and deed you do, must be done over the top of your own corpse or reaching over it in your preaching to others. Then it can only be Jesus that comes over and no one else. And I believe that every preacher must bear the mark of that death. Your life must be signed by the Cross, not just Christ's Cross (there is really no other) but your cross in his Cross, your particular and unique cross that no one ever died—the cross that no one ever could die but you and you alone: your death in Christ's death.[16]

The Power of Christ's Resurrection

As much as Paul had to say about knowing Christ in his sufferings and death, he also understood that union with Christ entails exaltation. His ministry was a *gospel* ministry—grounded in both crucifixion and resurrection. And in the summary statement for his theology of the ministry of preaching, the apostle did not begin with suffering, but with glory, "that I may know [Christ] and the power of his resurrection" (Phil 3:10).

What *is* the power of Christ's resurrection? Specifically and explicitly, it is the life-giving power of God the Holy Spirit. The Scripture teaches that "according to the Spirit of holiness" Christ "was declared to be the Son of God in power ... by his resurrection from the dead" (Rom 1:4). The Holy Spirit therefore is the effective transforming agent of God's resurrection power. What was true for Christ remains true for the Christian. As Paul later wrote, "If the Spirit of him who raised Jesus from the dead dwells in you, he who raised Christ Jesus from the dead will also give life to your mortal bodies through his Spirit who dwells in you" (Rom 8:11). The self-same Spirit who brought Jesus back to life also vitalizes and revitalizes the believer. To know the power of the resurrection, therefore, is to know the power of the Holy Spirit, which the church received at Pentecost (Acts 2:1–4).

The resurrection alone gives power for gospel ministry. This was true in the ministry of Jesus Christ. It was not until Jesus was raised from the dead that his preaching achieved its lasting effect. Prior to the resurrection, his followers remained uncertain of his identity and thus lacked the courage to live

---

16. Still, *Dying to Live*, 136.

for his kingdom. It was only when Jesus rose from the dead that they began to experience resurrection-empowered success in ministry.

As soon as the apostles became eyewitnesses to the risen Christ, they began to preach the risen Christ. The resurrection was not simply the basis for their message; it was also the source of their success. Their proclamation of the risen Christ became the performative act that brought the dead back to spiritual life. Michael Horton observes that after Pentecost "the apostles, deputized by the Son and empowered by the Spirit, became witnesses whose preaching did exactly what was prophesied by Ezekiel. By preaching—and not just by preaching anything, but by preaching the gospel—the dead were raised."[17] Here is another compelling way to connect our theology to our proclamation: preaching is raising the dead!

As we have seen, the ministry of the Old Testament prophets was marked primarily by humiliation. The same can be said of Jesus Christ—up until the time of his death. But everything changed with the resurrection and ascension, when the Spirit was unleashed in all his saving power and as a result the ministry of the gospel revealed God's power to save sinners. In union with Christ, therefore, fulfilling the preacher's calling includes exaltation as well as humiliation.

After Lawrence Zoch had been imprisoned following his conversion to Lutheranism—and when he had suffered further loss through the death of his beloved wife—Martin Luther wrote these words to encourage his friend:

> It is with heartfelt sorrow that I learn of the great misfortune and grief that has come to you.... Thus it appears as if God himself has now attacked you, and your enemies can boast and say, "So fare these Christians; this is the reward of your new gospel." This is more than suffering and dying; it is being buried and descending into hell. But, my dear doctor, be steadfast. This is the time for firmness. Remember that Christ also had this experience, and even worse. But God, who seemed to be assailing him, did not forsake him, but raised him up in honor. So God will also raise us up with him.[18]

Union with Christ means suffering. It also means exaltation to such glory that all the attendant suffering will seem as nothing in comparison.

How Preaching Comes to Life

The life-giving power of the Holy Spirit is the source of everything good that happens through preaching. The Holy Spirit has the power to regenerate (see

17. Horton, *Covenant and Eschatology*, 267.
18. Luther, *Letters of Spiritual Counsel*, 66.

John 3:5). It is only by the Spirit that anyone ever comes to say, "Jesus is Lord" (1 Cor 12:3). Through the proclamation of a risen Savior, sinners are granted the blessings of resurrection life. The Holy Spirit also has the power to sanctify. By way of example, one church member testified that he was delivered—totally delivered—from lifelong bondage to same-sex transgressions as the result of a single sermon from Gal 2. Until his promotion to glory, he would mark the occasion every year by celebrating the anniversary of his landmark deliverance—something he celebrated as a gift of the Holy Spirit.

This is what everyone needs in the proclamation of God's word: the resurrection power of God's Spirit. It is what people need when they are trying and failing to escape the enslavement of addictive sins, drowning in oceans of grief, seeking healing from a history of abuse, crying out for the reconciliation of broken relationships, and struggling with all the other agonies of a fallen world. It is what the artist needs to avoid despair, the businessperson to resist greed, the homeless person to overcome oppression, and the churchgoer to be healed from hypocrisy. Everyone needs a fresh and powerful work of God the Holy Spirit, who alone is able to bring the dead back to life.

When Charles Spurgeon mounted each of the fifteen steps of London's Metropolitan Tabernacle pulpit saying, "I believe in the Holy Ghost," he was exercising his ministry in union with Christ.[19] Without this divine perspective, preaching gets reduced to a merely human enterprise. Ministers wrongly come to regard natural gifting—which of course the Spirit can and does use for gospel purposes—as the crucial factor in ministry. Without the Spirit, ministry becomes a distraction, or worse, a manipulation. By contrast, what expands the Spirit's work is the kind of self-forgetfulness that Luther practiced when he said, "I simply taught, preached, and wrote God's Word; otherwise, I did nothing. And then while I slept, . . . the Word did it all."[20]

Thankfully, the Spirit is at work not only in a minister's evident successes, but also in apparent failures. In every struggle, there is also consolation in the inescapable presence of the risen Christ. Perhaps this is the best place to emphasize that dying and rising with Jesus are not two successive stages in gospel ministry but constantly present as inter-related experiences. As William R. Edwards explains in his essay on suffering in pastoral ministry, for Paul, "the dimensions of death and resurrection in ministry" are "not experienced sequentially but simultaneously. . . . Paul does not describe an experience of death that is then followed by an experience of resurrection. They are

---

19. Recounted in Stott, *Between Two Worlds*, 334.
20. Luther, quoted in George, "Reading the Bible," 28.

not separate moments or distinct occasions. . . . It is not first death and then resurrection. The pattern is *always* death and *also* resurrection."[21]

The apostle repeatedly testifies to this gospel paradox in his epistles. Whenever he faced difficulty in ministry, as he often did, Paul was compelled to depend more completely on the Holy Spirit. In his public proclamation of the gospel, he claimed that although he often preached "in weakness and in fear and much trembling," nevertheless his message came "in demonstration of the Spirit and of power, so that your faith might not rest in the wisdom of men but in the power of God" (1 Cor 2:3–5; cf. 2 Cor 1:8–9). In this way, the story of Christ's death and resurrection was displayed in Paul's ministry. And it was humiliation that compelled him to rely more completely on the exalting power of God's Spirit. "Therefore," he said, "I will boast all the more gladly of my weaknesses, so that the power of Christ may rest upon me" (2 Cor 12:9; cf. 4:7). Paul's ministry really was the message: it portrayed the same gospel that he proclaimed.

Attaining to the Resurrection of the Dead

When the final resurrection finally comes, the church will witness the Holy Spirit's power to glorify. Here it must be emphasized that most of the greatest glories of preaching ministry are deferred benefits. As ministers suffer the cross, they are waiting for the crown. This was true in the ministry of the promised Christ. As noted previously, the Suffering Servant said, "I have labored in vain; I have spent my strength for nothing and vanity." Yet the Servant went on to declare his expectation of his coming exaltation: "Yet surely my right is with the Lord, and my recompense is with my God" (Isa 49:4; cf. 53:10–12). Isaiah's suffering Messiah looked forward in faith and believed that he would be fully rewarded for his gospel labors. This is exactly what God the Son did when he gave up his spirit on the cross (Luke 23:46): he entrusted his Father with the results of his ministry.

The hope of deferred glory is of particular encouragement whenever preachers are discouraged by apparent fruitlessness in ministry. As it was for Christ, so it is for his ministers: exaltation comes only after humiliation. Thus, pastors labor in their fields with the hope of a harvest that will not be reaped until eternity, when a ministry of suffering will be revealed as a ministry of glory. Lesslie Newbigin writes,

> Our faith as Christians is that just as God raised up Jesus from the dead, so will He raise up us from the dead. And that just as

---

21. Edwards, "Participants," 462.

all that Jesus had done in the days of his flesh seemed on Easter Sunday to be buried in final failure and oblivion, yet was by God's power raised to new life and power again, so all the faithful labor of God's servants which time seems to bury in the dust of failure, will be raised up, will be found to be there, transfigured, in the new Kingdom. Every faithful act of service, every honest labor to make the world a better place, which seemed to have been forever lost and forgotten in the rubble of history, will be seen on that day to have contributed to the perfect fellowship of God's Kingdom. As Christ, who committed Himself to God and was faithful even when all ended in utter failure and rejection, was by God raised up so that all that He had done was found to be not lost, but alive and powerful, so all who have committed their work in faithfulness to God will be by Him raised up to share in the new age, and will find that their labor was not lost, but that it has found its place in the completed Kingdom.... In that day it will all be found to be there raised up, transfigured.[22]

In view of this coming transfiguration, the Puritan Richard Sibbes wisely advised ministers to wait patiently for the rewards of their ministry. "Let us commit the fame and credit, of what we are or do to God. *He will take care of that*, let us take care to be and to do as we should, and then *for noise and report*, let it be good or ill as God will send it.... Therefore, let us labour to be good *in secret*.... We should be carried with the Spirit of God, and with a holy desire to serve God and our brethren, and to do all the good we can, and never care for the speeches of the world.... We'll have glory enough BY-AND-BY."[23]

The apostle Paul was looking for glory by-and-by. His definition of success in ministry was future oriented. "Our citizenship is in heaven," he wrote, "and from it we await a Savior, the Lord Jesus Christ, who will transform our lowly body to be like his glorious body, by the power that enables him even to subject all things to himself. Therefore, my brothers, whom I love and long for, my joy and crown ... my beloved" (Phil 3:20—4:1; cf. 1 Pet 5:4).

Paul was trusting in the power of the Holy Spirit to achieve the ultimate goal and crowning glory of any preaching ministry: to present people unto God ready to receive their eternal inheritance. "For what is our hope or joy or crown of boasting before our Lord Jesus at his coming?" he asked the Thessalonians. "Is it not you? For you are our glory and joy" (1 Thess 2:19–20; cf. 2 Cor 1:14; 2 Tim 4:8). Here the apostle describes future glory as present reality. He was counting on the co-inherent practical/theological connection

---

22. Newbigin, *Signs Amid the Rubble*, 47, 50.
23. Sibbes, *Works*, 1:xxiii–xxiv.

between proclamation and glorification, by which his preaching of the risen, ascended, and glorified Christ would serve as the Spirit-empowered preparation of the risen, ascended, and glorified church.

Bibliography

Anyabwile, Thabiti. *The Faithful Preacher: Recapturing the Vision of Three Pioneering African-American Pastors*. Wheaton, IL: Crossway, 2007.

Calvin, John. *Institutes of the Christian Religion*. Translated by Ford Lewis Battles. Library of Christian Classics 20–21. Philadelphia: Westminster, 1960.

Dunnam, Maxie. *Exodus*. The Communicator's Commentary. Nashville: W, 1987.

Edwards, William R. "Participants in What We Proclaim: Recovering Paul's Narrative of Pastoral Ministry." *Themelios* 39 (2014) 455–69.

Edwards, William R., et al. *Theology for Ministry: How Doctrine Affects Pastoral Life and Practice*. Phillipsburg, NJ: P&R, 2022.

Ferguson, Sinclair B. "The Reformed View." In *Christian Spirituality: Five Views of Sanctification*, edited by Donald L. Alexander, 47–76. Downers Grove, IL: InterVarsity, 1988.

George, Timothy. "Reading the Bible with the Reformers." *First Things* 211 (2011) 27–33.

Goetz, David L. "Tour of Duty: A Day with Stu Weber." *Leadership* 17 (1996) 22–30.

Horton, Michael S. *Covenant and Eschatology: The Divine Drama*. Louisville: Westminster John Knox, 2002.

Lane, Bo. "Why Do So Many Pastors Leave the Ministry? The Facts Will Shock You." ExPastors, January 27, 2014. http://www.expastors.com/why-do-so-many-pastors-leave-the-ministry-the-facts-will-shock-you/.

Lillback, Peter, ed. *The Practical Calvinist: An Introduction to the Reformed Heritage*. Fearn, Ross-shire: Mentor, 2002.

Luther, Martin. *Luther: Letters of Spiritual Counsel*. Edited and translated by Theodore G. Tappert. Library of Christian Classics 18. London: SCM, 1955.

Nation, Hannah, and Ruth Gordon. "Imaginations Awakened in the PCA." byFaith, October 23, 2023. https://byfaithonline.com/imaginations-awakened-in-the-pca/.

Newbigin, Lesslie. *Signs Amid the Rubble: The Purposes of God in Human History*. Grand Rapids: Eerdmans, 2003.

Oden, Thomas. *Pastoral Theology*. San Francisco: Harper & Row, 1983.

Robinson, Marilynne. *Home*. New York: Farrar, Straus & Giroux, 2008.

Schneider, John R. "Why Does Creation Groan?" *Christianity Today*, March 13, 2023. https://www.christianitytoday.com/ct/2023/april/why-does-creation-groan-animal-suffering-pain-evolution.html.

Sibbes, Richard. *The Works of Richard Sibbes*. 7 vols. Edited by Alexander Grant. London: Banner of Truth Trust, 1973.

Still, William. *Dying to Live*. Fearn, Ross-shire: Christian Focus, 1991.

Stott, John R. W. *Between Two Worlds: The Art of Preaching in the Twentieth Century*. Grand Rapids: Eerdmans, 1982.

Thomas à Kempis. *The Imitation of Christ*. Translated by Ronald Knox and Michael Oakley. New York: Sheed and Ward, 1959.

Whitefield, George. *The Works of the Reverend George Whitefield*. 21 vols. London: Edward and Charles Dilley, 1771.

5

The Answer

Revelation 5

NICOLE MASSIE MARTIN

UNPACKING THE QUESTION

THERE IS SO MUCH in life that we just do not understand. We have more information now than we have ever had before. We are more educated as a people than we have ever been before. We have access to more knowledge than we have ever experienced in any generation before now. And yet, there is still so much about life that we just do not get.

I know that we are not entitled to our lives, but I do not understand why life for some of us is so much harder than it is for others. I know that money comes and money goes, but I do not understand how some can be so wasteful and still have wealth while others can be so resourceful and yet so poor. I know that we are all born and we must all die, but I do not understand why some people have to die so quickly. I do not understand why children have to suffer. I do not understand why evil gets to exist. I do not understand why bad people experience good things and I still do not understand why bad things happen to good people. I have my degrees, I have been around a few years, I have met some of the smartest people in the world, and yet there are still so many things that I just cannot wrap my head around.

There is just so much that I do not understand about justice and equality, so much I do not understand about wealth and poverty. There is so much I do not understand about death and dying. I do not understand why we have so much money and so many medical advances, but we still do not have a cure for cancer. I do not know why we have so much innovation and so many prescriptions, but we still do not have a way to reverse brain damage. We are the most advanced military in the world, but we still do not know how to stop wars that seem like they will never end.

I know that all things work together for our good. I know that weeping may endure for a night and joy comes in the morning. I know that God is good all that time. I know that joy comes in the morning. But there are some things in this world, some tragedies in our walk, some traumas in our communities, some pains in our lives that make it hard for me to understand God. Since God is still sovereign and since he is still in complete control, it makes me wonder: God, what is this all for? I know you have plans to prosper us and not to harm us, but why so much pain? I know that you are the Alpha and the Omega, but when will it all end? I believe that you have the whole world in your hands, but when will it all make sense?

When we are dealing with things we do not understand, we tend to do one of two things: we either simplify or we dismiss. We either try to boil it all down into small, simple pieces that are easier to digest, or we sweep it under the carpet and try to live like it does not exist. This is exactly how the enemy wants us to deal with our discomfort of the unknown. He wants us to simplify our realities so that we start to think that everything has an easy answer. Why did my marriage not work? God just has better things for you. Why did God not answer my prayers? It just was not his timing. Why did my loved one die? God wanted your loved one more than you did.

Sometimes a simple answer is the answer. But, more often than not, complex questions demand complex answers. While these trite and simple answers may work for a little while and might even be enough for some, they certainly will not work for long, and they will not work for younger people. This generation is full of questions that we cannot answer simply. And when you give a simple answer to a complex question, you end up simplifying and minimizing God. Simple answers make God look inept, like he is unable to do anything beyond what humanity can understand. And when we are not simplifying God with things we do not understand, we often swing the pendulum to a dismissal of God. When we are unable to explain why bad things happen, we just pretend like they did not happen or like God was not there. God has power over all things, but just not the bad things. God is everywhere at all times, but not in the places of our deepest pain.

Seeking the Answer

There is so much in life that we do not understand. We have so many complex questions that need to be answered and so many painful problems that need to be resolved. In times like these, we do not just need a word from God, we need a revelation. We do not just need to hear from God, we need to see him in action. For times like these, we need the book of Revelation. Like the complexity of our times, we often treat this book with either simplicity or dismissal. We either distill it down to John's hallucinations on an isolated island or we dismiss the book altogether. But God loves us too much to allow us to simplify or dismiss the vision of who he is.

John's revelation about God was intended to help people overcome dark times. John's revelation of Jesus was written to give hope to people who struggled to make sense of their realities. This revelation was a vision that clarified that Jesus Christ was and is still Lord of all. Because God knows that if the people have a vision of who Christ is, then they can have strength to endure until the end when Christ will make it all clear. Brian Blount described Revelation like a Quentin Tarantino movie.[1] Like *Pulp Fiction*, *Django Unchained*, or *Kill Bill*, the book is filled with gory and difficult images described in almost glorious and poetic fashion. And, just like these movies, Blount suggests that it is not the content of the book that matters, but the plot.[2]

In chapter 5, this revelation is specifically linked to the opening of a scroll that holds the answers to all the questions that have ever been asked, are being asked, and will ever be asked for all of humanity. It holds the solutions to the deepest problems facing human life and tells us exactly how everything will be resolved in the end. This scroll represents the key to understanding everything we cannot understand on earth. It holds so many secrets that it is written on both sides, which is rare for a scroll, and it is sealed, not just with one or two, but with seven seals. In other words, what John saw in his vision, upheld in the right hand of God, was the secret to the answer of life for all time.

Can you imagine, standing there before the throne of God and seeing him hold the answers to all the questions humanity has ever asked, is asking, and will ever ask, wrapped up in one simple scroll? While we might find comfort in knowing that this scroll was in God's hand, the plot thickens and tension builds when the angel calls out, "Who is worthy to break the seals and open the scroll?" (Rev 5:2 NIV). All the answers, all the solutions, were right there. The end of our angst was right there before John's eyes, but there was no

---

1. Blount, "Revelation," 523.
2. Blount, "Revelation," 523.

one, John said, not in the heavens, not on the earth, not even under the earth, who could open the scroll!

With oppression and fear lurking behind him and the answers to the future waiting, unopened in front of him, John began to weep. He weeps and weeps until an elder appears in the vision and consoles him, letting him know that there is one who can open the scroll. There is one who is worthy. With these words, the plot thickens again with the entrance of the only one in all the heavens and in all the earth who is worthy to open the scroll that holds the answers for all humankind.

Friends, we stand like John with the fears of the world beside us, the unexplained issues of the past behind us, and the unknown future before us. We stand, like John, looking at God on the throne, knowing that he has the answers, but knowing there is only one who can lead us to the truth. And because this book is the end of all books, we know that this one is Jesus. But what is it about Jesus that makes him the only one who can open the scroll? What is it about Jesus that qualifies him above every being, every deity, every religion, and every faith?

THE SLAIN LAMB

There is so much in life that we do not understand and will never understand without Jesus. But, if we understand who Jesus is, we will have strength to endure until he makes it all clear. What was it about Jesus that made him worthy to open the scroll? The first thing that the text points out about Jesus is that *he is the lamb who was slain*. As John weeps over the knowledge that no one could open the scroll, the elder said to him, "Do not weep! See, the Lion of the tribe of Judah, the Root of David, has triumphed. He is able to open the scroll and its seven seals" (Rev 5:5).

As if watching a movie, we look around the scene and wait with anticipation for a brave lion to enter. We are waiting for Aslan to enter as he did in *The Chronicles of Narnia*. We are waiting for Mufasa to enter with strength and power as he mounted the cliff overlooking his kingdom. But the plot thickens again. Instead of a lion, we witness the entrance of a lamb. And this is not just any lamb, this was a lamb that, John said, looked like it was slain—slaughtered, executed. In biblical times, the priests would slaughter the lamb by slitting its throat with a sharp knife, letting the blood drip on the altar, and then either burn the flesh or hang it on a hook to be eaten later. This was a vivid and common image for the people of Israel because they saw it daily through the practice of the *Tamid*.[3]

The *Tamid* sacrifice was made up of the morning and evening offering of an unblemished young lamb at the entrance of the tent of meeting. The Israelites understood the image of the blood as it dripped on the altar. They understood the scent of death as it daily crept upon their camp. They understood the contrast of color as the near-white wool became saturated with the dark red blood. But they also understood that the blood of the lamb was required for the protection, presence, and pleasure of God. In Exod 12, the blood of the lamb was placed on the doorframes to protect them from death. In Exod 29, the blood of the lamb made it possible for the priests to meet with God. In Lev 4, the blood of the lamb was required for the sin offering. In Num 28, the blood of the lamb was necessary to please God. The elder in Revelation spoke of a Lion, but John saw the Lion as the bloody Lamb, slain for our sins, and therefore worthy to open the scroll.

As in the Old Testament, so in the New: the blood of the Lamb is required for the protection, presence, and pleasure of God. Without the blood of the Lamb, there is no passing over. Without the shedding of blood, there is no remission of sin. Without the slaughter of the Lamb, there is no entering in. Without the Lamb's willingness to die, his willingness to shed his blood and cover our sins, we could never approach the throne of grace!

The Slain Lamb, Standing

The vision does not stop there. Jesus was worthy not only because he was the slain Lamb, but because *he was slain and standing*. John did not just see a lamb lying on the ground in pool of its own blood. He did not see the weakness of a lamb while it was being killed. John wrote, "Then I saw a Lamb, looking as if it had been slain, standing" (Rev 5:6). This is a miracle. Slaughtered animals do not stand. When they are slaughtered, they go limp and weak because their strength has been drained. But in this vision, the conquering Lamb who was slain is seen standing. He was executed, but he still stood firm. He was bloodied, but still standing fast. He was murdered, and yet still alive. The Lamb may have been slain, yet he stood.

The resurrection was an act of defiance. Jesus got up from the grave. He stood up. He defied death. While death forces us down, life raises us up. Through his resurrection, Jesus demonstrated his defiance of death. He may have been knocked down, but he refused to be knocked out. He may have

---

3. *Encyclopaedia Judaica*, "Tamid."

been bloodied, but he was still alive. He stood up. And he was not resurrected on weak, unsteady feet. He was resurrected with all power! And because he stood, all those covered by his blood will keep standing too!

Standing is an act of resistance. It is a reminder to your opponent that the match is not over and there is still a chance you will win. Your opponent, the devil, is trying to knock you out. He is trying to hit you so hard that even if you do get up, you will not stand on steady feet. But he keeps forgetting one important thing: you are *covered* by the blood of the Lamb that was slain yet still stands.

This is why the devil does not like you. No matter what he does to you, you have the nerve to stand back up. He tried to knock out your job, but God still provided for you. He tried to challenge your health, but God still healed you. He tried to take your sanity, but God still gave you peace. He tried to destroy your family, but God still made a way. The devil is trying to knock you out, but I dare you to shout, "I am still standing! I might be wounded, but I am still standing. I might be weary, but I am still standing. I might be slain, but because of the Lamb, I am still standing!"

The Slain Lamb, Standing, and Centered

John's vision gives us courage to endure until the end because he saw the Lamb who was slain. It gives us courage to press on because John saw this Lamb slain and standing. But there is more to say. John says he saw the "Lamb, looking as if it had been slain, standing at the center of the throne" (Rev 5:6). Jesus was the only one who could open the scroll because *he was the Lamb slain, standing, and centered.* John saw not just the perfect Lamb, but the bloody one. He did not see the Lamb lying down but standing firm. And he did not see the Lamb on the margins, blending in with the elders or even off to the side of the throne. No, John saw this bloodied Lamb standing right in the center of the throne, surrounded by the elders and the angels. He saw that the Lamb had seven eyes and seven horns, representing the all-surpassing power and perfection of the one who was worthy to open the scroll.

John says that Jesus, as the perfect and powerful Lamb, stood at the center of the throne room. And when he took the scroll, as the only one who could, all those who surrounded him fell down in worship. The four living creatures bowed down in worship. The twenty-four elders fell down and, holding the prayers of the people that had been prayed for centuries, they worshiped him and sang a new song. *But it does not stop there.*

With Jesus at the center of the throne room, John says that millions of angels began to worship in a loud voice saying, "Worthy is the Lamb, who was slain, to receive power and wealth and wisdom and strength and honor and glory and praise!" (Rev 5:12) *But it does not stop there.*

With Jesus at the center, John says that he heard "every creature in heaven and on earth and under the earth and on the sea, and all that is in them, saying, 'To him who sits on the throne and to the Lamb be praise and honor and glory and power, for ever and ever!'" (Rev 5:13) And everybody, everywhere fell down and worshiped the Lamb.

This centering of the Lamb is symbolic of the centrality of Christ for all creation. He is the source of all things. He is the ruler over all things. He is the core from which everything flows. Paul writes in Col 1:17, "He is before all things and in him all things hold together." He is the Lamb who was slain and he stands at the center of it all. And, like a series of dominos that cascade down from center to the perimeter, John said that everyone, from the nearest to the farthest, fell down and worshiped him. They worshiped him as the center of the throne. They worshiped him as the center of the story. They worshiped him as the center of the plan. They worshiped him as the center of the world.

Our worship of the Lamb declares that the devil is not the center. Angels and demons are not the center. The president is not the center. Your pastor is not the center. Your boss is not the center. Even *we*—our jobs, intellects, children, money—are not the center. Jesus Christ is the center of it all. And because he is the center, we do not have to worry about the future. Because he is the center, we do not have to fear what is to come. Because the Lamb who was slain stands at the center as Lord of all, we can rest. And since he is the center, he is worthy of our praise. He is "worthy to receive power and wealth and wisdom and strength and honor and glory and praise" (Rev 5:12). In other words, Jesus is worthy of everything we have because he is the center of it all. Jesus is the answer. May we respond to this revelation with praise!

Bibliography

Blount, Brian K. "Revelation." In *True to Our Native Land: An African American New Testament Commentary*, edited by Brian K. Blount et al., 523–58. Minneapolis: Fortress, 2007.

Encyclopaedia Judaica. "Tamid." Jewish Virtual Library, 2007. https://www.jewishvirtuallibrary.org/tamid.

Part Two

THE HUMILITY OF THE PULPIT

6

Is Your Preaching Pain-Full?

Adopting Paul's Theology of Homiletical Weakness

MATTHEW D. KIM

INTRODUCTION

I DO NOT HAVE to tell those reading this collection of essays that the Bible can be a rather painful book. But I will. I am not just referring to slogging through the books of Leviticus or Numbers in our annual Bible reading plans. It is painful because it is littered with pain-filled examples of biblical persons who, whether deservedly or not, experienced pain and suffering. One minor character who stands out and does not get much press, or pulpit time for that matter, is poor Eutychus in Acts 20:7–12.

Have you ever wondered what the headlines of the *Troas Times* might have said on the morning after young Eutychus fell out the third-floor window? Extra, extra, read all about it: "A young man falls from a third-story window due to a never-ending sermon and lives to talk about it!" Perhaps it did not make headline news, but the event was recorded by Luke in the Book of Acts.

Eutychus, whose name, ironically or providentially, can mean "lucky" or "fortunate," generously makes the long trek, probably after a long day of work, to attend an evening gathering to hear precious and significant words from the apostle Paul.[1] Doctor Luke records,

---

1. Barry et al., "Eutychus."

PART TWO: THE HUMILITY OF THE PULPIT

> On the first day of the week we came together to break bread. Paul spoke to the people and, because he intended to leave the next day, kept on talking until midnight. There were many lamps in the upstairs room where we were meeting. Seated in a window was a young man named Eutychus, who was sinking into a deep sleep as Paul talked on and on. When he was sound asleep, he fell to the ground from the third story and was picked up dead. Paul went down, threw himself on the young man and put his arms around him. "Don't be alarmed," he said. "He's alive!" Then he went upstairs again and broke bread and ate. After talking until daylight, he left. The people took the young man home alive and were greatly comforted (Acts 20:7–12 NIV).

Is this the longest dinner ever recorded, the longest sermon, a needlessly prolonged recitation of Paul's comprehensive ministry plan, or something else?

It is uncertain whether Paul physically resurrected Eutychus from death or if he was just as good as dead. Regardless, the fact that Eutychus lived is a miraculous event and an act of mercy by God. While witnesses were still picking up their jaws from the ground, Luke tells us that Paul nonchalantly reentered table fellowship as if nothing had happened! How painful this moment must have been for Eutychus and those bystanders.

Why do I begin with this minor account from Acts? While the title for this chapter insinuates that our preaching can be painful or difficult for listeners to hear, à la Eutychus, another way to view the word painful—following the story of Eutychus—is to spell it "pain-full." Even in a seemingly dismissible or "throw away" biblical narrative, God shows us in his word that he cares about the pain of people, significant or small.

In this chapter, I would like to raise the following question that addresses our times: Might an antidote to our broken and disheartened world be that a theology of preaching includes preachers incorporating our pains and the pains of our people into our sermons? Could we entertain the notion that both theological homiletics or homiletical theology requires acknowledging and addressing those who are hurting within the fold of God and beyond? My goal is to introduce a theology of preaching that embraces two Christian qualities: humility and weakness. In the doctrine of suffering, I propose that those who preach need to communicate sermons that are attentive, compassionate, and empathetic toward our listeners, their situations, their communities, their struggles, their pain, and perhaps even our own.

My Testimony

My involuntary admission into the world of preaching began in 1990 at the tender age of thirteen. Born and raised in Chicagoland, we attended a church in the northern suburbs. At a church youth retreat, the college leaders decided to hold an impromptu, unsolicited—might I say gratuitous—sermon competition. Oxymoronic, right? Three vulnerable and *most* unqualified youths were selected to preach a short sermon with only a few hours to prepare. There was no time for exegetical, theological, or homiletical marination. Whether it was a moment solidifying my calling or just a well-intended idea gone wrong on the part of our leaders, I was one of the victims—I mean, preachers—selected. We made the young Timothy, the youthful minister of First Christian Church of Ephesus, look mature and well-experienced!

A recent convert myself, I had no clue how to prepare or preach a sermon. I did not know much about the Christian faith. Had these leaders not read and understood Paul's teaching, "[The preacher] must not be a recent convert, or [the preacher] may become conceited and fall under the same judgment as the devil" (1 Tim 3:6)? In any event, having never missed a Sunday worship service since birth, I had heard my share of sermons—some memorable, many forgettable. But why do this now at a youth group retreat? And what kind of sermon would I craft?

Between the seventh grade and senior year of high school, our youth group had a slew of seminarians—part-time youth pastors—who came and went for various reasons. Without a modicum of exaggeration, in a span of six years we encountered and experienced a total of eight different youth pastors. Here today, gone tomorrow, without any explanation from the church's leadership about their departures.

As a young Christian, the explicit and implicit theology conveyed in Sunday youth messages taught me that preaching could be categorized into three clusters. The first was what Bonhoeffer referred to as a theology of shame in his book *Ethics*. Some youth pastors preached shame-ridden/guilt-inducing sermons that made us feel horrible about ourselves, leaving us thinking, "We are the worst Christians ever to walk planet earth. How could God ever love us? I am such a disgusting, terrible person." It was theology tacked on to anthropology, targeted not on the love and grace of the triune God, but focusing solely on our sinfulness, a hamartiology of sorts.

The second type was humor-centered sermons, comedic and at times bordering on heresy. This was preaching couched in telling funny anecdotes, jokes, and sheer entertainment. It was self-aggrandizing and self-promoting at best. At worst, it was a mockery of the pulpit. The preacher was the hero of every sermon—full of humor but sans the Holy Spirit.

A third category was extemporaneous, off-the-cuff sermons—otherwise known as winging it! These were ill-prepared sermons: impromptu and untethered to the Scripture text. This type of sermon wandered away from the Bible like a rebellious two-year-old toddler at Target, never to return to the passage at hand. It was a homiletic that rejected the authorial intention of the passage.

Unbelievably, thirty-three years have passed since preaching that first sermon. I do not claim homiletical brilliance, but my observation over these decades as I have preached and taught homiletics is that current approaches to preaching have not changed all that much in many pulpits and congregations. These approaches can be grouped into the following three categories:

1. "More of me, less of you." These are sermons that elevate the preacher and intentionally or unintentionally make less of Jesus. We might call this the flipside of John the Baptist's sobering self-assessment: "I must increase while Jesus must decrease" (see John 3:30).
2. "Scripture-lite." These are sermons that make little of and/or belittle the Scriptures. Some have described this as preaching which dances around the text but never actually holds hands with one's dance partner—the Scripture passage. Sadly, this is far more common than we think.
3. "Sacred." These are sermons that are faithful to authorial intention and make much of the triune God through exposition, illustration, and application of the very word of God to the people of God. This is always our ambition. And, thankfully, such faithful proclamation does happen.

Most sermons on a given Sunday can be grouped into one of these three categories. But what would theological proclamation look like if we introduced a fourth? What if preaching intentionally addressed the hurting, broken, vulnerable, voiceless, and weak among us: a theological homiletic of *humilitas* and weakness, catered particularly to those who are in pain and suffering? Before we get there, it may be helpful to take a bird's eye view of homiletics and theology.

A Homiletical-Theological Prolegomena

We might start by adapting Tertullian's famous question. "What hath theology to do with preaching?" The late British preacher Ian Pitt-Watson quipped, "Preaching cannot be divorced from pastoring." Likewise, preaching cannot be divorced from theology. That is, preaching is a theological act, and the telos of theology is homiletical.

These two seemingly disparate disciplines do not have to be siloed. They form a symbiotic relationship. Chase R. Kuhn argues in a recent essay that "preaching in its most biblically faithful form is deliberately theological."[2] Similarly, Douglas O'Donnell and Leland Ryken helpfully remind preachers, "In each sermon, give your people the theoretical and practical theology they need to know to live as his people in his world. And on the top of the list of theological truths they need to understand, and be weekly reminded of, is God's gospel."[3] In her Parchman Lectures given at Truett Seminary, Fleming Rutledge identified one of the main contributors to the weakening of modern preaching: "Preachers have forgotten how to be theological." That is, as Robert Dean notes concerning the lecture, "The anthropological turn in preaching leaves preachers with much to say about human potential and possibility, but very little to say about God."[4]

The problem has been observed, yet what is a leading cause of the tenuous and at times fractured relationship between preaching and theology? Richard Lischer observes, "Although preaching is central to the life of the church, it has had to struggle continually against its exclusion from the church's self-reflection, its theology."[5] The importance of preserving the unity and collaboration between preaching and theology cannot be overstated. To do so, I would like to propose a homiletical-theological prolegomena.[6]

One might argue that the telos of intertwining preaching and theology is doxology. To develop a homiletical theology or a theological homiletic, we begin with the cooperative relationship witnessed in the triune God: Creator Father, Creator Son, and Creator Spirit. The genesis of humankind, described for us in Gen 1:26–28 alludes to the fact that the Trinity existed prior to the physical creation of the world in Gen 1:1. Scott Swain writes, "Christians praise the triune God not only in response to the greatness of his being, beauty, and beatitude. We also praise him in response to the wonder of his works of creation, redemption, and consummation. The thrice-holy God is

---

2. Kuhn, "Theology for Preaching," 1.
3. O'Donnell and Ryken, *Beauty and Power*, 131.
4. Dean, "Powerful Preaching."
5. Lischer, *Theology of Preaching*, 1.
6. While the word prolegomena is typically reserved for theology proper, a word might be said about the need for a homiletical-theological prolegomena. Theologians and biblical scholars could benefit from practitioners most tangibly in the form of homiletical discovery and doxology, while preachers likewise benefit from more intentional and circumspect theological discourse with theologians and biblical scholars.

worthy 'to receive glory and honor and power' because he 'created all things' (Rev. 4:11)."[7] Since Gen 3, however, and the ensuing sin of Adam and Eve, creation and humankind has forever been marred. Pain and suffering were introduced to humanity and have never left. Some might argue that it has only gotten worse.

Yet the holy and triune God has not abandoned us in our pain and suffering. Just the opposite. Our earthly and eschatological hope resides in the hope offered to us in the gospel of our Lord and Savior Jesus Christ. As we construct sermons in our day, preachers need not only theologize about God, wondering what God is like somewhere out in the distance. Rather, the preacher reminds the people, the listeners, that God is here. He is present. He is Immanuel. He is the incarnation. He indwells us. He speaks in and through us, the preacher. He speaks into our pain and suffering.

A homiletic of humility and weakness begins with this God and his presence with us. But what might it look like in the twenty-first century? Our Lord Jesus and the apostle Paul offer examples for preachers to follow today. As we look to them as exemplars, we will ask the following questions: Can preaching be accomplished apart from a position and posture of humility and weakness? Is our preaching pain-full? Does it acknowledge the various pains felt in the room? Is the act of preaching one of dependence and weakness which give space for the power of Christ to shine through?

HUMILITAS AND WEAKNESS ARE THE WAY OF CHRIST

I often begin each new semester by letting the students in the class know that I have been praying for them. This is a true statement. I then proceed to tell them what exactly I have been praying for them. A few eager ears lean in to hear. My foremost prayer for students pursuing pastoral ministry is that they would never become famous or seek to be famous. At this point, I usually get a few dirty looks and unkind glares from those who entered seminary with the very opposite prayer request: that God would grant them fame and celebrity as ministers of the gospel and become the next well-known pastor/preacher/teacher.

We are living in a world of Christian celebrity.[8] But I wonder where humility and weakness fit into the homiletical equation. Where do we, as pastors and teachers, take our cues in shepherding the flock to which we have been entrusted by the Lord Jesus Christ? When did pastoral ministry and preaching become more interested in who I am reaching "out there" rather than "in

---

7. Swain, *Trinity*, 15–16.
8. See Beaty, *Celebrities for Jesus*; and Kirby, *PreachersNSneakers*.

here" within our own congregations? For some, why do I care more about the virtual external flock out in the distance and not the flesh and bones sheep to whom I have been entrusted and called to pastor? Might it be the case that preaching and pastoring need an overhaul in many places across the globe? What if it begins by pursuing humility and weakness?

Over the course of a year, Richard Foster took notes from the Gospels regarding Jesus's example of humility. These notes became his recent book *Learning Humility*. Foster encourages his readers to meditate on the humility of Christ in this powerful passage:

> By meditating on Jesus' life we see humility take on flesh and blood. A humble birth in an obscure village. The growing-up years in quiet obscurity. Magnificent teachings to "the sat upon, the spat upon, the ratted on." The twelve chosen without regard to position or status or title. The wonder-filled miracles that did indeed draw enormous attention. And note carefully how Jesus handles all this fame without manipulation, without control, without domination. The borrowed donkey for his entry into Jerusalem; the borrowed room for his Last Supper. The disciplined silence throughout a mock trial and conviction. The enormous courage of suffering for the sins of the whole world. This has to be the supreme example of humility. The cry of abandonment, "Eli, Eli, lema sabachthani, My God, My God, why have you forsaken me?" The cry of humble triumph, "It is finished." As I look at this all it begins to dawn on me that Jesus is indeed the divine paradigm for conjugating all the verbs of humility.[9]

Is it not apropos that in Matt 4, even Jesus's entrance into his three-year earthly ministry began not from a position of strength but from a station of weakness? Thomas Long writes, "The testing of Jesus, the testings of Israel before him, and the testing of the church today are not primarily temptations to do what we would really like to do, but know we should not; they are temptations to *be* someone other than who God calls us to be, to deny that we are God's children."[10] The accuser's temptation and testing, in this case, are bound to Jesus's identity and seeking for him to doubt his identity as the Son of God. "If you are the Son of God . . ." (Matt 4:3, 6).

Notice the devil preys on Jesus's moment of physical weakness after having fasted for forty days and forty nights. I confess that I am a terrible faster. Like many of us, I have fasted from food for twenty-four hours and even occasionally forty-eight hours. But let me tell you, it was not pretty. But Jesus was

9. Foster, *Learning Humility*, 7–8.
10. Long, *Matthew*, 37.

without food for "forty days and forty nights," which is nearly one thousand hours (Matt 4:2). Unlike me, Jesus was not counting down the time. He had a greater mission to launch and complete.

Jesus began ministry in a posture of lack rather than abundance. Nothing in Jesus's earthly ministry shouted "health, wealth, and prosperity." Jesus says, "Foxes have dens and birds have nests, but the Son of Man has no place to lay his head" (Matt 8:20). He did not have an apartment, condo, townhouse, or single-family home to crash in at the end of his long days of ministry. Rather, his ministry was clearly a life marked by suffering, culminating in the cross.[11]

In battling the devil in the wilderness, Jesus overcame weakness and demonstrated power by knowing and quoting Scripture. He used Scripture simultaneously as his shield and his sword. "It is written: 'Man shall not live on bread alone, but on every word that comes from the mouth of God'" (Matt 4:4). "It is also written: 'Do not put the Lord your God to the test'" (Matt 4:7). "Away from me, Satan! For it is written: 'Worship the Lord your God, and serve him only'" (Matt 4:10). It is written. It is written. It is written.

Have we been preaching sermons from a posture of strength rather than weakness, of celebration only and not from lament? If I focus on technique, mechanics—putting in the work of exegesis, translation, word studies, hermeneutics, sentence diagramming, studying the historical, grammatical, literary, and cultural context—preaching should work out okay and I should never preach a stinker. Better yet, if I am well-coiffed, wear trendy clothes, showcase clever wordsmithing, develop engaging storyteller-abilities, and become comedic, I will not only keep them awake but even give them a few laughs along the way. Why is it that many preachers fill their sermon time with less Scripture and holy exposition and more of themselves and heroic exposé? Is that what preaching is and has become? When did we set the hermeneutical and homiletical bars so low?

Have we forgotten as pastors and preachers that our strength in the Christian life and in the pulpit comes only from God's holy and perfect word, not from being clever, slick, or professional in our speaking? Preaching derives from a humble heart, a blind-Bartimaeus type of desperation, a clinging to the Holy Spirit on account of our powerlessness to transform hearts, a homiletic of weakness and humility. This brings us to a lesson from the apostle Paul's homiletics classroom found in various letters.

---

11. Long, *Matthew*, 39.

Paul's Homiletical Theology of Weakness

Who is Paul the homiletician? What are his distinguishing preaching traits? When can we say, "Now that's an apostle Paul sermon!"? What can we learn from his preaching content and style? The truth is we do not know all that much. But here is a quick summary: Saul converted and preached boldly in the name of Jesus (Acts 9). As we explore the Pauline epistles, the central themes of the cross, the gospel, and weakness emerge regarding his sermonic emphases.

The Cross

"But we preach Christ crucified: a stumbling block to Jews and foolishness to Gentiles" (1 Cor 1:23).

The Gospel

"For Christ did not send me to baptize, but to preach the gospel—not with wisdom and eloquence, lest the cross of Christ be emptied of its power" (1 Cor 1:17). "For when I preach the gospel, I cannot boast, since I am compelled to preach. Woe to me if I do not preach the gospel!" (1 Cor 9:16)

Follow Paul's example. Give your listeners a clear presentation of the gospel: the salvific and atoning work of Christ, his perfect and sacrificial life, his death, burial, resurrection, ascension, and return. The gospel is for us and for every person listening. Today is the day of salvation. Let us turn now to Paul's embrace of weakness.

Weakness

Paul argues, counter-culturally, that weakness is an asset. It is in our weakness that we are made strong in God.

> In the same way, the Spirit helps us in our weakness. (Rom 8:26)

> But God chose the foolish things of the world to shame the wise; God chose the weak things of the world to shame the strong. (1 Cor 1:27)

> If I must boast, I will boast of the things that show my weakness. (2 Cor 11:30)

> But he said to me, "My grace is sufficient for you, for my power is made perfect in weakness." Therefore, I will boast all the more

gladly about my weaknesses, so that Christ's power may rest on me. (2 Cor 12:9)

The irony of preaching in Paul's time, as Duane Litfin observes, is that "powerful speakers gained repute, while weak speakers suffered not only defeat but ridicule. . . . Paul's written efforts are effective enough, the critics grant, but his physical presence is weak and his speech is contemptible."[12] Reflecting on this posture of weakness, Richard Bauckham writes,

> If God's definitive salvific act occurred through the weakness of the crucified Jesus, then it should be no surprise that the saving gospel of the crucified Jesus should reach the Gentiles through the weakness of his apostle. . . . The impressiveness of his ministry will not be his own impressiveness, but that of his message which matches up to the experience of human weakness and makes it the vehicle of God's power.[13]

In short, Paul was not much to look at, he was perhaps weak in the art and craft of homiletics, but this did not make his preaching ministry any less effective because his *dunamis* came from his homiletical theology of humility and weakness.

A Testimony of Humility and Weakness

The unspoken Western philosophy of ministry is: Do all you can in your own strength and when all else fails, ask God for help in your weakness! But weak is what I am. I am a broken sinner in need of God's grace. To illustrate this, I would like to share my testimony.

In the year 2022, I almost died twice. Not to sound overly dramatic, but it is true. But, before I get to these stories, I want to give you a little background on personal pain and suffering which were unexpectedly introduced to me more than a decade ago.

On March 20, 2013, I was playing basketball with my seminary students when I did not see the ball that was passed at full speed toward the left side of my head. Since that spring day in 2013, I have been dizzy (from post-concussion syndrome) every moment I am awake. Nearly four thousand days have passed, not that I am counting. In addition, for nearly twenty years I have suffered from severe tinnitus in both ears. So, basically, I am losing my vision and hearing and am dizzy all the time.

---

12. Litfin, *Paul's Theology of Preaching*, 59, 135.
13. Bauckham, "Weakness," 5, 6.

Yet, nothing would prepare me for the profound grief I experienced when my younger brother, Timothy D. Kim, was brutally murdered in Manila, Philippines, on November 7, 2015. He had been living in Asia for ten years and in the Philippines for three as a businessman. Claiming it was an accident, the police, local detectives, and workers at the condo where he lived conspired together to fabricate a false story. Local corruption prevented us from getting justice. He was celebrating his thirty-sixth birthday on the day he was killed. It was clearly foul play. We believe he was targeted for his money. There is not a day that goes by that I do not think of him. I loved him and miss him so much.

Now back to 2022. I spent the first half of that difficult year seeking improvement from COVID-pneumonia (including hospitalization and needing a home oxygen machine). By June 2022, long COVID led to chronic insomnia for five months, resulting in a medical leave from Truett Seminary at Baylor University for fall of 2022 after my family and I moved to Waco, Texas. I had yet to step foot on campus when I was institutionalized for ten days for insomnia, depression, psychosis, and suicidal ideation. Due to the inability to sleep, I completely fell apart. After a few months of insomnia, I was no longer able to think, walk, talk, or do anything. I sat on the couch wondering if God had abandoned me. Long story short, through much prayer intercession from others, Christian counseling, and medication, God has healed me. After five months of insomnia, I slowly began to sleep again around Thanksgiving of 2022. It has been a miraculous act of God to bring me back from this condition over the last twelve months. To God alone be praise and glory!

Why do I share my pain and suffering with you? It is not to throw a pity party or to manipulate you. Rather, I want to illustrate what pain-full preaching can do. As I have boasted in my weakness and shared these hardships with others in my preaching ministry, God has used my pain for his glory and to encourage others. Paul writes to the Corinthian believers, "Praise be to the God and Father of our Lord Jesus Christ, the Father of compassion and the God of all comfort, who comforts us in all our troubles, so that we can comfort those in any trouble with the comfort we ourselves receive from God" (2 Cor 1:3–4).

A theological homiletic or homiletical theology invites us to explore human suffering, broadly, and more specifically, personal suffering. The common denominator we share with fellow Christians is not success but suffering. Guest preaching one Sunday, as I shared my testimony about having glaucoma and losing significant peripheral vision, about eight elderly congregants came up to me and related the pain of vision loss with me. They encouraged me as I sought to encourage them.

On another Sunday, as I was using my brother's murder as a sermon illustration, an older lady came up to me after the worship service and was weeping. She proceeded to tell me that two years ago her daughter had been murdered. She shared how she felt like no minister understood her pain. We cried and prayed together in the sanctuary. People usually do not connect with us in our success but in our suffering. This leads to three final encouragements for adopting a homiletic of weakness.

Three Encouragements from Adopting Paul's Homiletic of Weakness

First, a homiletic of weakness will encourage intentional prayerfulness. When we recognize our weakness and utter dependence on God's power, it will cause us to pray more. Effective preaching is connected to prayerful engagement. Jesus made this clear when he said, "I am the vine; you are the branches. If you remain in me and I in you, you will bear much fruit; apart from me you can do nothing" (John 15:5). When we are suffering, we will pray more for ourselves, our sanctification, our loved ones, our parishioners, our communities, our preaching, our teaching, our counseling, our leadership, our pastoring. I would like to embolden you today to pray even more for your preaching ministry. No amount of hermeneutical or homiletical savvy can transform us and our hearers; only God can. A homiletic of weakness challenges us to pray.

Second, a homiletic of weakness encourages us to preach God's word more than ourselves. Paul's charge to Timothy applies to us: "In the presence of God and of Christ Jesus, who will judge the living and the dead, and in view of his appearing and his kingdom, I give you this charge: Preach the word; be prepared in season and out of season; correct, rebuke and encourage—with great patience and careful instruction" (2 Tim 4:1–2). What if our preaching was marked by more Scripture and less self? A student in class once gave this helpful example: "We can think of interpersonal conversations as 'time of possession' in football. How much time do we spend talking about ourselves and how much time is spent asking questions and listening to the person in front of us?" In the same way, how much time is spent talking about the triune God and about the particular Scripture text versus time on other less important matters?

Will you try an experiment in the coming weeks? Listen back on a recent sermon and calculate the time. How much pulpit time did you give to teaching, expositing, and applying God's word and how much was spent on yourself, what you did that week, telling other stories, and commenting on the culture? A homiletic of weakness encourages more Scripture and less self.

Third, a homiletic of weakness calls for discipleship through obedience. Jesus expected full obedience from his disciples. Jesus's instructions are straightforward in the Great Commission, leaving no wiggle room from discipleship as obedience: "[Teach] them to obey everything I have commanded you. And surely I am with you always, to the very end of the age" (Matt 28:20). Discipleship occurs not just through practicing spiritual disciplines of prayer, giving, Scripture reading, and fasting, but through obedience. In our weakness, may God's power help us to live out our faith through complete obedience to the Lord in all things.

Conclusion

Some of you reading this may be wondering at this point, What did he preach on for the sermon competition on that frigid winter day in Wisconsin at the age of thirteen? I do not remember much, but I do recall selecting one of my favorite Bible verses: "Now to him who is able to do immeasurably more than all we ask or imagine, according to his power that is at work within us, to him be glory in the church and in Christ Jesus throughout all generations, for ever and ever! Amen" (Eph 3:20–21). I wonder if leaning into a homiletical-theological prolegomena can nurture closer ties between preaching and theology, and perhaps even humility and weakness.

So, let me ask, is your preaching pain-full, humble, full of weakness? Does it rely on Scripture and on the power of the Holy Spirit? Is it steeped in prayer? Does it seek to empathize with the suffering of our people? Does it lead to doxology? We might have a few pew sleepers along the way, no matter what we do, but the future of preaching, I believe, rests in a theological homiletic of humility and weakness. As we grow in these countercultural Christian attributes, following in the way of the incarnate Lord and the apostle Paul, may the triune God's power be manifest in our weakness, meeting us in our prayer closets, and emboldening and empowering our pulpits and pews. To God be the glory.

Bibliography

Barry, John D., et al., eds. "Eutychus." In *The Lexham Bible Dictionary*. Bellingham, WA: Lexham, 2016. Digital Logos Edition.
Bauckham, Richard. "Weakness—Paul's and Ours." *Themelios* 7 (1982) 4–6.
Beaty, Katelyn. *Celebrities for Jesus: How Personas, Platforms, and Profits Are Hurting the Church*. Grand Rapids: Brazos, 2022.
Bonhoeffer, Dietrich. *Ethics*. New York: Touchstone, 1995.
Dean, Robert. "Powerful Preaching: Fleming Rutledge's Parchman Lectures." Thinking After, September 30, 2019. http://thinkingafter.com/powerful-preaching-fleming-rutledges-parchman-lectures/.

PART TWO: THE HUMILITY OF THE PULPIT

Foster, Richard J. *Learning Humility: A Year of Searching for a Vanishing Virtue.* Downers Grove, IL: InterVarsity, 2022.

Kirby, Ben. *PreachersNSneakers: Authenticity in an Age of For-Profit Faith and (Wannabe) Celebrities.* Nashville: Thomas Nelson, 2021.

Kuhn, Chase R. "Theology for Preaching, Preaching for Theology." In *Theology Is for Preaching: Biblical Foundations, Method, and Practice*, edited by Chase R. Kuhn and Paul Grimmond, 1–17. Bellingham, WA: Lexham, 2021.

Lischer, Richard. *A Theology of Preaching: The Dynamics of the Gospel.* Eugene, OR: Wipf & Stock, 2001.

Litfin, Duane. *Paul's Theology of Preaching: The Apostle's Challenge to the Art of Persuasion in Ancient Corinth.* Downers Grove, IL: IVP Academic, 2015.

Long, Thomas G. *Matthew.* Westminster Bible Companion. Louisville: Westminster John Knox, 1997.

O'Donnell, Douglas Sean, and Leland Ryken. *The Beauty and Power of Biblical Exposition: Preaching the Literary Artistry and Genres of the Bible.* Wheaton, IL: Crossway, 2022.

Swain, Scott R. *The Trinity: An Introduction.* Wheaton, IL: Crossway, 2020.

7

From Bully Pulpits to Kata-pulpits

*Preaching with Well-Tempered Boldness
in the Economy of Divine Communication*

KEVIN J. VANHOOZER

INTRODUCTION: SOWING INTO THE AIR

CAN WE BY SPEAKING into the air, from pulpits, change the world? Paul uses the phrase "speaking into the air" pejoratively in 1 Cor 14:9 to compare the futility of speaking in tongues without translation to a boxer who, because he cannot land a punch, is only "beating the air" (1 Cor 9:26 ESV). In context, "speaking into the air" signifies powerless, ineffectual, and incoherent speech—simply put, a short-circuited communication.

Speaking into the Air is also the title of John Durham Peters's excellent study of the idea of communication: its nature, history, and challenges.[1] I call it "general communications theory" because Peters does not treat the "special communications theory" that preaching requires and exemplifies. Preaching, I want to argue, is more, but not less, than a form of human communication. My purpose in what follows is to explicate that *more*.

Jesus's parable of the Sower (Matt 13:3–8, 18–23) likens speaking into the air to throwing seeds into the air. Speakers can sow, but they cannot control where the words land or whether they take root. In some cases, the sown

---

1. Peters, *Speaking into the Air*.

word is remarkably effective, yielding understanding, and a crop a hundred times larger. We can read the entire book of Acts as an enacted parable of the sower, "as a drama which has this [preached] word as its protagonist. It is the story of the [preached] word's advance."[2] For Luke and the authors of the New Testament, the pulpit—the place from which the word is sown—leads the world, for "preaching stood as the event through which God works."[3]

To preach the word of God is to speak truth into the air. This is how Augustine thought about communication in general: "When there is an idea in your heart, [it] . . . clothes itself in the sound, somehow gets itself into this vehicle, travels through the air, comes to me . . . through my ear your thought descended into my heart."[4] Jesus taught with parables, but the medium of his communication was open-air preaching, as it was for later evangelicals like George Whitefield, Charles Spurgeon, and Billy Graham. Speaking into the air is arguably the core activity of ministers of the word.

My topic is not communication in general but preaching, understood as a theological act. I begin by contrasting public speech in general with that speech peculiar to the gathered church: the ministry of the word's proclamation. This leads to reflection on Heinrich Bullinger's claim in the Second Helvetic Confession that the preaching of the word of God *is* the word of God. I turn next to my primary aim: to provide a theology of preaching, specifically, a dogmatic description of the (speech) act of preaching. I then consider some implications for our theme of the power and authority of the pulpit and give some suggestions as to how this theological account of preaching ought to bear on the preacher's boldness of speech. But we begin with bully pulpits.

A Tale of Two Pulpits

Bully Pulpits: Speaking into the Air to Persuade

I wonder if there has ever been a more precarious time to speak into the air than the present day. An idle comment captured on social media can destroy a person's career. Communication is fraught with danger. That is because it involves, not simply a transfer of information but "social interaction through messages,"[5] an interaction that can establish, nurture, disrupt, or ruin relationships. We speak into the air in the hope of breaking through racial, social, and generational barriers, but according to Peters, "Humans are hardwired by the

---

2. Higton, *Life of Christian Doctrine*, 78.
3. Robinson, *Biblical Preaching*, 2.
4. Augustine, *Tractates* 37.4.
5. Fiske, *Introduction to Communication Studies*, 2.

privacy of their experience to have communication problems."[6] Our polarized political environment is a further complication.

Still, the idea of having a bully pulpit—a platform from which to advocate for one's ideas and beliefs—is attractive. It was Theodore Roosevelt who coined the term *bully pulpit*, referring to the presidency as a particularly prominent platform for promoting causes and influencing public opinion. In context, "bully" meant "excellent" or "superb," as in "bully for you." But these days it may be just as common for people to view any public platform as "bully" in the other sense, a platform for exercising coercive communicative power. The postmodern suspicion—that speaking into the air from a position of privilege is always for the purpose of maintaining privilege—may explain the widespread distrust of politicians, and why so few voters change their minds after hearing candidates speak.

Sadly, it is becoming increasingly challenging (some would say futile) to speak into the air, or to preach, in our age of widespread distrust and cynicism. One recent book on preaching bemoans the folk postmodernism that makes even those who have never heard of Derrida suspicious of authorities and authoritative claims: "to be postmodern is to be post-certain."[7]

Pastors who speak into this poisonous public air on a weekly basis may understandably want to empower their bully pulpits by honing their communication skills. Some theorists distinguish between "tactical" and "strategic" approaches. Some speakers rely primarily on tactics, desiring to craft and deliver sermons with insights from general communication studies, messages that persuade people to believe or do certain things, or succeed in being relevant or entertaining. By way of contrast, speaking into the air is strategic if it aims at influencing a person's sense of what is real, their social imaginary.

It is tempting to use every new technology that comes along in the hope that, like the printing press, new media might speed our ministry of the gospel and help us to out-communicate the opposition. Is it wise to want to be like the other digital nations? Augustine, a classically trained rhetorician, encouraged Christians to "plunder the Egyptians," particularly their persuasive techniques—as long as one deployed them to speak what is true and for building up the communion of saints, not for career purposes, like increasing your number of Facebook friends and social media followers. Augustine knew that pastors speak into the air in vain but for the grace of God. Before we say more about God's gracious activity, though, I want to explore another kind of pulpit.

---

6. Peters, *Speaking into the Air*, 4.
7. Allen, *Theology for Preaching*, 28.

PART TWO: THE HUMILITY OF THE PULPIT

Kata-pulpits: Curating the Word of God

The kata-pulpit. No, it is not a weapon for flinging one's own ideas into the air in the arena of public opinion. Nor is it a stage for the pastor to display his talents, sense of humor, or good looks. That is what TV is for. By "kata-pulpit," I mean to call attention to preaching being "in accordance with" a prior subject matter to which it is accountable. I am thinking in particular of 1 Cor 15:3, where Paul says he delivered to the Corinthians a message of first importance, "that Christ died for our sins in accordance with (*kata* + the accusative) the Scriptures." A kata-pulpit is a holy place, a set-apart platform for speaking into the air words that are in accordance with the Scriptures.

The pulpit is not the place to exercise one's First Amendment right to freedom of speech, at least not if that means freedom *from* the written word of God. It happens. I remember one particular evensong at King's College Chapel during my time in Cambridge when instead of a Bible passage we had a reading from D. H. Lawrence's *Sons and Lovers*—a novel about a young man's troubled relationships with his mother and two very different women.

It is imperative that preaching be in accordance with (*kata*) the subject matter of the Scriptures, even when it is not popular to do so: "For the time is coming when people will not endure sound teaching, but having itching ears they will accumulate for themselves teachers to suit their own passions" (2 Tim 4:3). The noun that follows the preposition *kata* typically "specifies the criterion, standard, or norm in the light of which a statement is made or is true."[8] For example, Luke tells us in Acts 2:23 that Jesus was delivered up "according to [*kata*] the definite plan and foreknowledge of God." Paul in Rom 16:25 says that his gospel and preaching of Christ is "according to [*kata*] the revelation of the mystery that was kept secret for long ages." In Col 2:8, he contrasts the deceptive philosophy which is *kata* human tradition with his own preaching which is *kata* Christ. Preaching from a kata-pulpit is thus preaching that corresponds to or is in conformity with an external standard, the will of God, revealed in the word of God, living and written.

What we proclaim from a kata-pulpit is therefore *bound* speech. Both our conscience and our discourse must be captive to the word of God. However, our speech is not so bound that preachers can only repeat a biblical passage word-for-word. For the genesis of understanding begins only with the exodus from verbatim repetition. I have used various metaphors to describe the work of the pastor theologian: farmers of men (and women); bodybuilders; theater directors of the company of the gospel; artisans in the house of God.[9] Let

---

8. *NIDNTE*, "κατά," 2:633.
9. Vanhoozer, "Introduction," 23–24.

me now share another metaphor that is especially apt in thinking about the kata-pulpit: the curator.

I am aware that the image of the person in charge of various collections—like the twenty-two thousand sets of condiment dispensers at the Salt and Pepper Shaker Museum in Gatlinburg, Tennessee, the antique Dog Collar museum in Leeds Castle, United Kingdom, or the National Museum of Roller Skating in Lincoln, Nebraska—may not generate much excitement. Accessioning and cataloging are hardly superpowers. But the essence of the curator's vocation has everything to do with the pastor's kata-pulpit.

The term curator comes from the Latin *cura* ("to take care of"). Whatever the collection, a curator has two main tasks: preservation and presentation. Pastor theologians are responsible for *preserving* the collection of books that comprise the Old and New Testaments. Pastors preserve not the physical objects so much as the content, a process that involves study and research, often in collaboration with others, in order to understand the items in the collection. Like the Jews, pastors have been entrusted with the "oracles of God" (Rom 3:2), like Paul, with the good deposit of the gospel (1 Thess 2:4; cf. 1 Tim 1:11; 6:20; 2 Tim 1:14).

The pulpit comes into its own, however, when we consider the curator's second task: *presenting*. The curator is the person who interprets and exhibits the items in the collection to the public. A curator has to decide which items to display, how to arrange them, and how to communicate their significance.

Think of the pulpit as the place where pastors make the word of God accessible and intelligible to a gathered assembly. Interestingly, Paul describes not only the gospel but the *preaching* that brings God's word to light as itself that with which he has been entrusted (Titus 1:3). If the pastor theologian is the curator of the word of God, preaching is the principal public exhibit, the pulpit its exhibit case. Good curators also serve as advocates for their collection by showing their continued relevance and significance. In addition to preserving and presenting, then, they must also promote the value of the gathered assembly's continued attention and participation. They must communicate their own passion for the subject matter to others so that their enthusiasm becomes infectious. In preserving, presenting, and inviting reflection on and response to God's word, pastor-curators lead others in their congregations to care about participating in the story of Scripture as much as they do. In sum: preaching is word-care (preservation), word-craft (presentation), and word-cheer (promotion).[10] If you are still not convinced by my new metaphor, consider the etymology of "curator": it is the same root as the old English term

---

10. Cf. Augustine's claim that a Christian orator must aim to teach, delight, and persuade. Augustine, *Teaching Christianity* 4.12.27.

for pastor—curate, one who cares for the people in his parish. We curate the people of God by serving as curators of the word of God.

Text: "The Preaching of the Word of God is the Word of God"

And with that insight we arrive at my central topic: a theology of preaching, by which I mean a dogmatic account of the pastor theologian's preaching. Let me state the question I hope to answer: Are sermons delivered from a well-curated kata-pulpit the word of God? Does it follow from God having spoken *behind* the text (in history) and *in* the text (via inspiration) that God also speaks *in front of* the text, namely, through preaching?

Bullinger's Rule

The Bible is replete with examples of human messengers appointed by God to deliver his word: "Long ago, at many times and in many ways, God spoke to our fathers by the prophets" (Heb 1:1). Jesus is greater than those servants, for he is the Son and Word of God, yet the risen Christ anoints the apostles with his Spirit, empowering them to be his witnesses, and sends them to preach "in his name to all nations" (Luke 24:47). According to the book of Acts, the church grew because believers received the word that begets faith not directly from Christ, but from those who preached him. Paul asks his Roman readers "to become the 'feet' of the Isaianic servant who brings good news (Rom 10:15; cf. Isa 52:7)."[11] Paul also charges Timothy, "Preach the word" (2 Tim 4:2).

The "text" of this essay is Bullinger's claim, stated in the Second Helvetic Confession: *Praedicatio verbi Dei est verbum Dei* ("The preaching of the Word of God *is* the Word of God"). What follows provides a little nuance: "Wherefore when this Word of God is now preached in the church by preachers lawfully called, we believe that the very Word of God is preached, and received by the faithful."[12] As Edward Dowey points out, Bullinger here corrects the enthusiasts who claimed to have direct revelations from God.[13] Though God can use other means to bring about faith (Barth mentions God speaking "through Russian Communism, a flute concerto, a blossoming shrub, or a dead dog"[14]), preaching is the ordinary ordained means of doing so. Scripture

---

11. Chan, *Preaching*, 110.
12. Bullinger, "Second Helvetic Confession," 1.4.
13. Dowey, "Word of God," 8. See also Scharf, "Was Bullinger Right?"
14. Barth, *Doctrine of the Word*, 1.1, 55.

remains normative, but "the preaching of the Word becomes the instrumental means that the Holy Spirit uses as he causes the faithful to hear the very voice of God."[15] Bullinger's formation may be the best known, but Luther and Calvin made similar claims.

Related Formulations

Martin Luther

Martin Luther made the sermon the centerpiece of Protestant Christianity, even if it was Zwingli who first recommended moving the pulpit to the center of the church. Luther explained the power of the pulpit in effecting the Reformation, saying, "I simply taught, preached, wrote God's Word; otherwise I did nothing . . . the Word of God did it all."[16]

Commenting on Rom 10:15 ("And how are they to preach unless they are sent?"), Luther says we recognize whether a preacher has been sent from God if he speaks "only what is commanded to him and not what he likes or has invented."[17] Nevertheless, even those who have a mandate to preach must acknowledge their limits. In Luther's words, "I can get no farther than to men's ears; their hearts I cannot reach. . . . That is God's work alone. . . . We have the *jus verbi* [right to speak], but not the *executio* [power to do]."[18]

To preach God's word is to preach the gospel of Jesus Christ, which for Luther means both the message Jesus proclaimed and the message about what God has done in Christ. It is a liberating message which should be "so presented that you hear your God speak to you."[19] Both the written and proclaimed word of God present Christ—talk about curating!

John Calvin

I began by asking whether we can change the world by speaking into the air. Calvin thought so. He viewed preaching "as the primary means by which God's work is accomplished in individual life and the community."[20] And he gave the Lord plenty of opportunity to work, preaching more than two

---

15. Baines, "*Praedicatio Verbi Dei*," 38.
16. Luther, "Eight Wittenberg Sermons," 399–400.
17. Luther, *Lectures on Romans*, 297.
18. Luther, "Eight Wittenberg Sermons," 397–98.
19. Luther, "Freedom of a Christian," 359.
20. Leith, "Calvin, John," 60.

thousand sermons. In all of them, Calvin kept in mind the voice that spoke from the cloud at Jesus's transfiguration: "Listen to him [i.e., Christ]" (Matt 17:5). The prophets proclaimed only what had been spoken to them by God, and even Jesus said, "My teaching is not mine, but his who sent me" (John 7:16). Preachers do well to remember this.[21]

On the other hand, Calvin responds in no uncertain terms to those who think God's word is distorted or diluted "by the baseness of the men called to teach it" and thus consider preaching superfluous: "It is a singular privilege that [God] deigns to consecrate to himself the mouths and tongues of men in order that his voice may resound in them."[22] This is part of divine accommodation, God stooping and lisping: God wills to speak to us through human means.[23]

Karl Barth

For Karl Barth, himself a pastor theologian, the sermon was the minister's prime problem.[24] The challenge is to proclaim the Word of God, which for him meant primarily Jesus Christ himself, not a set of statements about Jesus Christ. The Word of God is the commission, content, and criterion of proclamation. A hundred years ago, Barth wrote an open letter to his former teacher Adolf von Harnack, insisting that "the task of theology is one with the task of preaching."[25] In the same year, he urged Reformed churches to recover the theme of God speaking: *Deux dixit*.[26]

For Barth, the word of God has three forms: the making known of God in Jesus Christ, the witness to that event in Scripture and, finally, the proclamation of that witness in the church. It has been said that Barth's life work "was one grand single meditation on the presupposition of the sermon—not on the (secondary, homiletical) question, 'How *does* one do it?,' but on the (primary, theological) question, 'How *can* one do it?' That is, 'How does God enable human discourse about God?'"[27] The short answer: God freely, graciously, and miraculously chooses to make himself present in faithful proclamation. "God is Lord in the wording of his Word."[28]

21. Calvin, *Institutes*, 4.8.4.
22. Calvin, *Institutes*, 4.1.5.
23. Calvin, *Institutes*, 4.1.5.
24. Barth, *Word of God*, 100.
25. Barth, "Answer," 48.
26. Barth, *Word of God*, 252.
27. Stoevesandt, "Barth, Karl," 27.
28. Barth, *Doctrine of the Word*, 1.1, 139.

The Question

Bullinger's axiom raises an important theological question: "When is preaching the word of God, and how is [it] to be discerned?"[29] Peter Adam worries that if we equate "any one sermon as a word of God, we are beginning to treat human explanations and ideas as God's words."[30] We need to wax analytic for a moment to further clarify the key issues: is *all* preaching the word of God or only *some* preaching? Is preaching *always* the word of God or only *sometimes*?

Consider the logical possibilities: (all/some/no) preaching is *always* the word of God; (all/some/no) preaching is *never* the word of God; (all/some/no) preaching is *sometimes* the word of God. I think we can eliminate the extreme views, namely, that preaching is *never* the word of God or that preaching is *always* the word of God. We are left with the option that *some* preaching is *sometimes* the word of God. This generates further questions: *when* is preaching the word of God, under *what* conditions, and when these conditions are met does preaching convey the same authority and power as God's word? And finally: How can we recognize preaching that is the word of God, and is it still the word of God if it is not so recognized? If a sermon falls in a chapel and there are no ears to hear it, is it still the word of God?

Exposition: Towards a Dogmatic Account of Preaching

Deux dixit. God speaks. A dogmatic account of preaching must begin here, with the astounding claim that the Creator of heaven and earth has spoken in human language. Consider: If God did not actually speak, with words, then we would not know what he is up to. But he has spoken, through the prophets and apostles, in Scripture (the word written) and, definitively, through his Son (the living Word). Is God's word still living and active if we confine it to the past, to propositional revelation? The danger here is a peculiarly Christian version of deism: not the claim that God created and then withdrew from the world but, rather, that he inspired Scripture and then withdrew from the church. The question, then, is whether preaching is a means of God's speaking in the present: "Today, if you hear his voice, do not harden your hearts" (Heb 3:15).

---

29. Chan, *Preaching*, 6.
30. Adam, *Speaking God's Words*, 115.

Speech Act Accounts

Some commentators see a connection between Barth's idea that God's word is God in action and the philosophical notion of speech acts, a reminder that speakers are not simply uttering sounds (locuting) but, in saying something, are also performing actions (illocuting), and perhaps, *by* illocuting, bringing about further actions (perlocuting). For example, John in his Gospel is not simply writing Greek sentences but narrating the story of Jesus (the illocution), in order to persuade his readers (the perlocution).

Nicholas Wolterstorff

Nicholas Wolterstorff compares and contrasts two Reformed understandings of what it means to identify preaching with the word of God. First, he examines the Swiss liturgical theologian Jean-Jacques von Allmen who, drawing on Barth, views the minister as proclaiming the Word of God, *presenting* Christ. In Allmen's words, "[Preaching] prevents the petrifaction of the Word of God in the *illic et tunc* [there and then] . . . of its coming in Jesus Christ, and makes that *illic et tunc* newly operative in the *hic et nunc* [here and now]."[31] Strictly speaking, on this model the preacher does not speak for God. Rather, the word of God proclaims itself by means of the preacher's speech such that the sermon "becomes" the word of God, God's personal address.

In contrast, Calvin views the minister as a deputy of God and preaching as what Wolterstorff terms "deputized discourse."[32] Like the Old Testament prophets, the preacher locutes (provides the words and sentences), but the illocutionary act—promising, commanding, warning, etc.—is God's. Wolterstorff suggests that preaching, like prophesying, is an example of double-agency discourse: the word of the Lord in human discourse. At the very least, preachers must *undertake* to preach the word of God rather than air their own opinions.[33]

Sam Chan

The most ambitious attempt to use speech act theory to explain how preaching the word of God is the word of God is Sam Chan's *Preaching as the Word of God*. Viewing preaching as discourse—something someone says to someone about something for some purpose—allows Chan to discuss the preacher's

---

31. Allmen, *Worship*, 143.
32. Wolterstorff, *Divine Discourse*, 13.
33. Wolterstorff, "Preaching the Word," 267.

intentions and to draw on speech act theory's criteria for distinguishing between "happy" (felicitous) and "unhappy" (infelicitous) speech acts, between speech acts that hit their mark and those that misfire.

The gist of Chan's argument is that the preacher speaks at God's behest and on God's behalf, re-locuting and re-illocuting the divine speech acts previously locuted and illocuted by the prophets and apostles in Scripture.[34] Significantly, the human preacher "is not responsible for the perlocutionary effects."[35] Chan faults Barth for appearing to reduce the whole speech act to the perlocutionary act by identifying the word of God with the event of faith that comes from hearing. He faults expository preachers for exaggerating the locutionary dimension and for failing to recapture the illocutionary act.[36] Finally, he answers my earlier question about whether preaching that fails to be recognized as the word of God is still the word of God. It is, says Chan, if the sermon is a "happy" speech act. That is, if a commissioned speech agent satisfies certain "felicity" conditions and successfully re-locutes and re-illocutes the original scriptural speech act.[37]

Preaching in the Economy of Communication

"God has always been a communicator."[38] Speech act theory provides helpful ministerial concepts, but more is required to explicate Bullinger's formula. What follows is a more robust theological analysis of preaching—a dogmatic account that locates preaching in the broader triune economy of communication.

I have argued elsewhere that God's being is a being in communicative activity, namely, the perfect life of Father, Son, and Spirit whose loving communications issue in communion.[39] Preaching is not just a means to an end; it corresponds to the communicative character of God and to the communicative means God has appointed to bring about communion with himself and others. Preaching is a thoroughly theological activity, not simply because the gospel of God is its content but because the God of the gospel is also its

---

34. Chan, *Preaching*, 211.
35. Chan, *Preaching*, 211.
36. Chan himself assigns priority to the locutionary aspect on the grounds that it is foundational to the other two. Chan, *Preaching*, 213.
37. On felicity conditions, see Chan, *Preaching*, 205–9.
38. Thompson, "Declarative God," 19.
39. Vanhoozer, *Remythologizing Theology*, 241–59.

communicative *agent*: "The ministry of the church is, by the Holy Spirit, a sharing in God's ministry to and for us in, through, and as Jesus Christ."[40]

"Jesus came . . . [preaching] the gospel of God" (Mark 1:14). Of course he did. Our God is a communicating God. The Father initiates, the Son executes, and the Spirit perfects the communicative action. In particular, the Son performs his threefold office as prophet, priest, and king. Jesus commissions witnesses who will minister the stuff of life, "every word that comes from the mouth of God" (Matt 4:4). He also commands preachers to "feed my sheep" (John 21:17). What sets preaching from the kata-pulpit apart from every other form of human speech is, first, its service to the written word and, second, its participation in the Father-sent, Spirit-empowered, Son's prophetic ministry.

Paul says in Eph 4:11 that the risen and ascended Christ gives gifts to the church to equip all the saints for the work of ministry. These gifts are church officers—apostles, prophets, evangelists, and pastor-teachers. Each of these divinely appointed offices represents a different form of the ministry of the word, a different God-ordained means by which God communicates his light and life in love in order "to equip the saints for the work of ministry, for building up the body of Christ" (Eph 4:12). This is the broader economy of communication in which we should locate preaching, the pastoral proclamation of the word and gospel of God.

Preachers have a place in the pattern of divine communication, for preaching "is located within the plans and purposes of God for his world."[41] Think about it: God ordains that the words pastor theologians speak into the air achieve his ordained purpose. At least this is what I think Bullinger means: "For God himself alone, by sending his Holy Spirit into the hearts and minds of men, doth open our hearts, persuade our minds, and cause us with all our heart to believe that which we by his word and teaching have learned to believe."[42] Perhaps we too often look for divine action in the wrong place. It is not in the chaos of the thunderstorm, or the quirkiness of the quark. Perhaps it begins in the pulpit, which Herman Melville famously compares in *Moby Dick* to the prow at the front of a ship: "The pulpit leads the world." Or, as Edwin Chr. van Driel states, "The church . . . is itself a place where the ascended Christ enacts his eschatological reclaiming and transforming of creation."[43]

Preachers participate in what is ultimately Christ's work. Bullinger writes, "That thing which Christ . . . worketh in his Catholic Church inwardly,

---

40. Purves, *Reconstructing Pastoral Theology*, 4.
41. Kuhn and Grimmond, "Preface," xx.
42. Bullinger, *First and Second Decades*, 84–85.
43. Van Driel, "What Is Jesus Doing," 7.

... the very same outwardly he declareth and testifieth by his ministers."[44] May we not say, with Calvin, that Christ is "really present" not only in the sacraments, but also in the ministry of the word, that "the pulpit is his throne" and preachers his emissaries and heralds?[45] For preaching, viewed theologically, does not simply proclaim the God of the gospel but *presents* him, or rather, serves as an occasion for his self-presentation. D. A. Carson describes this as "re-revelation": "There is a sense in which God, who revealed himself by that word in the past, is re-revealing himself by that same word once again."[46]

We are used to asking "What would Jesus do," but a recent collection of essays poses another question—"What is Jesus doing?"—and goes on to answer, "Jesus is gathering himself a church."[47] This is arguably the end of the economy of communication, an end planned by the triune God "before the foundation of the world," as we learn from Eph 1, where we read that God chose to bless us with a heavenly inheritance in Christ. This, too, is the economy of communication: the Father predestines to adopt us as sons and daughters in the Son through the Holy Spirit. And it is God's will that preaching from the kata-pulpit must proclaim, inhabit, and explore this reality: "Jesus Christ does not want to do his prophetic work alone. He desires human participation."[48]

Preaching is therefore the seriously joyful practice "by which the church is taken into the very life of God."[49] Speaking invites another person into our space, "to exist with us, to associate with us . . . in real time."[50] Similarly, preaching invites us to become communicants in the economy of God's self-communication: "The actual context for preaching is the divine agency of the triune God."[51] "Ministry," says Andrew Root, "is the movement into being (of neighbor and God) through act."[52] It is a participation in the economy of communication that comes from the Father through the Son in the power of the Spirit.

---

44. Bullinger, *Fifth Decade*, 96–97.

45. Parker, *Calvin's Preaching*, 27. Cf. the discussion of Christ's active presence in preaching in Orr, "New Testament Clarity," 128–41, esp. 130.

46. Carson, "Challenges," 176.

47. Van Driel, "Rethinking Church," 48.

48. Hancock, "Prophetic Agency," 285.

49. Owens, *Shape of Participation*, 67.

50. Schultze, *Habits*, 175.

51. Johnson, "Preaching in Context," 295.

52. Root, "Ministry," 203.

PART TWO: THE HUMILITY OF THE PULPIT

Application: The Peculiar Power of the Kata-pulpit

I turn now to the application section of my essay on the theology of preaching. In time-honored fashion, I have three points. Each one concerns the posture of the preacher as curator of God's word in the kata-pulpit.

Humility of Spirit: Recognizing the Locus of Authority

First, whatever authority a sermon carries derives not from the force of a preacher's personality or academic degrees, but from the office of the ministry of word and sacrament to which one has been appointed or, as Calvin says, "to the Word, whose ministry is entrusted to them."[53] People do not go to museums or art exhibits to meet the curator, but to see the art. Moreover, as curator of God's word, "The preacher is not one who applies an old word to new situations, but . . . a servant and an instrument of the living Word, the *viva Vox Dei*, for its effective operation in the world."[54] John Piper acknowledges the privilege and responsibility of speaking from a kata-pulpit: "The Bible-oriented preacher wants the congregation to know that *his* words, if they have any abiding worth, are in accord with *God's* words. He wants this to be obvious to them. That is the root of his humility and authority."[55]

Boldness of Speech: Remembering the Source of Kata-pulpit Power

Second, preaching that is in accordance with Scripture is a species of bold or fearless speech. The power of the pulpit is, in Calvin's words, the power to "dare boldly to do all things by God's Word . . . to compel all worldly power, glory, wisdom, and exaltation to yield to and obey [God's] majesty."[56] Here I stand, in the pulpit, an ordained minister of the word and ambassador of Christ. As John Webster reminds us, to hear the word exposited is to hearken to the address of Christ in and through his commissioned witnesses: "At his glorification to the Father's right hand, Jesus Christ does not resign his office of self-communication."[57] Boldness of speech therefore stems, not from self-confidence in one's own ratiocination or rhetoric but from the encouragement of the Spirit who, in "couraging" us, gives us a spirit of fearlessness, and from the conviction that preachers are the *porte-paroles* of the risen Christ, heralds and bearers of

---

53. Calvin, *Institutes*, 4.8.2.
54. Muller, *Dictionary*, 328.
55. Piper, *Supremacy of God*, 125.
56. Calvin, *Institutes*, 4.8.9.
57. Webster, "Visible Attests the Invisible," 109.

the king's speech. The apostle Paul is the paradigm of one who proclaimed the gospel boldly, and boldness of speech was surely in his mind when he encouraged the Corinthians, "Be imitators of me" (1 Cor 4:16).

Vivacity of Imagination: Recapturing the Eyes of the Heart

Third, when preachers proclaim the king's speech, they tap into the peculiar power of the kata-pulpit, namely, the power to fling not stones but stories into the air, the better to take captive what Paul terms the "eyes of [the heart]" (Eph 1:18)—every thought, imagination, and social imaginary. Those who proclaim the king have the power to turn the world upside down (cf. Acts 17:6) as did Jesus's parables of the kingdom. The great Scottish preacher James Stewart knew that it is not enough to believe something theoretically "without ever seeing it, imagining it, realizing it in its exciting dramatic reality."[58] Preachers have, in Calvin's words, the power to "build up Christ's household and cast down Satan's."[59] The power of the pulpit consists in exhibiting the already/not-yet reality of a new humanity in Christ. "According to Calvin, preaching is the instrument God uses to span time and space and to bring Christian, Christ, and cross together."[60] Rembrandt does just this when he painted himself into the scene in his 1633 work *The Raising of the Cross*. A picture may speak a thousand words, but the words preachers utter from the kata-pulpit are the means the Spirit uses to arrest attention, form consciousness, and capture the imagination. John Piper observes that even a sentence can change your life insofar as it offers "a new glimpse into reality or truth."[61]

Conclusion

It is the privilege and responsibility of all Christians, and not preachers only, to "proclaim the excellencies of him who has called [us] out of darkness into his marvelous light" (1 Pet 2:9). The power of the pulpit is not in competition with the congregation's embodied witness, but its enabler: its template and catalyst—its concentrate.

Can preachers by speaking into the air change the world? Yes, they can! Through ordinary human words, God can intrude into the intimate realm of

---

58. Stewart, *King for Ever*, 39.
59. Calvin, *Institutes*, 4.8.9.
60. Davis, *This Is My Body*, 99.
61. Piper, "1 Percent."

our imagination, present Christ, and begin to reshape our world.[62] Preaching is the cutting edge of the word's forward progress as, empowered by the Spirit, it continues to increase (Acts 6:7), multiply (Acts 12:24), and prevail mightily (Acts 19:20), communicating Christ and, in so doing, turning the world upside down one heart and mind at a time.

Bibliography

Adam, Peter. *Speaking God's Words: A Practical Theology of Expository Preaching*. Leicester: IVP, 1996.

Allen, Ronald J., et al. *Theology for Preaching: Authority, Truth, and Knowledge of God in a Postmodern Ethos*. Nashville: Abingdon, 1997.

Allmen, Jean-Jaques von. *Worship: Its Theology and Practice*. London: Lutterworth, 1965.

Augustine. *Teaching Christianity*. Translated by Edmund Hill. Hyde Park, NY: New City, 1995.

———. *Tractates on the Gospel of John 28–54*. Translated by John W. Rettig. Washington, DC: Catholic University Press of America, 2002.

Baines, Ronald. "*Praedicatio Verbi Dei est Verbum Dei*: 'The Preaching of the Word of God is the Word of God'—Heinrich Bullinger and the *Second Helvetic Confession*." *Journal of the Institute of Reformed Baptist Studies* 2 (2015) 25–42.

Barth, Karl. "An Answer to Adolf von Harnack's Open Letter." In *The Essential Karl Barth: A Reader and Commentary*, edited by Keith L. Johnson, 44–56. Grand Rapids: Baker Academic, 2019.

———. *The Doctrine of the Word of God*. Vol. 1.1 of Church Dogmatics. Translated by G. W. Bromiley. Edinburgh: T&T Clark, 1975.

———. *The Word of God and the Word of Man*. Gloucester, MA: Peter Smith, 1978.

Bullinger, Heinrich. *The Decades of Henry Bullinger: The First and Second Decades*. Edited by Thomas Harding. Cambridge: Parker Society, 1849.

———. *The Decades of Henry Bullinger: The Fifth Decade*. Edited by Thomas Harding. Cambridge: Parker Society, 1852.

———. "Second Helvetic Confession." https://creedsandconfessions.org/second-helvetic-confession.html.

Calvin, John. *Institutes of the Christian Religion*. Library of Christian Classics. Edited by John T. McNeill. Philadelphia: Westminster, 1960.

Carson, D. A. "Challenges for the Twenty-First Century Pulpit." In *Preaching the Word: Essays on Expository Preaching in Honor of R. Kent Hughes*, edited by Leland Ryken and Todd A. Wilson, 172–89. Wheaton, IL: Crossway, 2007.

Chan, Sam. *Preaching as the Word of God: Answering an Old Question with Speech-Act Theory*. Eugene, OR: Pickwick, 2016.

Davis, Thomas J. *This Is My Body: The Presence of Christ in Reformation Thought*. Grand Rapids: Baker Academic, 2008.

---

62. I am paraphrasing Juel's description of how a student's words tore a gaping hole in his class's imagination: "Through ordinary words, God intruded into the intimate realm of our imagination and began reshaping our world." Juel, *Shaping the Scriptural Imagination*, 25.

Dowey, Edward A., Jr. "The Word of God as Scripture and Preaching." In *Later Calvinism: International Perspectives*, edited by W. Fred Graham, 5–18. Sixteenth Century Essays and Studies. Kirksville, MO: Northwest Missouri State University, 1994.
Fiske, John. *Introduction to Communication Studies*. 3rd ed. London: Routledge, 2010.
Hancock, Angela Diehard. "The Prophetic Agency of Jesus Christ and the Task of Preaching." In *What Is Jesus Doing? God's Activity in the Life and Work of the Church*, edited by Edwin Chr. van Driel, 270–92. Downers Grove, IL: IVP Academic, 2020.
Higton, Mike. *The Life of Christian Doctrine*. London: T&T Clark, 2020.
Johnson, Trygve D. "Preaching in Context." In *What Is Jesus Doing? God's Activity in the Life and Work of the Church*, edited by Edwin Chr. van Driel, 293–318. Downers Grove, IL: IVP Academic, 2020.
Juel, Donald. *Shaping the Scriptural Imagination: Truth, Meaning, and the Theological Interpretation of the Bible*. Waco, TX: Baylor University Press, 2011.
Kuhn, Charles R., and Paul Grimmond. "Preface." In *Theology Is for Preaching: Biblical Foundations, Method, and Practice*, edited by Chase R. Kuhn and Paul Grimmond, xix–xxi. Bellingham, WA: Lexham, 2021.
Leith, John H. "Calvin, John." In *Concise Encyclopedia of Preaching*, edited by William H. Willimon and Richard Lischer, 60–64. Louisville: Westminster John Knox, 1995.
Luther, Martin. "The Eight Wittenberg Sermons, 1522." Pages 387–428 in vol. 2 of *Works of Martin Luther*. Translated by A. Steimle. Philadelphia: A. J. Holman, 1915.
———. "The Freedom of a Christian." Pages 356–79 in *The Basis of the Protestant Reformation*. Edited by Bertram Lee-Woolf. Vol. 1 of *Reformation Writings of Martin Luther*. New York: Philosophical Library, 1952.
———. *Lectures on Romans*. Translated by Wilhelm Pauck. Philadelphia: Westminster, 1961.
Muller, Richard A. *Dictionary of Latin and Greek Theological Terms: Drawn Principally from Protestant Scholastic Theology*. Grand Rapids: Baker, 1985.
New International Dictionary of New Testament Theology and Exegesis (*NIDNTE*). 2nd ed. Edited by Moisés Silva. 5 vols. Grand Rapids: Zondervan, 2014.
Orr, Peter. "New Testament Clarity: The Presence of Christ in the Proclamation of the Word." In *Theology Is for Preaching: Biblical Foundations, Method, and Practice*, edited by Chase R. Kuhn and Paul Grimmond, 128–41. Bellingham, WA: Lexham, 2021.
Owens, L. Roger. *The Shape of Participation: A Theology of Church Practices*. Eugene, OR: Cascade, 2010.
Parker, T. H. L. *Calvin's Preaching*. Edinburgh: T&T Clark, 1992.
Peters, John Durham. *Speaking into the Air: A History of the Idea of Communication*. Chicago: University of Chicago Press, 2001.
Piper, John. "1 Percent of a Book Can Change Your Life." Ask Pastor John, March 8, 2023. https://www.desiringgod.org/interviews/1-percent-of-a-book-can-change-your-life.
———. *The Supremacy of God in Preaching*. Rev. ed. Grand Rapids: Baker, 2015.
Purves, Andrew. *Reconstructing Pastoral Theology: A Christological Foundation*. Louisville: Westminster John Knox, 2004.
Robinson, Haddon. *Biblical Preaching*. 3rd ed. Grand Rapids: Baker Academic, 2014.
Root, Andrew. "Ministry and the *Concursus Dei*." In *What Is Jesus Doing? God's Activity in the Life and Work of the Church*, edited by Edwin Chr. van Driel, 201–20. Downers Grove, IL: IVP Academic, 2020.

Scharf, Greg R. "Was Bullinger Right About the Preached Word?" *Trinity Journal* 26 (2005) 3–10.
Schultze, Quentin J. *Habits of the High-Tech Heart: Living Virtuously in the Information Age*. Grand Rapids: Baker, 2002.
Stewart, James S. *King for Ever*. Nashville: Abingdon, 1975.
Stoevesandt, Hinrich. "Barth, Karl." In *Concise Encyclopedia of Preaching*, edited by William H. Willimon and Richard Lischer, 26–27. Louisville: Westminster John Knox, 1995.
Thompson, Mark D. "The Declarative God: Toward a *Theological* Description of Preaching." In *Theology Is for Preaching: Biblical Foundations, Method, and Practice*, edited by Chase R. Kuhn and Paul Grimmond, 18–33. Bellingham, WA: Lexham, 2021.
Van Driel, Edwin Chr. "Rethinking Church in a Post-Christian Age." In *What Is Jesus Doing? God's Activity in the Life and Work of the Church*, edited by Edwin Chr. van Driel, 47–72. Downers Grove, IL: IVP Academic, 2020.
———. "What Is Jesus Doing? Christological Thoughts for an Anxious Church and Tired Pastors." In *What Is Jesus Doing? God's Activity in the Life and Work of the Church*, edited by Edwin Chr. van Driel, 1–23. Downers Grove, IL: IVP Academic, 2020.
Vanhoozer, Kevin J. "Introduction: Pastors, Theologians, and Other Public Figures." In *The Pastor as Public Theologian: Reclaiming a Lost Vision*, edited by Kevin J. Vanhoozer and Owen Strachan, 1–27. Grand Rapids: Baker, 2015.
———. *Remythologizing Theology: Divine Action, Passion, and Authorship*. Cambridge: Cambridge University Press, 2010.
Webster, John. "The Visible Attests the Invisible." In *The Community of the Word: Toward an Evangelical Ecclesiology*, edited by Mark Husbands and Daniel J. Treier, 96–113. Downers Grove, IL: InterVarsity, 2005.
Wolterstorff, Nicholas. *Divine Discourse: Philosophical Reflections on the Claim That God Speaks*. Cambridge: Cambridge University Press, 1995.
———. "Preaching the Word of God." In *What Is Jesus Doing? God's Activity in the Life and Work of the Church*, edited by Edwin Chr. van Driel, 247–69. Downers Grove, IL: IVP Academic, 2020.

8

The Pasteurization of the Pastorate

Preserving Pastoral Authority in the Wake of Pastoral Abuses

LAURIE NORRIS

Introduction

PASTEURIZATION OF MILK IS an interesting process. On one hand, it kills dangerous bacteria and prevents potential spoilage. On the other hand, it kills many important nutrients in the process. As one website so vividly puts it, "All the living food in raw milk—delicate enzymes, probiotic bacteria, and various other nutrients—is bombed with extreme high heat and left for dead. Left in its wake is a trail of lost vitamins and minerals, altered flavor and texture and denatured proteins. Simply put, pasteurization is an absolute disaster for human health because it kills many of the nutrients in milk that our bodies need in order to process it." The situation supposedly arose when "big scale farmers began to commercially sell their milk and had less than desirable conditions of cleanliness."[1] To guarantee consumer safety, the milk was heated to remove potential contaminants, killing the bad along with the good. Might this also provide an apt description of current developments in the American church, and the pastorate in particular? In addressing the pastoral abuses of our present day—abuses perhaps catalyzed (like the milk industry) by large-scale

---

1. Golden Rule Dairy, "Pasteurized Milk Is Bad." The purpose of this paper, of course, is not to engage in debate over raw milk versus pasteurization but rather to note a helpful and perhaps analogous parallel.

commercialization of the church—what good and life-sustaining nutrients might we also be destroying? In addressing abuses of pastoral authority, are we also undermining pastoral authority altogether? Are pastors being put out to pasture?

Let's be clear: There is a problem that must be addressed. In recent years, we have witnessed the fall of prominent pastors. We have heard reports of shepherds failing to protect the sheep, either through their own predation or their passivity in confronting the wolves. We are daily, it seems, bombarded by staggering new stories of scandal—from viral podcasts to popular blogs to formal, large-scale denominational investigations and reports. These abuses have ranged in kind and degree, from sexual abuse and misconduct to bullying and domineering leadership to financial exploitation and other abuses of power. When perpetrated by those in spiritual leadership, that power dynamic is only intensified. The confusion and damage are significant. Certainly, the church cannot and must not remain silent or passive amidst such abuses.

The Concern: Dismantling of Pastoral Authority on the Altar of Abuse

The impetus for this paper arose out of last year's CPT conference theme, "Reconstructing Evangelicalism." The question surfaced in my mind: If much of our "reconstruction" of evangelicalism is driven, to some degree, in response to abuses and scandals by those in pastoral authority, what place does ecclesial authority have in this "reconstructed" evangelical church? Are there potentially unintended consequences in *how* we address the problem? Might the reaction against pastoral abuses pose a new threat—namely, the silencing and cancelling of pastoral authority? Put simply, could evangelicalism be reforming in ways that functionally undermine pastoral authority altogether?[2]

In an age of polarization and cancellation, where so many things are labeled as abuse, what narrative does the church embrace as a corrective? Desiring to right these wrongs, do we inadvertently appropriate a cultural narrative of power, wherein abuses of power are remedied through a *reversal* of power? In this narrative, pastoral abuses are potentially mitigated by dismantling pastoral authority, sacrificing pastoral authority for the perceived greater good—namely, the eradication of abuse. And the language of abuse, applied with increasing subjectivity, becomes a new and powerful weapon to wield against church leadership.

---

2. Various pastoral anecdotes come to mind as I observe the cultural landscape of today's churches.

This question, of course, also emerges within our broader cultural context—a context that is experiencing a crisis of authority in all spheres of life. We see this, for example, in the sciences, in the field of law (and law enforcement), and in the family structure.[3] These cultural waves relentlessly pound against the very *concept* of authority, eschewing authority in pursuit of revolutionary freedom while subtly succumbing to forms of totalitarianism.[4] In addition, there is a culture of fear—fear of liability, fear of cancellation, fear of social media exposure. Will one's *true* words be experienced by another as violence or hate speech, simply because they dare to confront this cultural narrative?

How can we address the present ills of pastoral authority without imbibing the anti-authority cultural waters in which we swim? How do we swim upstream, rather than surrendering to the cultural currents of our age? How do pastors shepherd people in a context where authority is viewed with suspicion and distrust, or, where authority itself is viewed as inherently *abusive*?[5]

---

3. This broader topic was addressed at length during the recent Touchstone Conference in Chicago, October 13–14, 2023, addressing the nature of authority and crisis of authority relative to science/scientism, law, politics, technology, and the fine arts.

4. On this crisis of authority, see the in-depth analysis by late Italian philosopher Augusto Del Noce in *The Crisis of Modernity*, especially 189–246. Addressing what he called an "eclipse of authority" in the West, Del Noce observed that while the etymology of the word "authority" is positively associated with "growth" ("to make or help grow"), present conceptions of authority largely associate it with "repression," i.e., that which stops and opposes growth, thereby "reversing what the etymology implies" (190). Del Noce explained this monumental conceptual shift by noting that authority historically has been connected to the invisible and transcendent; as such, it has led to potential for growth and ultimately, for freedom. The crisis of modernity, however, with its focus on the imminent and material and its dismantling of authority, has led to a construal of *freedom apart from authority*—tied to concrete rather than metaphysical realities. So then, freedom has come to be defined through revolution, through the absence of authority, which in turn ironically has become its own form of totalitarianism. Del Noce writes, "Revolution means radical liberation from authority, but such a rejection implies also the rejection of tradition, and the rejection of tradition implies the rejection of meta-physical-religious thought" (217). All that is left is power—strength or force, which manifests "visibly and outwardly . . . by the use of external means." "Today's reality," he argues, "shows us that the eclipse of authority does not coincide at all with the advent of liberation, but rather with that of *power*, and totalitarian systems are the tangible expression of this substitution" (229). He asks, "What is pure power, when it is not subordinated to morals? Force" (233). And, with no appeal to the transcendent or universal, there can be no rational dissent (230). I wonder to what degree this power paradigm has seeped into the modern church as well, leading to the equivalent of totalitarian *ecclesial* regimes that sacrifice transcendence for pragmatic immanence.

5. Some might consider it self-serving for pastors even to raise such questions because it reinforces these entrenched power dynamics. Note Mike Cosper's valid caution in "Don't Make."

PART TWO: THE HUMILITY OF THE PULPIT

Survey results from Barna offer an interesting perspective. According to Barna's 2017 *State of Pastors* report, only about one in five Americans thought of a pastor "as very influential in their community," while about one in four did not think pastors are "very influential or influential at all." In addressing important cultural issues, a 2016 Barna study found that "nearly half of American evangelicals don't see their pastors as being an authoritative voice for navigating current affairs." Fast-forward to a more recent Barna study in 2020, in which a mere 23 percent of Americans and only 31 percent (less than a third) of Christians said they "definitely" see a pastor as a "trustworthy source of wisdom." *That is less than "a third of Christians [and only 4 percent of non-Christians!] who said they 'definitely' consider a pastor a 'trustworthy source of wisdom.'"*[6] Causation, of course, is difficult to establish. However, this decline in pastoral credibility is noteworthy. Addressing the erosion of pastoral credibility and the reshaping of our view of authority, Barna senior fellow Glenn Packiam concludes, "Yes, there are cultural headwinds that have changed the social standing or cultural power of a pastor. But we have made a mess of things too. From small country churches to uber-megachurches, many pastors have been found to be bullies and hypocrites, alcohol abusers, and womanizers. The crisis of credibility is a symptom. The misuse of authority is the root cause."[7]

This misuse of authority has led to a present crisis of authority. Packiam further observes, "In one sense, the internet has been a great equalizer, disrupting traditional hierarchies of power and granting anyone the access and the potential to amass a following." However, it is also "a double-edged sword. It does not simply tear down or destabilize existing structures of authority. It creates new ways of establishing authority and gives rise to new authority figures . . . and] new 'tribes.' This can lead to the dangerous assumption that all views are equally valid. Each person becomes their own arbiter of religious truth . . . doing what is right in their own eyes—or in the eyes of the podcaster they listened to this morning." He concludes, "The declining credibility of pastors is bad news for the church."[8]

A cursory survey of literature in the last decade further points to this downward trend. Note this flurry of book titles ranging from 2010 to 2016:

---

6. Cited in Packiam, "As Pastoral Credibility Erodes," 34; see also Packiam, *Resilient Pastor*, 107–8; emphasis mine.

7. Packiam, "As Pastoral Credibility Erodes," 37. This may reflect a tragic cycle, wherein modernity's loss of authority has led to greater spiritual abuse, resulting in a further decline of authority.

8. Packiam, "As Pastoral Credibility Erodes," 34.

- *Up With Authority: Why We Need Authority to Flourish as Human Beings* (2010)
- *Playing God: Redeeming the Gift of Power* (2013)
- *Embracing Shared Ministry: Power and Status in the Early Church and Why It Matters Today* (2013)
- *Authority: God's Good and Dangerous Gift* (2016)

Then consider these titles from the last few years:

- "Humility and Narcissism in Clergy" (2018)
- *When Narcissism Comes to Church: Healing Your Community from Emotional and Spiritual Abuse* (2020)
- *Redeeming Power: Understanding Authority and Abuse in the Church* (2020)
- *A Church Called Tov: Forming a Goodness Culture that Resists Abuses of Power and Promotes Healing* (2020)
- *Let Us Prey: The Plague of Narcissist Pastors and What We Can Do About It* (2020)
- *Powerful Leaders? When Church Leadership Goes Wrong and How to Prevent It* (2022)
- *Bully Pulpit: Confronting the Problem of Spiritual Abuse in the Church* (2022)

The first wave of titles examines authority and power structures more constructively, while the second wave highlights abuses of power and authority.

Where will this trajectory lead us—toward a needed *re-visioning* of pastoral authority or toward an *undermining* of the same? Will the church uphold pastoral authority or practically discard it as an archaic relic of the past, vilified as the source of present abuses? And how will pastors respond to these shifting realities? Will they retreat in fear? Will they respond in militant aggression? Or will they contend for the sheep with cruciform humility and strength? In the remainder of this paper, I want to propose a way forward that broadly addresses two dimensions: first, our construal of pastoral authority in the church, and second, the appropriate pastoral response amidst such challenges to that authority.

PART TWO: THE HUMILITY OF THE PULPIT

The Way Forward

A Biblical Response: The Shepherd

The problem of pastoral abuse is the symptom of a deeper illness—a misconstrual of pastoral authority and the perceived honor that accompanies it, along with contemporary ministry models and church structures that perpetuate distorted conceptions of authority.[9] Much has been much written in recent years on the topic of narcissism among clergy and the cultural or institutional influences that cultivate it.[10]

However, spiritual abuse by religious leaders certainly is no new phenomenon. In Ezek 34 and Jer 23, the prophets utter scathing indictments against those false shepherds who prey on rather than protect the sheep, who exploit the sheep and feed themselves while the sheep go hungry. In a tragically ironic twist, the shepherds have become the wolves. The prophets look to a day when the Lord himself will emerge on the scene to care for his people. Such is the weight and audacity of Jesus's claim in John 10: "I am the good shepherd" (ESV). He is the one with rightful claim over the sheep, who enters by the gate. He is the one who knows the sheep intimately and personally, who leads ahead by his voice rather than harshly driving the sheep from behind (as we typically conceive of herding in the West). Unlike the hired hand, who bears no legal liability to risk his own safety for another's sheep, Jesus declares that he lays down his very life for the sheep, the sheep who belong to him. He is the shepherd *par excellence*—God, in flesh, dwelling with his people to fulfill the prophetic promises of covenantal protection and care. And he entrusts this mantle to Peter in John 21: "If you love me, then feed my sheep." Thus, Peter later writes in 1 Pet 5:1–4,

> So I exhort the elders among you, as a fellow elder and a witness of the sufferings of Christ, as well as a partaker in the glory that is going to be revealed: shepherd the flock of God that is among you, exercising oversight, not under compulsion, but willingly, as God

---

9. In this paper, the language of "pastoral authority" applies to wherever pastoral authority resides within a particular ecclesial system of governance. We also must acknowledge how cultural differences may influence the expression of pastoral authority in different cultural contexts.

10. See, for example, DeGroat, *When Narcissism Comes*, 102–17, for a discussion of narcissistic systems. Especially instructive is a study by Ruffing et al., which addresses a heightened correlation between clergy and narcissism and potential reasons for that correlation, given the complexities of spiritual leadership. See Ruffing et al., "Humility and Narcissism in Clergy," 525–45. We should also acknowledge that pastoral accountability, while certainly important, is not a guarantee; abusive pastors may cultivate enabling organizational systems in which supposed accountability is functionally ineffective.

would have you; not for shameful gain, but eagerly; not domineering over those in your charge, but being examples to the flock. And when the chief Shepherd appears, you will receive the unfading crown of glory.

John Chrysostom, writing in the late fourth century, echoed a similar sentiment:

> What greater advantage could there be, than to be obviously doing what Christ himself declared was proof of love for Christ? . . . It will be equally obvious that a great, indescribable reward will be in store for the man who works hard at the tasks which Christ values so highly. . . . What gift, then, will he give as a reward to those who shepherd his flock which he purchased, not for money or any such thing, but by his own death when he gave his blood for his flock's ransom.[11]

The temptation remains the same in every generation: self-aggrandizement rather than cruciformity. But spiritual authority exercised through faithful *servant*-shepherds is a gift to the church, for her flourishing.[12] As Heb 13:7 declares, "Remember your leaders, those who spoke to you the word of God. Consider the outcome of their way of life, and imitate their faith." Pastoral authority expresses a non-coercive, delegated responsibility and accountability under the lordship and word of Jesus Christ, the Great Shepherd, for the protection, growth, and flourishing of his body, the church, in submission and conformity to Christ, who is the head. The exercise of such authority is no mere transaction. It is *incarnation*. Such incarnation reflects the very heart of God as divine minister. And it is participation, not mere performance.[13] As Andrew Root aptly observes, "To give and receive ministry is the shape of God's very being." Put simply, "the shape of divine action reveals that God *is* a minister."[14] In our secular age, human beings need to reencounter the "real

---

11. Chrysostom, *Six Books*, 52, 54, 60.

12. See Austin, *Up with Authority*. See also Andy Crouch's stimulating work in *Playing God*, in which he argues that power (both individually and institutionally) is a gift for creation, not coercion, bestowed on image bearers within the Christian story. The abuse of power simply reflects a distortion and diminishment of this gift, which always leads to idolatry and injustice (cf. Pasewark, *Theology of Power*).

13. In my research for this paper, I was struck by the consistent defining of pastoral authority in mostly functional or structural categories.

14. Root, *Pastor*, 230. Drawing on Foucault, Root explains that "Israel uniquely, in contrast to the Greco-Roman world, experienced God as *shepherd*, asserting that divine action itself is ministry. God came to the world not as raiding king or ruler but as a shepherd who acted pastorally, keeping and overseeing his people. It is little wonder that when Israel wanted a king like the other nations, God refused (1 Sam 8). God reminded them

being of the shepherd God" through pastors who, first and foremost, embody and participate in the personal and ministerial action of God.[15]

But perhaps we have confused authority with power—or rather, a certain kind of power that looks more like corporate management, entrepreneurship, or celebrity than it does the cross, more like the culture of Christendom than the kingdom of God.[16] Again, this is nothing new. Consider the so-called "super-apostles" in Corinth. These polished individuals profited off the church, whereas Paul humbled himself by preaching the gospel free of charge (2 Cor 11:7). In 11:20, Paul writes, "You even put up with anyone who enslaves you or exploits you or takes advantage of you or puts on airs or slaps you in the face."

But such was not the way of Paul, whose ministry was marked by union and solidarity with the crucified and resurrected Christ—by a countercultural logic of power and status, articulated most profoundly in Phil 2: exaltation via humiliation. Refusing to leverage or exploit his status and position as a "social commodity" for personal advantage, as Hellerman observes, Jesus progressively descended in status—from equality with God, to incarnation, and ultimately, to crucifixion (vv. 6–8).[17] Early detractors of the Christian faith were quick to draw a direct connection between the dishonor of Jesus's

---

that kings 'lord over,' and they are but people of a shepherd. A king would corrupt the pastoral and ministerial at the heart of God's own being, which they were to reflect. It is little surprise that when God relented and allowed them a king, the king after God's own heart was a shepherd boy. This sense that there is but one God, and that this God is a pastor who ministers, [was] shockingly unique to the Greco-Roman mind" (155). He is the God who sees, who seeks, who listens, and who ministers in ways uniquely directed to the human need (224–25; cf. Gen 16).

15. Root, *Pastor*, 168–69. Root attributes this need to a shift in pastoral identity pre- and post-Reformation. Whereas pre-Reformation pastors focused on the cultic—"handling holy things" and mediating ontological encounter with God—the Reformation elevated "epistemology over ontology" in pastoral practice. "Pastoral power was bound in epistemological consent rather than ontological encounter," prodding the mind, encouraging devotion, and encouraging people to seek God for themselves, emphasizing pastoral service over sacrifice (i.e., mediating God himself in the real body of Jesus) (163). Root contends that in our secular age—an age which has exchanged the transcendent for the immanent—pastoral identity and function need to reunite service with divine encounter, that is, to frame pastoral service in terms of divine action (164, 168–69). This accords well with Del Noce's point explained in note 4 concerning authority and transcendence, though Mike Cosper's caution also should be heeded with respect to the danger of seeking the transcendent in our leaders. See Cosper, "Don't Make," 27.

16. Concerning the "systemic pitfalls of corporate Christianity"—that is, "ways that we structure and organize our churches" that "particularly lend themselves to the abuse of pastoral authority" rather than the servant leadership embodied by Jesus in Phil 2, see Hellerman, *Embracing Shared Ministry*, 228, 231. On addressing confusion about the nature of God's kingdom, see Langberg, *Redeeming Power*, 145–58.

17. Hellerman, *Embracing Shared Ministry*, 162.

crucifixion and the dishonorable social status of Jesus's followers. And yet, as Paul argued, "The only One in the universe with the indisputable authority to do so had completely redefined what counted for honor in the grand scheme of things."[18] This is the model of cruciform ministry—and the proper exercise of authority—that Paul commends. His conception of authority is neither "romanticized or idolized," as Longenecker and Still rightly observe, but rather is concerned with the "theological purification of authority through the gospel"—authority rooted in a vision of God's glory as uniquely revealed in the face of Christ (2 Cor 4:6).[19]

Service to God can be a seductive pursuit that lures one away from devotion and submission to Jesus Christ, exchanging his glory for our own.[20] Under-shepherds among God's flock, however, must maintain a proper posture of humility, servanthood, and submission—remembering that they, too, are sheep—lest they forget the delegated nature of their authority, the cruciform shape of their ministry, and the upside-down kingdom they represent.[21]

An Historical-Ecclesial Response

The nature and scope of pastoral authority has been a question for the church since its inception and in every subsequent generation, influenced by the cultural headwinds that threaten to define standards of church leadership either against cultural norms or in subtle (or not so subtle) alignment with the powers of the day—that is, in *conformity to* or *resistance against* cultural norms. Back and forth the pendulum swings, reflecting cultural values, then reacting against the same. Power is seductive, especially when wielded for honorable purposes, and we have much to learn from church history as it pertains to the delicate dance between spiritual authority and worldly power (a dance in which power always pulls and strives to lead). Clearly that history is fraught with many missteps, reflecting the pastor's own battle of Spirit versus flesh.[22]

---

18. Hellerman, *Embracing Shared Ministry*, 162.
19. Longenecker and Still, *Thinking Through Paul*, 157.
20. See Gregory the Great's *Book of Pastoral Rule* (ca. 590), describing those "who through the temptation of authority in the holy Church aspire to the glory of honor." Gregory, *Book of Pastoral Rule*, 29; cf. 210.
21. See Castaldo, *Upside-Down Kingdom*.
22. To this end, I recommend the work of Burgess et al., *A Pastoral Rule for Today*. The authors survey historical figures from Augustine to Bonhoeffer to consider central Christian practices and disciplines that "can help sustain pastoral ministry and contribute to the formation of faithful and vibrant Christian communities," calling Christian leaders to walk worthily of their pastoral vocation. Burgess et al., *Pastoral Rule for Today*, 181.

PART TWO: THE HUMILITY OF THE PULPIT

The patristic writings of Gregory of Nazianzus, John Chrysostom, and Gregory the Great are instructive in addressing these challenges.

A Pastoral Response

How should pastors respond to this shifting terrain? Certainly, we need to re-evaluate and perhaps even reform our models of ministry to mitigate against such abuses, but what is the appropriate pastoral response to an evacuation of (if not outright assault on) pastoral authority and the pastor's diminished credibility amidst these abuses? How should pastors respond to these shifts in cultural perceptions—as they feel increasingly marginalized and pigeonholed, and as their authority as ministers of the word is not so readily granted? Many good men and women have found themselves in the crosshairs of cancellation. How should biblically faithful shepherds respond who seek to reflect the humility and servanthood of Christ? In this age of polarization, it seems we are confronted with two extremes: flight or fight. Both responses are rooted in fear—fear of losing one's position amidst these cultural changes. And both have significant implications for how we understand "power and the pulpit."

Pastoral Compromise

Perhaps the easiest choice is flight. Remain silent. Soften the hard word or avoid it altogether. Acquiesce to the sirens of moral compromise in the name of Christian love. Avoid confrontation of sin and never speak of church discipline. Shun "hard conversations" that would inflict momentary pain in hopes of future restoration. Evade disagreement or potential confrontation which could be perceived as emotionally abusive or domineering. Such reactions may reflect weakness, or perhaps rather, weariness. Many pastors feel discouraged and worn. In a somewhat ironic reversal, shepherds now find themselves in an increasingly vulnerable position as well—at risk of public accusation, cancellation, or litigation for speaking unpopular truths that are deemed by the culture intolerant at best and hateful at worst, for bringing private matters to light, or for confronting sin (whether privately or publicly). Not to mention the pastor's own finitude and limitation in navigating complex topics and situations, which certainly will entail a margin of pastoral error and require grace; after all, the pastor is only human. How many pastors today walk on eggshells, continually aware of every possible misstep? This can lead to a kind of pastoral paralysis.

Consider the strong words of Paul, Peter, and John confronting false teachers who had infiltrated the church, or their direct confrontation and unequivocal condemnation of sinful attitudes, immoral behavior, and relational divisions. Could there ever be a "third letter to the Corinthians" written in our context today—the "painful letter" from Paul that inflicted great pain but produced a godly grief leading to repentance (2 Cor 7:8–12)? Certainly, that would be "Exhibit A" for pastoral bullying and domineering leadership. And yet, Paul's words were expressly motivated by love and free from coercion (he even avoided another personal visit to lessen the blow, 2 Cor 1:23—2:1). He explains in 2 Cor 2:4, "For I wrote to you out of much affliction and anguish of heart and with many tears, not to cause you pain but to let you know the abundant love that I have for you." How many pastors today are willing to take that risk, at the peril of being misunderstood, to exercise that kind of love as part of their pastoral vocation?

For sake of illustration: consider the shepherd's primary tools, the rod and staff. With these instruments, the shepherd both directs and protects the flock—nudging the sheep in desired directions, stabilizing the sheep on rough terrain, pulling them back from danger, and defending against predators. Certainly, the shepherd's rod and staff can be used against the sheep as a tool of abuse, as we have seen. But can shepherds function without that same rod and staff—the staff by which they pull back a wayward sheep (against its will) about to hurl itself over a cliff, or keep it from wandering down dangerous paths, or fend off those wolves who would infiltrate the flock to feed on the sheep? If the shepherd's staff and rod are discarded as potential tools of abuse, can the shepherd truly *shepherd*? And, what of the "power of the pulpit" if the sharper edge of the two-edged sword has been dulled? In this scenario, the sheep may suffer abuse through a form of pastoral abandonment.

Pastoral Combativeness

There is a second potential response to opposition, opposite of pastoral passivity or paralysis—that is, a more reactive posture of aggression and combativeness, what we might call "pastoral pugnacity" or belligerence. Acutely aware of rising cultural opposition and trending "post-Christian" rhetoric, pastors must now envision ministry leadership against a very different cultural backdrop, one in which Christianity holds a less privileged position and experiences increased marginalization or even cancellation.[23] In this embattled state,

---

23. This may partially account for the resurgence of political theologies like theonomy and Christian Reconstruction in certain contexts.

pastors may feel called to arms. Feeling the loss of voice, they may stridently demand their voice be heard. When faced with existential threats, they may be tempted to fight power with power, to become defensive or argumentative, to become a militant and authoritarian presence in the world, to sacrifice charity in their commitment to truth—to protect their own authority in ways that reflect self-interest more than submission to the lordship of Jesus Christ. They may even come to reflect the arrogant and "abusive" patterns of coercive leadership that we have recently witnessed in several well-known ministries. In this scenario, the sheep may suffer through pastoral severity or insensitivity.

To this point, David Wells incisively observes that "some pastors and Christian leaders, sensing the current chaos in society, and the vacuum that underlies it, have been tempted to step in and fill that vacuum. They do so by becoming *authoritarian* in their ways of relating to people. They develop a domineering style. Some have even become like cult leaders." He notes that while "this style does appeal to some people, especially to those who are filled with uncertainty and who are glad for someone else to make their decisions," it is a false and therefore destructive use of authority. What *is* needed, he argues, are not "not more authoritarian preachers but more *authoritative* sermons"—sermons "incubated in the godly life of the preacher," who speaks "out of Scripture, before God, and into life."[24]

Contending with Cruciformity

How, then, might pastors avoid these two extremes of passivity on one hand and militancy on the other? Certainly it begins with humble acknowledgment of failures and a renewed commitment to integrity and accountability, to character formation. Restored credibility of voice must begin with credibility of character. But what about pastors' more particular response to changing perceptions of pastoral authority? We must remember that, while not called to be *contentious*, pastors do have a calling to *contend* for the gospel and for the sheep. And there is a need to contend for pastoral authority in the church today. Despite protests to the contrary, the sheep need accountability. And the church desperately needs genuine shepherds who are both tender and tough in serving, leading, and protecting the sheep through faithful instruction and admonition, who can bear up under opposition—external and internal (both wolves and difficult sheep). As John Chrysostom rightly noted, the spiritual shepherd's ultimate "fight is not with wolves; his fear is not of robbers; his care is not to protect the flock from pestilence." Rather, the shepherd of Christ's

24. Wells, "Thinking Biblically About Authority."

flock wrestles against spiritual powers—a "terrible host of enemies," a "cruel and savage army . . . lying in wait for this flock."[25]

So then, what arms should be taken up? Second Corinthians 10:3–4 reminds us that "for though we live in the flesh, we do not wage war according to the flesh. The weapons of our warfare are not the weapons of the world. Instead, they have divine power to demolish strongholds." Pastors must guard their integrity in *how* they "fight." When we play dirty like our enemy, we get dirty too. Our souls become soiled. Taking up their weapons, we may come to resemble our opponent and assume their manner of speech, spirit, and strategies—a posture of pride that tears down, slanders, destroys reputations, and demolishes people (instead of arguments); such is the "cancel culture" of our day. The very thing you react against begins to form you (like the child intent on *not* becoming like their parents). *You* become increasingly polarized, embattled, fixated on what you are fighting against.

Spiritual leaders can begin to speak and act unbecomingly, dressing in ways unbecoming of one who is holy and beloved in Christ rather than clothing themselves with humility, kindness, compassion, patience, and forbearance (Col 3:12–14). They reflect the demonic and divisive "wisdom from below" (see Jas 3:14) rather than the wisdom from above that bears the fruit of peace. They become cunning and strategic, political more than prayerful. They are tempted, baited even, to seize the low-hanging fruit and respond *in kind*, to deal in the cultural currency of power that is antithetical to the gospel of Jesus Christ. They are tempted to change out of their spiritual clothes for the fight.

As a leader in the Ephesian church, Timothy faced dangerous opponents. These men were sowing false doctrine, and their teaching spread like gangrene; they were argumentative, greedy, and stirring up dissension; they had swerved from the truth and shipwrecked their faith and sought to lead others down a similar path of destruction (or in our case, "deconstruction"). Paul strongly, unequivocally, exhorted Timothy to rebuke and to oppose these false teachers. In both of his letters, Paul uses strong language of "contending for the faith" and "fighting the good fight of faith," guarding the teaching entrusted to him. *And yet*, Paul also warns Timothy not to emulate the character of these men by engaging on their terms. He tells Timothy to guard both *himself* and his teaching (1 Tim 4:16)—to watch not only his doctrine, but also his character. Note Paul's instruction in 2 Tim 2:24–26: "The Lord's bond-servant must not be quarrelsome, but be kind to all, skillful in teaching, patient when wronged, with gentleness correcting those who are in opposition, if perhaps God may grant them repentance leading to the knowledge of the truth, and

---

25. Chrysostom, *Six Books*, 54–55.

they may come to their senses and escape from the snare of the devil, having been held captive by him to do his will."

There was a risk for the younger Timothy—a risk that in contending for the truth, in fighting for the faith as a good soldier, Timothy may be tempted to engage his opponents by *their* rules—with quarrelling, selfish greed, ego, intent to destroy. But such is not the way of God's servant. Yes, he must teach and correct, but he must do so with kindness, patience (even when wronged), gentleness, and humility. To what end? Conviction. Repentance. Redemption. Restoration. Paul calls Timothy to recognize the true enemy. While confronting falsehood and threats to gospel fidelity, he must recognize the true spiritual condition of his opponents and not respond in kind—they are blind, enslaved, in need of deliverance from their bondage to the evil one. They are those for whom Jesus pleaded from the cross, "Father, forgive them, for they know not what they do" (Luke 23:34). In contending for the faith, pastors seek to warn, not to wound; to deliver, not destroy; to rescue and restore, not ruin reputations.

In sports, there can be a tendency to "play down" to the competition—to get sloppy, make unforced errors, lose focus. As under-shepherds, however, pastors must "play *up*" to the standard of the Great Shepherd, Jesus Christ. He alone is the standard of imitation. Though the spirit of pragmatism is an alluring siren, especially when contending for the *right things*, servants of Christ must contend in the *right ways*, with integrity and blamelessness, in fervent prayer—not picking up the enemy's weapons but following the countercultural rules of engagement Jesus laid out in Matt 5–7, which recalibrate the arsenal of our hearts. This is a "theology of the cross," whereby God has defeated the powers of darkness and redeemed the world by turning worldly wisdom, status, and power on their head, and continues to do so, even today.

We are called to *cruciformity*—that is, the "cross-shaped" life, in identification with our Savior. Facing what is ultimately a spiritual battle, we are called not to take up the weapons of this world, but rather, to deny ourselves, take up our *cross*, and follow *him*. So, Jesus concludes the Beatitudes in Matt 5:10–12, "Blessed are those who have been persecuted for the sake of righteousness, for theirs is the kingdom of heaven. Blessed are you when people insult you and persecute you, and falsely say all kinds of evil against you because of me. Rejoice and be glad, for your reward in heaven is great; for in this same way they persecuted the prophets who were before you."

Power and the Pulpit

This, of course, also means rendering faithful instruction without compromise. Like the prophets of old—who typically were *persona non grata*, delivering unwanted messages and upsetting *status quo* sensibilities—embracing cruciformity sometimes means saying the hard thing and risking one's reputation out of sacrificial love for the sheep instead of self-protection. There will be a cost *on all sides* to preaching the truth in love. However, power from the pulpit entails reproducing the illocutionary acts from the whole counsel of Scripture—even those speech acts that historically put prophets and apostles in the crosshairs of social alienation, public scorn, and even physical danger.

Consider, for example, New Testament warning passages, addressed to all professing believers in the church, admonishing them to persevere in faith in the face of heterodoxy, suffering, persecution, and/or moral apathy. There is no caveat offered, no word of comfort or exemption. The warning makes no distinction between regenerate or unregenerate members of the audience. With equal force, it calls each hearer to steadfastness and continuance in the faith, in right doctrine and practice. So then, in submission to Holy Scripture, pastors must faithfully represent both functions—the promise of assurance and the warning of admonition—in their teaching and preaching.[26] They must not soften or suppress the power inherent within these performative and world-constructing texts; they must not compromise, diminish, or neglect the function of the authors' language. They must not blunt the force of this "two-edged" sword, even if that sword brings potential discomfort, uneasiness, or judgment alongside words of comfort, assurance, and confidence. The preacher will faithfully confront the listener with warnings to persevere and comfort the listener with promises of divine preservation, in order that God's people might be transformed by the unmitigated living word of God.

Contending for the faith in a spirit of cruciformity demands cruciformity behind the pulpit—identifying with Christ and faithfully replicating the divine speech acts of Scripture, both in word and life, regardless of their potential reception.[27] This is not a new challenge. It has always been the mantle for all who would faithfully bear the word of the Lord.[28] Shepherding has never been a "safe" endeavor.

26. Schreiner and Caneday, *Race Set Before Us*, 44–45.

27. There of course are many significant implications for cruciformity in preaching; see, e.g., John Koessler's excellent work in *Folly, Grace, and Power*.

28. In his introduction to John Chrysostom's *Six Books on the Priesthood*, Graham Neville describes the ministry context and concerns of Gregory of Nazianzus in apt terms for today: "But his [Gregory's] attention turns from the ideal of the priesthood to the harsh realities, not of the world, but of the Church. How can he take on himself the guidance of others in such troubled times—the Church profaned, invective prized, personal rivalries flourishing, all in chaos and confusion? Priests and influential laymen are involved in the strife. Pagans hate us for our dissensions. Our own best people are scandalized. The Christian is even lampooned on the stage. His own disciples make Christ's name to be blasphemed. In these circumstances the probability of failure is great. . . . He [Gregory]

PART TWO: THE HUMILITY OF THE PULPIT

Conclusion

In recent years, patterns of pastoral abuse have been brought to light. These abuses have engendered appropriate scrutiny and response. However, the recognition of pastoral abuses in unhealthy church systems may also serve to undermine pastoral authority in the church more broadly *if* the church responds according to the spirit of the age. We must take care to avoid replacing one culturally flawed model with another that leaves us virtually "shepherdless." In our deconstruction of unhealthy ministry models and targeting of specific abuses, we must resist the dismantling of pastoral authority altogether. We must avoid the pasteurization of the pastorate.

What do the shepherd's staff and rod look like when wielded by Christ for the good of the sheep rather than the self-interest of the shepherd? The cross is part of that answer—in addressing both the question of authority and the question of credibility. As the apostle Paul defended his own apostolic credibility with *bold humility* by pointing to his fellowship of suffering with and for Jesus, and on behalf of the church, so should the pastor.

Perhaps there is a correlation in our American context between the decline in pastoral credibility and the relative comfortability versus cost (culturally speaking) that pastors have enjoyed in recent decades. Perhaps these more recent cultural shifts, while unsettling and disruptive to our equilibrium, will prompt needed purification of the pastoral office—deterring false shepherds who abuse the sheep and drawing under-shepherds who submit to Christ and are called to lay down their lives for the sheep in a spirit of selfless humility, who are willing to suffer in fulfillment of their vocation. As Gregory the Great rightly recognized, there is both value in adversity and danger in prosperity: "[Jesus] fled the glory of exaltation offered to him. He chose instead the penalty of a shameful death so that his [followers] might also learn to flee the applause of the world, to fear not its terrors, to value adversity for the sake of truth, and to decline prosperity fearfully. This final concern [prosperity] often corrupts the heart through pride, while adversities purge it through with suffering. In the one, the soul becomes conceited," whereas in the other, it is humbled.[29] These changing circumstances remind us of our exilic identity as

---

recalls the stringent demands of the Scriptures for purity alike in priest and sacrifice. . . . With such an exalted view of the spiritual qualities and the preparation needed for the work of the priestly ministry, Gregory's natural inclination had been to refuse ordination. He had no opinion at all of those who, though not yet able to take up the Cross, eagerly accepted the priesthood. . . . But in the end his fears and his preferences give way to what he cannot avoid regarding as his duty" (12–13).

29. Gregory the Great, *Book of Pastoral Rule*, 33.

aliens in a foreign land and confront our bent toward comfortability, conformity, and kingdom building in this present world.

In the face of shifting cultural realities, will pastors be silenced? Will they compromise or acquiesce under pressure? Will they become bitter or combative? Indeed, their response must entail a counterintuitive ethic befitting ministers of God's kingdom and wielding the power of the cross—one that restores pastoral integrity and credibility while refusing to yield pastoral authority, for the good of the church and the glory of Christ.

Bibliography

Austin, Victor Lee. *Up with Authority: Why We Need Authority to Flourish as Human Beings*. London: T&T Clark, 2010.

Burgess, John P., et al. *A Pastoral Rule for Today: Reviving an Ancient Practice*. Downers Grove, IL: IVP Academic, 2019.

Castaldo, Chris. *The Upside-Down Kingdom: Wisdom for Life from the Beatitudes*. Wheaton, IL: Crossway, 2023.

Chrysostom, John. *Six Books on the Priesthood*. Translated by Graham Neville. Popular Patristics Series 1. Edited by John Behr. Crestwood, NY: St. Vladimir's Seminary Press, 1977.

Cosper, Mike. "Don't Make the Leadership Crisis Worse." *Christianity Today* 66 (2022) 27.

Crouch, Andy. *Playing God: Redeeming the Gift of Power*. Downers Grove, IL: InterVarsity, 2013.

DeGroat, Chuck. *When Narcissism Comes to Church: Healing Your Community from Emotional and Spiritual Abuse*. Downers Grove, IL: InterVarsity, 2020.

Del Noce, Augusto. *The Crisis of Modernity*. Edited and translated by Carlo Lancellotti. McGill-Queen's Studies in the History of Ideas 64. Montreal: McGill-Queen's University Press, 2021.

Golden Rule Dairy. "Why Pasteurized Milk Is Bad for You." July 23, 2018. https://www.goldenruledairy.com/new-page-2.

Gregory the Great. *The Book of Pastoral Rule*. Translated by George E. Demacopoulos. Popular Patristics Series 34. Crestwood, NY: St. Vladimir's Seminary Press, 2007.

Hellerman, Joseph H. *Embracing Shared Ministry: Power and Status in the Early Church and Why It Matters Today*. Grand Rapids: Kregel, 2013.

Honeysett, Marcus. *Powerful Leaders? When Church Leadership Goes Wrong and How to Prevent It*. Downers Grove, IL: InterVarsity, 2022.

Koessler, John. *Folly, Grace, and Power: The Mysterious Act of Preaching*. Grand Rapids: Zondervan, 2011.

Kruger, Michael J. *Bully Pulpit: Confronting the Problem of Spiritual Abuse in the Church*. Grand Rapids: Zondervan, 2022.

Langberg, Diane. *Redeeming Power: Understanding Authority and Abuse in the Church*. Grand Rapids: Brazos, 2020.

Longenecker, Bruce W., and Todd D. Still. *Thinking Through Paul: A Survey of His Life, Letters, and Theology*. Grand Rapids: Zondervan, 2014.

McKnight, Scot, and Laura Barringer. *A Church Called Tov: Forming a Goodness Culture That Resists Abuses of Power and Promotes Healing*. Carol Stream, IL: Tyndale Momentum, 2020.

Nelson, Tom. *The Flourishing Pastor: Recovering the Lost Art of Shepherd Leadership*. Downers Grove, IL: InterVarsity, 2021.

Neville, Graham. "Introduction." In *John Chrysostom, Six Books on the Priesthood*, edited by John Behr, 12–34. Crestwood, NY: St. Vladimir's Seminary Press, 1977.

Packiam, Glenn. "As Pastoral Credibility Erodes, How Can We Respond? Perhaps God Wants to Reshape Our View of Authority." *Christianity Today* (2022) 32–37.

———. *The Resilient Pastor: Leading Your Church in a Rapidly Changing World*. Grand Rapids: Baker Books, 2022.

Pasewark, Kyle A. *A Theology of Power: Being Beyond Domination*. Minneapolis: Fortress, 1993.

Puls, Darrell. *Let Us Prey: The Plague of Narcissist Pastors and What We Can Do About It*. Rev. ed. Eugene, OR: Cascade, 2020.

———. "Narcissistic Pastors and the Making of Narcissistic Churches." *Great Commission Research Journal* 12 (2020) 67–92.

Root, Andrew. *The Pastor in a Secular Age: Ministry to People Who No Longer Need a God*. Ministry in a Secular Age 2. Grand Rapids: Baker Academic, 2019.

Ruffing, Elizabeth G., et al. "Humility and Narcissism in Clergy: A Relational Spirituality Framework." *Pastoral Psychology* 67 (2018) 525–45.

Sayers, Mark. *A Non-Anxious Presence: How a Changing and Complex World Will Create a Remnant of Renewed Christian Leaders*. Chicago: Moody, 2022.

Schreiner, Thomas R., and Ardel B. Caneday. *The Race Set Before Us: A Biblical Theology of Perseverance and Assurance*. Downers Grove, IL: IVP Academic, 2001.

Wells, David. "Thinking Biblically About Authority: An Interview with David Wells." 9Marks Journal, March 15, 2017. https://www.9marks.org/article/thinking-biblically-about-authority-an-interview-with-david-wells/.

9

"Treasures from an Earthen Pot"

How the Pastor-Poet George Herbert Can Inform Our Theology and Practice of Preaching

Stephen Witmer

> Judge not the preacher; for he is thy Judge:
> If thou mislike him, thou conceiv'st him not.
> God calleth preaching folly. Do not grudge
> To pick out treasures from an earthen pot.
> The worst speak something good: if all want sense,
> God takes a text, and preacheth patience.
>
> —GEORGE HERBERT

Introduction

SOMETIME IN THE YEAR 1630, having recently become rector of the tiny church in Bemerton, England, George Herbert preached his first sermon to the congregation. That sermon was described several decades later by Isaak Walton, one of Herbert's first biographers.[1] Walton's account is significant

---

1. Although Walton's biography is sometimes historically suspect, his account of this

because it is about as close as we can come to experiencing a George Herbert sermon. In stark contrast to Herbert's friend, godfather, and fellow pastor-poet John Donne, 160 of whose sermons have been preserved, not a single Herbert sermon remains. Walton tells us that Herbert's inaugural sermon was based on the words of Prov 4:23—"Keep thy heart with all diligence." Herbert "gave his parishioners many necessary, holy, safe rules for the discharge of a good conscience both to God and man, and delivered his sermon after a most florid manner, both with great learning and eloquence."[2]

That Herbert preached with learning and eloquence, in an ornate, embellished, "florid" style, is unsurprising. At the time, he was best known as the former public orator of the University of Cambridge, a coveted and prestigious position in which he had addressed the king and many other famous people. Born into a wealthy and socially prominent family, Herbert was well-trained at elite academic institutions (Westminster School; Trinity College, Cambridge) and regarded as a superb Latinist and an accomplished speaker. So, it is perhaps expected that he would address the people of Bemerton with polish and learning.

But two features of Walton's vignette are surprising. First is the fact that Herbert was in Bemerton at all. It was a small village outside of Salisbury, and the parishioners were largely farmers, very unlike the learned and elite company that Herbert had kept in Cambridge. Why was an accomplished and highly regarded scholar serving as the new rector of such a parish? Second, toward the end of his eloquent sermon, Herbert informed his congregation that they would not be hearing such preaching from him again. He told them, "That should not be his constant way of preaching; for since Almighty God does not intend to lead men to heaven by hard questions, he would not therefore fill their heads with unnecessary notions; but that for their sakes his language and his expressions should be more plain and practical in his future sermons."[3]

It is intriguing to speculate on Herbert's reasons for preaching his inaugural sermon in "a most florid manner," only to then immediately reassure his congregation that going forward he would preach more plainly and practically. Why the instant about-face? Did he observe his congregation's bored or confused response, and realize that his words were not getting through? Walton provides no further details. However, it is significant that the reason Herbert offered for preaching with "plain and practical" expressions was God's own example of not placing unnecessary obstacles in the way of those whom he was

---

particular sermon fits well with what we know from other sources about Herbert's understanding of preaching.

2. Walton, "Life," 365.
3. Walton, "Life," 365.

leading to heaven. Herbert committed to use simpler language in preaching to his congregation, "for their sakes." In other words, his commitment to clarity and simplicity was a matter of attentive concern and loving accommodation. This desire to serve the people in front of him squares with Herbert's stated aim in his pastoral handbook *The Country Parson*, to please God by feeding "my flock diligently and faithfully, since our Saviour hath made that the argument of a pastor's love."[4] Love is central to Herbert's vision of how a pastor is to relate to his people. The "business and aim" of a pastor is to see love flourish among the people of his parish.[5] So, how does a loving pastor preach to his congregation? One answer is: He preaches understandably.

In Herbert's day, preaching was both spiritually and politically significant. The developing Laudian party and the Crown were aware of the ability of sermons to create discord among the people. Through their preaching, Puritans could continue their work of reforming the church. In 1622, less than a decade before Herbert became the rector of the Bemerton church, King James issued "Letters and Directions to Preachers," which required preachers to be licensed, preach in agreement with the Thirty-Nine Articles, and avoid the topic of predestination. This was a time in which the very act of preaching required careful thought. George Herbert devoted sustained attention to preaching, and this is evident in both his prose and poetry.

My aim in this chapter is to highlight several ways in which Herbert's thought can inform our contemporary theology and practice of preaching. In particular, I will focus on Herbert's vision of preaching as embodied, local, and limited. Each of these emphases provides a corrective (or at least a check) for homiletical trends in our day. In some cases, Herbert *assumes* (rather than arguing for) his view of preaching. But because of his chronological distance, even his assumptions can be helpful, because they reveal that our own assumptions and default understandings are not inevitable. There are other options available.

Embodied Preaching

In our podcast world, many people experience preaching aurally rather than visually. In our post-COVID, live-stream world, many also experience preaching through a screen rather than in person. Podcast or live-stream sermons are often preached by someone they do not personally know. There are obvious advantages to digital dissemination and consumption of sermons, including

---

4. Herbert, *Country Parson*, 196.
5. Herbert, *Country Parson*, 251.

the remarkably broad reach of podcasts or video sermons preached by gifted and well-known pastors and the opportunity for many people to hear God's word proclaimed in the course of their everyday lives (e.g. while walking the dog, running on the treadmill, or commuting).

But it is important to consider what is lost. Herbert helps us here because his vision of preaching consistently assumes *the embodied presence* of the preacher. Of course, the technological means of physically separating a sermon from its preacher were more strictly limited in Herbert's day, but the separation was not impossible—sermons were being printed for distribution.[6] Throughout his work, Herbert clearly sees great value in the physical presence of the preacher with his congregation.

This was part of Herbert's larger reckoning with the embodied presence of a priest within his local parish in *all* his pastoral responsibilities. Leading the Eucharist is an activity that evokes stupefied wonder from Herbert, since a created being is tasked with serving the elements to the congregation. "When God vouchsafeth to become our fare, / Their hands convey him, who conveys their hands."[7] The priest's hands, together with the rest of his body, were to be fully employed in the ministry. Herbert instructs a pastor, when he leads public services, to lift up "his heart and hands and eyes" and to use "all other gestures which may express a hearty and unfeigned devotion."[8] Additionally, the pastor is to instruct his *congregation* "how to carry themselves in divine service," not allowing them to talk, sleep, gaze, lean, or half-kneel, but instead having them "to do all in a straight and steady posture" without huddling, slubbering, gaping, scratching the head, or spitting while they speak.[9] Clearly, for Herbert, the external behavior and physical posture of a parson matters a great deal, as does the physical posture of the congregation, because both are inextricably linked to spiritual realities.[10]

This close connection between external and internal realities helps to address a perceived deficiency of Herbert's chapter on preaching in *The Country Parson*. Chapter 7, "The Parson Preaching," is the longest statement on preaching

---

6. Additionally, many listeners of sermons took careful notes, with the intent of discussing the sermon throughout the week. And the emphasis upon memorization in the education of the time meant that many listeners could recall large portions of sermons for recounting to others. Cf. Rundell, *Super-Infinite*, 223.

7. Herbert, "Priesthood," lines 27–28.

8. Herbert, *Country Parson*, 202.

9. Herbert, *Country Parson*, 203. It seems that such instruction was necessary. Rundell tells of the fate of one person in Norwich Cathedral upon whose gown someone in the gallery "did conspurcate and shit." Meanwhile, someone else in the balcony let his shoe fall, narrowly missing the mayor's head. *Super-Infinite*, 222–23.

10. Cf. Wolberg, "Posture and Spiritual Formation," 57–72.

we have from Herbert. Somewhat disappointingly, it includes no clear theology of preaching. Instead, it focuses on what some might consider superficial matters. For example, Herbert urges preachers to procure the attention of their congregations "by all possible art." Preachers are to speak earnestly, because it is "natural to men to think that where is much earnestness there is somewhat worth hearing."[11] Preachers are to aim for a holy character in their sermons, and one way of doing this is to speak often and directly to God in the course of the sermon. "Oh Lord, bless my people and teach them this point." "Oh my Master, on whose errand I come, let me hold my peace, and do thou speak thyself, for thou art Love, and when thou teachest all are scholars."[12]

One might think that Herbert is concerned merely with artifice and rhetorical technique. But that view would be seriously mistaken. In this same chapter, he urges preachers to preach holy sermons "by dipping and seasoning all our words and sentences in our hearts before they come into our mouths, truly affecting and cordially expressing all that we say, so that the auditors may plainly perceive that every word is heart-deep."[13] He clearly cares about what is happening *beneath* the words. In his view, a crucial means of communicating the heart of the preacher, in order to affect the hearts of the hearers, is *how* the preacher says what he says.[14] Herbert's manifest concern for the preacher to use his words and manner to capture the congregation's attention and convey a tone of holiness assumes the embodied nature of preaching. For Herbert, personal presence and the use of the body (face, voice, arms) matters for spiritual formation.

As a good, attentive pastor, Herbert is well-aware that embodied people grow tired and distracted. So he suggests that pastors should not preach for more than an hour (!), because doing so will become counterproductive in reaching the congregation. "He that profits not in that time, will less afterwards, the same affection which made him not profit before making him then weary, and so he grows from not relishing to loathing."[15]

---

11. Herbert, *Country Parson*, 204.

12. Herbert, *Country Parson*, 205.

13. Herbert, *Country Parson*, 205.

14. Cf. Herbert's counsel in "The Parson Praying," *Country Parson*, 202. Since the majesty of God is the true reason for the pastor's inward fear, "so he is content to express this outwardly to the utmost of his power; that being first affected himself, he may affect also his people, knowing that no sermon moves them so much to a reverence . . . as a devout behaviour in the very act of praying."

15. Herbert, *Country Parson*, 206. The residents of Shadwell took their rector before an ecclesiastical court in order to lodge a complaint about the excessive length of his prayers and sermons, which often went so late that it was difficult for his parishioners to give proper attention to their cattle back home. Cf. Rundell, *Super-Infinite*, 222.

Herbert's view of preaching as an embodied activity is also indicated by the reciprocity he envisions between the preacher and congregation. He urges preachers to observe the congregation during the sermon and to let them know (in real time!) that he sees who is—and is not—paying attention.[16] In one of his few (semi-)negative comments, Herbert's very positive biographer Izaak Walton says, "And to this I must add that if he were at any time too zealous in his sermons, it was in reproving the indecencies of the people's behaviour in the time of divine service."[17] In preaching, the congregation sees the preacher *and the preacher sees the congregation* and *reminds them that he sees them.*

In fact, transformative preaching requires active, diligent participation and collaboration by the congregation, not just the preacher. It is a cooperative effort. In "The Church-Porch," the sequence of poetic instruction which prepares readers for Herbert's collection of poems *The Temple*, Herbert instructs listeners of sermons how to receive preaching.

> Let vain or busy thoughts have there no part:
> Bring not thy plough, thy plots, thy pleasures thither.
> Christ purg'd his temple; so must thou thy heart.
> All worldly thoughts are but thieves met together
> To cozen thee. Look to thy actions well:
> For churches are either our heav'n or hell.[18]

Because worldly thoughts will defraud and cheat ("cozen") the listener from benefiting during the service, attentiveness is necessary. Churches can be either "heav'n or hell," and that is true for sermons, too. The word of God will either benefit the receptive hearer or judge the hard-hearted. Herbert advises preachers frequently to tell their people "that sermons are dangerous things, that none goes out of the church as he came in, but either better or worse; that none is careless before his Judge, and that the Word of God shall judge us."[19]

In fact, in Herbert's view, there is always some way to benefit from the preached word, even if the preacher is far from gifted. Members of the congregation can "pick out treasures from an earthen pot."[20] Even when there's nothing of worth in the sermon, at least "God takes a text, and preacheth

---

16. Herbert, *Country Parson*, 204.
17. Walton, "Life," 370.
18. Herbert, "Church-Porch," lines 421–26.
19. Herbert, *Country Parson*, 204.
20. Herbert, "Church-Porch," line 430.

patience."[21] And "He that gets patience, and the blessing which / Preachers conclude with, hath not lost his pains."[22]

Herbert's understanding of the importance of what the congregation actually *sees* the preacher doing during the sermon and of the physical presence and posture of the congregation itself is important in constructing a theology of preaching in our day. So is the reciprocity experienced in real time between preacher and people. Although we perhaps should not implement Herbert's advice to reprove congregants' behavior during our sermons, his instincts are helpful. Is it not a good thing for the preacher to be able to see someone responding with strong emotion to a particular point in the sermon, someone consistently sleepy, someone who appears bored or offended or angry or convicted or enthused or joyful? These are opportunities to know our people more deeply. Though we may not engage with them directly during the sermon itself, we can follow up later. This embodiment, observation, and reciprocity is not possible over a podcast or a screen.

Moreover, it is worth asking how the ways in which we use our bodies while listening to a sermon affect our reception of it. Does it matter whether we are jogging, walking in the woods, stuck in traffic, or sitting alongside other believers? How does it affect our reception of a sermon when we can pause it at any time, or turn it off altogether? How is our hearing shaped through the regular interruption of podcast advertisements?

LOCAL PREACHING

Herbert's vision of embodied preaching is closely linked to his understanding of preaching as highly local and personal.[23] The country pastor preaches frequently in his own parish, for "the pulpit is his joy and his throne."[24] He steps out of the pulpit only when necessary for health reasons, or to give his congregation an opportunity to hear someone else for a change, or on certain special occasions. Because his own parish is "all his joy and thought," he is careful about when to leave it for a time in order to attend to other duties.[25]

Herbert advises preachers to particularize their sermons to the specific groups of people in front of them: the young and old, the poor and rich. "This is for you, and This for you; for particulars ever touch and awake more than

21. Herbert, "Church-Porch," line 432.
22. Herbert, "Church-Porch," lines 433–34.
23. "Herbert understood that preaching, however universal and eternal in matter, was also a very local thing." Drury, *Music at Midnight*, 241.
24. Herbert, *Country Parson*, 204.
25. Herbert, *Country Parson*, 220.

generals."²⁶ He also counsels preachers to take note of God's judgments that have happened temporally and geographically close to the parish, "for people are very attentive at such discourses, and think it behoves them to be so, when God is so near them, and even over their heads."²⁷

One of the consistently striking features of *The Country Parson* is Herbert's attentiveness to rural people and his desire to minister effectively to them. This carries through in his advice for preaching. He encourages country pastors to tell stories and sayings of others as the Scripture text invites them, because people pay attention to stories and sayings, and remember them better than exhortations, which often die with the sermon. Herbert notes that this is especially true for country people, who "are thick and heavy, and hard to raise to a point of zeal and fervency, and need a mountain of fire to kindle them; but stories and sayings they will well remember."²⁸ Throughout *The Country Parson*, Herbert shows himself a close observer of his village parishioners. In this, he follows his own advice to fellow pastors to "carry their eyes ever open, and fix them on their charge."²⁹

Not only does Herbert expect pastors and preachers to observe their people; he anticipates that there will be an irreplaceable benefit to congregations who regularly observe the lives and actions of those who preach to them. In his poem "The Windows," Herbert writes,

> Lord, how can man preach thy eternal word?
>   He is a brittle crazy glass:
> Yet in thy temple thou dost him afford
>   This glorious and transcendent place,
>   To be a window, through thy grace.
>
> But when thou dost anneal in glass thy story,
>   Making thy life to shine within
> The holy Preacher's; then the light and glory
>   More rev'rend grows, and more doth win;
>   Which else shows watrish, bleak, and thin.
>
> Doctrine and life, colours and light, in one
>   When they combine and mingle, bring
> A strong regard and awe: but speech alone
>   Doth vanish like a flaring thing,
>   And in the ear, not conscience ring.

26. Herbert, *Country Parson*, 204.
27. Herbert, *Country Parson*, 204.
28. Herbert, *Country Parson*, 204.
29. Herbert, *Country Parson*, 234.

Here, Herbert assumes that a local congregation will be able to observe the life of a holy preacher. They will know and see him in the course of daily life. When "doctrine and life . . . combine and mingle," the people will stand in awe of the beauty of God and his gospel. Of course, this vision of preaching assumes, not a disembodied or distant preacher but a very present, personal one. It assumes, not a vast congregation drawn from a wide geographical region, with no opportunity to see the daily life of the preacher, but rather a smaller church in a smaller setting, in which parishioners can see God's light shining within the life of "the holy Preacher." Herbert himself, along with the members of his household, gathered with his parishioners every day for morning prayer at ten o'clock and for evening prayer at four.[30] He lived across the street from the church. He was present with his people.

This local, congregation-specific preaching runs counter to the pressure contemporary preachers may feel to make their sermons accessible to the widest possible audience of anonymous podcast listeners or live-stream viewers who do not know them, will never meet them, and may live far away, with no knowledge of local affairs. Evergreen sermons work well for podcasts and live-streams. But that is not the kind of preaching Herbert envisions. Without downplaying the upsides of podcast sermons that spread far and wide and can potentially help many thousands of people, it is important to recognize the unique and crucial advantages of bespoke sermons, preached by a pastor with specific knowledge of a particular congregation which is "all his joy and thought," and received by people who know and regularly observe the daily life of that preacher.[31] There is a uniquely formative impact in such sermons.

Limited Preaching

Evangelical approaches to preaching have sometimes suffered from an inadequate anthropology that emphasizes the role of knowledge, cognition, and truth to the exclusion of a more fully embodied understanding of what it means to be human. If human beings are mainly "thinking things" (to use James K. A. Smith's phrase), it follows that the chief function of a sermon is to convey truth from one mind to another.[32] The *content* is what matters supremely, and it is less important how it is conveyed—whether in person from a local pastor the congregation knows well and sees often, or through cameras and screens from a preacher whose audience will never personally meet him.

---

30. Cf. Drury, *Music at Midnight*, 241.
31. Cf. Witmer, "Preach Bespoke Sermons"; and Witmer, "Best Preacher for You."
32. Smith, *What You Love*, 3.

PART TWO: THE HUMILITY OF THE PULPIT

Our anthropology also has implications for the role we accord to preaching within the life of a congregation. If the exclusive goal of Christian leaders is to convey biblical content (since human beings are most basically rational, thinking beings), the sermon may assume an outsized role in the life of the congregation, perhaps to the minimization or exclusion of other means of shepherding. This view sometimes leads to the all-too-common practice among congregants of exclusively listening to sermons rather than being involved in the life of a local congregation, or the practice of entering the sanctuary after the singing and readings just in time for the sermon.

In Herbert's view, the sermon was crucially important. But it never stood alone in the life of the pastor or the congregation. This is evident through two features of *The Country Parson*. First, Herbert tends to expand the meaning of the word "sermon" to "include the broad scope of liturgical and pastoral practice."[33] For example, he writes that when the parson experiences repentance himself and shares it with others, it "becomes a sermon."[34] The charity of a parson is "in effect a sermon."[35] As Susan Bell notes, "Consecrated pastoral practice not only authenticates the preached Word, but is itself also a vehicle of the Word. All exemplary pastoral and liturgical actions thus are lived sermons. Herbert's holistic understanding of the pastoral life integrates the goal of good preaching with the whole of a dedicated pastoral life."[36]

Second, Herbert repeatedly states that a sermon is necessarily surrounded by the numerous other means the pastor has of shepherding his congregation. It is helpful to compare Herbert's *The Country Parson* with a roughly contemporaneous book on pastoring: *The Faithful Shepheard*, published in 1609 by the Calvinist Richard Bernard, who subscribed to the Thirty-Nine Articles and remained in the Church of England. *The Faithful Shepheard* is 413 pages long and entirely devoted to preaching, with no discussion of liturgical ceremony or other pastoral duties. *The Country Parson*, by contrast, contains only seven and a half pages (out of 168 total pages) directly devoted to preaching.[37]

The important but limited role of preaching is evident in both Herbert's life and writing. Isaak Walton notes that when Herbert renovated the parish church in Layton Ecclesia, "by his order the reading pew and pulpit were a little distant from each other, and both of an equal height; for he would often say, They should neither have a precedency or priority of the other; but that

33. Bell, "Sermons Are Dangerous Things," 52.
34. Herbert, *Country Parson*, 247.
35. Herbert, *Country Parson*, 215.
36. Bell, "Sermons Are Dangerous Things," 52.
37. Bell, "Sermons Are Dangerous Things," 49.

prayer and preaching, being equally useful, might agree like brethren, and have an equal honour and estimation."[38] In *The Country Parson*, Herbert addresses praying and preaching in consecutive chapters.[39] And in "The Church-Porch," he advises congregants to, "Resort to sermon, but to prayers most: / Praying's the end of preaching."[40]

Herbert was clear that a pastor had a *range* of important ways to shepherd his people, including sacraments, daily living, and deeds of practical service (including advising on medicine). He suggests that the parson on Sunday afternoons/evenings should spend time "in exhortations to some of his flock by themselves, whom his sermons cannot or do not reach. And every one is more awaked when we come and say, *Thou are the man*. This way he finds exceeding useful and winning; and these exhortations he calls his privy purse, even as princes have theirs, besides their public disbursements."[41]

Catechizing was a particularly important tool for pastors. Herbert argues that "at sermons and prayers men may sleep or wander, but when one is asked a question he must discover what he is. This practice exceeds even sermons in teaching. But there being two things in sermons, the one informing, the other inflaming; as sermons come short of questions in the one, so they far exceed them in the other. For questions cannot inflame or ravish: that must be done by a set, and laboured, and continued speech."[42] In other words, because humans are more than empty brains waiting to be filled, because they are not just thinking things but embodied beings with emotions and affections that ought to be awakened for God, the parson has a range of shepherding responsibilities, including preaching and catechizing.[43]

Herbert's understanding of human persons as embodied, with minds and affections, properly challenges evangelical understandings that emphasize the sermon to the detriment or exclusion of other means of spiritual formation.

---

38. Walton, "Life," 353.
39. "The Parson Praying" is chapter 6 and "The Parson Preaching" is chapter 7.
40. Herbert, "Church-Porch," lines 409–10.
41. Herbert, *Country Parson*, 207.
42. Herbert, *Country Parson*, 226.
43. Herbert acknowledged that sometimes even sermons wouldn't stir the hearts of hearers. This was one of the reasons he wrote poems. "A verse may find him, who a sermon flies, / And turn delight into a sacrifice." And a poem may "make a bait of pleasure." See "Church-Porch," lines 4–6.

PART TWO: THE HUMILITY OF THE PULPIT

The Awesome Task of Preaching

In the lines cited at the beginning of this chapter, Herbert refers to the preacher as "an earthen pot." He is drawing on the words of the apostle Paul: "But we have this treasure in earthen vessels, that the excellency of the power may be of God, and not of us" (2 Cor 4:7). That description of course assumes that the preacher is an embodied being, like Adam, made of the dust of the earth. Further, it expresses the weakness, fragility, transience, and sheer ordinariness of the preacher. Herbert clearly felt this way about himself. "I am both foul and brittle; much unfit / To deal in holy Writ."[44] Before preaching in Bemerton on Sunday mornings, he would pray for God's blessing and confess himself "thy unworthy servant."[45] In "The Priesthood," he wrote:

> Only, since God doth often vessels make
> Of lowly matter for high uses meet,
> I throw me at his feet.
>
> There will I lie, until my Maker seek
> For some mean stuff whereon to show his skill:
> Then is my time. The distance of the meek
> Doth flatter power.[46]

The image of Herbert prostrate before God is reminiscent of a story Isaak Walton tells. On the night of Herbert's induction as a priest, a friend looked in the window of the Bemerton church and saw Herbert alone, lying prostrate on the ground before the altar.[47] Lines 6–10 of Herbert's poem "Aaron" demonstrate that a clear sense of personal sin and inadequacy was a recurring feature of Herbert's ministry:

> Profaneness in my head,
> Defects and darkness in my breast,
> A noise of passions ringing me for dead
> Unto a place where is no rest,
> Poor priest thus am I drest.

Herbert's sense of weakness and need for God's help is surely part of the answer to one of the questions posed at the beginning of this paper: Why would

---

44. Herbert, "Priesthood," lines 11–12.

45. Herbert, "Author's Prayer Before Sermon," 256: "Especially bless this portion here assembled together, with thy unworthy servant speaking unto them."

46. Herbert, "Priesthood," lines 34–40.

47. Cf. Drury, *Music at Midnight*, 209, who thinks this story is best read as an "illustrative vignette" for *The Temple*.

an accomplished public orator of the University of Cambridge deign to be the priest of a rural village such as Bemerton? It is clear that Herbert did not think himself too good for a tiny village church. Walton tells us that when Herbert was first offered the priesthood at Bemerton, he considered the offer for more than a month, because of "the apprehension of the last great account that he was to make for the cure of so many souls."[48] So *many* souls. Herbert was aware of the greatness of his task, even in a small parish—and of his own weakness in the face of that task.

His inadequacy was not the final word for Herbert, though. Yes, the preacher is merely "an earthen pot," but he represents God himself. Herbert warns his reader, "Judge not the preacher; for he is thy Judge."[49] The preacher has been commissioned by God. For this reason, Herbert advises congregants not to make jokes about the preacher's language or expression, for "God sent him, whatsoe're he be."[50] Before preaching, Herbert would pray to God, "Neither doth thy love yet stay here! for this word of thy rich peace and reconciliation thou hast committed, not to thunder or angels, but to silly and sinful men; even to me, pardoning my sins, and bidding me go feed the people of thy love."[51]

Herbert's awareness of personal inadequacy, coupled with his resting in God's call and provision, is an important corrective in our age of celebrity pastors. Strength and competency are frequently exalted, weakness is often minimized or hidden. Pastors, famous or otherwise, do not like to admit to being an "earthen pot." And this has all too often led to their eventual collapse under an unsustainable burden. Herbert points us to a more biblical way.

In this chapter, I have highlighted several significant features of George Herbert's understanding of preaching and preachers. There is much more to explore. Herbert provides a helpful corrective to some of our contemporary inadequate approaches to preaching and a positive vision we will do well to explore and embrace.

Bibliography

Bell, Susan. "'Sermons Are Dangerous Things': George Herbert, Richard Bernard, and the Politics of Preaching." *Toronto Journal of Theology* 1 (2010) 41–54.

Drury, John. *Music at Midnight: The Life and Poetry of George Herbert*. London: Penguin, 2013.

---

48. Walton, "Life," 359.
49. Herbert, "Church-porch," line 427.
50. Herbert, "Church-porch," lines 439–44.
51. Herbert, "Author's Prayer Before Sermon," *The Country Parson*, 255.

Herbert, George. "Aaron." In *George Herbert: The Complete English Works*, edited by Ann Pasternak Slater, 170. Everyman's Library. New York: Knopf, 1995.

———. "The Author's Prayer Before Sermon." In *George Herbert: The Complete English Works*, edited by Ann Pasternak Slater, 255–56. Everyman's Library. New York: Knopf, 1995.

———. "The Church-Porch." In *George Herbert: The Complete English Works*, edited by Ann Pasternak Slater, 9–21. Everyman's Library. New York: Knopf, 1995.

———. *The Country Parson*. In *George Herbert: The Complete English Works*, edited by Ann Pasternak Slater, 195–256. Everyman's Library. New York: Knopf, 1995.

———. "The Priesthood." In *George Herbert: The Complete English Works*, edited by Ann Pasternak Slater, 156–57. Everyman's Library. New York: Knopf, 1995.

———. "The Windows." In *George Herbert: The Complete English Works*, edited by Ann Pasternak Slater, 64–65. Everyman's Library. New York: Knopf, 1995.

Pasternak Slater, Ann, ed. *George Herbert: The Complete English Works*. Everyman's Library. New York: Knopf, 1995.

Rundell, Katherine. *Super-Infinite: The Transformations of John Donne*. London: Faber & Faber, 2022.

Smith, James K. A. *You Are What You Love: The Spiritual Power of Habit*. Grand Rapids: Brazos, 2016.

Walton, Isaak. "The Life of Mr. George Herbert." In *George Herbert: The Complete English Works*. Edited by Ann Pasternak Slater. Everyman's Library. New York: Knopf, 1995.

Witmer, Stephen. "The Best Preacher for You." Desiring God, April 4, 2023. https://www.desiringgod.org/articles/the-best-preacher-for-you.

———. "Small-Town Pastor, Preach Bespoke Sermons." The Gospel Coalition, November 6, 2019. https://www.thegospelcoalition.org/article/small-town-pastor-preach-bespoke-sermons/.

Wolberg, Kristine. "Posture and Spiritual Formation: Sanctification in George Herbert's *The Country Parson* and *The Temple*." *Christianity and Literature* 66 (2016) 57–72.

Part Three

THE PRACTICE OF THE PULPIT

10

The Philanthropic Pulpit

AHMI LEE

Introduction

THE ORIGINAL GREEK WORD *philanthropia* means "acting out of kindness and love for humanity." Care for humanity can be expressed in many ways—like sharing resources, showing hospitality, and meeting people's needs through service—but at its core, philanthropy is about promoting human flourishing. Despite the obvious points of contact between preaching and philanthropy, contemporary homiletical literature on their relationship is scarce. Moreover, culturally, preaching and philanthropy are generally seen as antithetical. One has to do with word, the other with deed. The former is about the proclamation of the gospel, the latter is about social justice. We see this tension when people imagine evangelism (or even evangelicalism) and social action as opposite ends of a spectrum. Such folks think pastors must choose between preaching biblical sermons or preaching on social justice. Beyond the pulpit, this ideological fault line divides people, churches, and denominations. This was not always the case for preachers in earlier centuries.

My aim in this essay is straightforward: *to show that preaching is a profoundly philanthropic activity.* To be clear, preaching and activities of philanthropy are not the same. Nor do I think that evangelism and social action can be collapsed into each other, for that reduces the distinctiveness of each and the importance of proclaiming the gospel both in word *and* in deed. But I do want to show that preaching encapsulates the essential meaning of philanthropy, which is acting out of love for humanity to promote flourishing. In this, the evangel and action are inseparable and inherent in the definition of preaching.

To demonstrate this, we will examine one of the richest portraits of Christian *philanthropia* from antiquity: *Oration 14: On Love of the Poor*, preached by the Greek church father, Gregory of Nazianzus, known as "the Theologian." This oration, or sermon, urges Christians in the fourth century to love and generosity toward the most vulnerable and excluded people in their society: lepers.

Lepers were alienated from social life and cut off from equal access to basic necessities such as food and a public water source where they could wash themselves. People feared that lepers' disease would pollute and spread to whatever they touched. Lepers were homeless and begged for a living. They sang for attention and pity, hoping for some leftover food or scraps of clothing. But more than anything, they longed to be seen as truly human. Their destitution was unrivaled: lepers were the most devastated and marginalized people of Gregory's day.

Gregory could easily have made a case for charity that is *humanistic*—if we define "humanism" as a belief system that centers on human ability and potential to achieve fulfillment without God—or for charity as *humanitarian* in its orientation; that is, "promoting human welfare and social reform"[1] as an end itself. But Gregory takes a very different approach to lepers by making a theocentric—especially Christocentric—appeal on the basis of the *imago Dei*.

Oration 14 is a fitting text for our investigation for three reasons. First, because of who Gregory was. Gregory of Nazianzus was many things: philosopher, poet, lover of the contemplative and ascetic life, archbishop of Constantinople, and a dear friend to Basil the Great and Gregory of Nyssa. But above all, he was a pastor theologian. He was a leading theologian in the fourth century in the Christian East and was instrumental in formulating clear doctrines of the Trinity, Christology, and pneumatology that led to establishing the Nicene Creed at the Second Ecumenical Council. Over and above all his theological roles and accomplishments, he was a pastor. He saw theology as a midwife to the church and so remained committed to shepherding the flock faithfully in all his different roles.

Second, among Gregory's forty-five extant sermons, *Oration 14* stands out because its purpose is explicitly philanthropic. The sermon may have been intended to support Basil the Great's initiative to build a leprosarium in the region. Two sermons by Gregory of Nyssa written sometime after Gregory of Nazianzus take up the same theme, which suggests that the Cappadocian

---

1. Merriam-Webster, "Humanitarian."

Fathers may have teamed up to campaign for Basil's medical project. It is highly likely, however, that Gregory Nazianzus had a bigger purpose and impact in mind when he penned *Oration 14*.[2] John McGuckin suggests that it was possibly "on a larger scale for [Gregory's] own work as Christian philanthropist and Bishop-*Philoptochos* (i.e., friend of the poor)."[3] Regardless of the occasion for this sermon, we can fairly conclude that *Oration 14* (along with the efforts of the other two Cappadocians) played a vital role in the rise of institutional Christian philanthropy in antiquity.

Third, while the charitable purpose of this oration is important, perhaps even more important is what Gregory models in it: a *homiletic theology* that thinks about *philanthropy* Christianly and *preaching* philanthropically. In other words, we are interested not only in the theology contained in Gregory's sermon but that he embodies that theology through preaching. *Oration 14* offers us a lens through which we can see how the pulpit can exercise power that glorifies God by inviting people to into a fuller humanity in Christ.

I explore our topic in three parts. Part 1 sketches the historical backdrop for Gregory's philanthropic appeal in *Oration 14* that both overlaps with and is distinct from the philosophical ideals of his day. This sets the stage for what follows in the next section. Part 2, which is the longest section, examines Gregory's theological anthropology, which is the foundation for his philanthropic appeal. Part 3 attempts to pull everything together by briefly considering a picture of the philanthropic pulpit that emerges from *Oration 14*.

Philanthropy in the Greco-Roman Tradition: The Historical Backdrop of *Oration 14*

Gregory's ideas cannot be separated from his culture and the influence of classical philosophy. Before we delve into the oration, we need to consider the historical setting with particular interest in how Gregory's vision of philanthropy overlapped and diverged from the ideals and customs of human flourishing in his day.

Social assistance was not uncommon in the fourth century. Philanthropy was a political means of achieving social stability by promoting harmonious relationships between citizens of different classes and statuses.[4] Benefactions were a civic responsibility to contribute to the city's welfare and order.[5]

---

2. McGuckin, *Saint Gregory of Nazianzus*, 145.
3. McGuckin, *Saint Gregory of Nazianzus*, 147.
4. Caner, "Clemency," 229.
5. Holman, *Hungry Are Dying*, 3–30. See also Veyne, *Bread and Circuses*.

Nevertheless, no formal concept of "almsgiving" existed, especially regarding the anonymous poor. Charitable gifts were normally bestowed on its own community members (where membership may be defined in terms of family, class, civic, and religious terms) who merited the aid on the basis of honor and status rather than financial need.[6] In spite of justice—or fairness in giving people their due—holding a high social value, it did not translate into a common practice of indiscriminate generosity toward all who lacked due justice. Gary Ferngren notes, "The classical world believed in the dignity of humans, but it was in the dignity of the virtuous person, the person who possessed *arete* (excellence, virtue)."[7] This meant that beggars, diseased people, and non-citizens existed on the peripheries.

The hierarchical Roman society did not function much differently. To them, inequality was an accepted fact of life. Those who belonged to the lower class served those on top, and in return, those of a higher status, power, and privilege bestowed favors and benefits to the ones who served them.[8] The Romans aspired to and encouraged the development of humane virtues (*humanitas*) through education, which included qualities such as kindness, courtesy, and devotion to others. However, they considered learned aristocrats (and not many others) to be capable of developing such virtues.[9] In a fixed social hierarchy governed by the rule of *quid pro quo*, extrinsic factors such as class, citizenship, and kinship tended to determine the scope and object of charity. The intrinsic worth of human beings was not a concern. Susan Holman asserts a person's "moral standing in society was judged on the basis of his class, his education, and his consequent ability to verbally express himself with eloquence within a given rhetorical structure."[10] By this standard, the poor and needy were simply inferior—meaning that those above them in the social hierarchy deemed them to lack ethical qualities such as industriousness, dignity, respectability, prudence, and even reciprocity to return the favor in equal or greater measure.

The criterion of honor not only determined who received provision but was also what motivated donors. Giving was a civic duty of the wealthy elites in Greco-Roman society, who donated voluntarily and involuntarily (due to social pressure) to meet the needs of their communities. For example, donations were solicited to subsidize the cost of new public infrastructures such as theaters. In return for their service, honorary inscriptions were set up to

---

6. Holman, *Hungry Are Dying*, 18.
7. Ferngren, *Medicine and Health Care*, 95.
8. Schultz et al., "Early Roman Society," 40–55.
9. Ferngren, *Medicine and Health Care*, 92, 95.
10. Holman, *Hungry Are Dying*, 22.

memorialize the donors' generosity. Benevolence was a widely recognized currency to acquire public recognition and prestige among the rich. Giving was a public affair, even a spectacle. Charitable impulse was often *philotimia*—"love of honor"—or *philodoxia*—"love of glory"—not *philanthropia*—"love of humanity."[11] Spontaneous personal giving—and to an extent corporate giving—to those outside one's obligatory community (however that community was defined) and to the "dishonorable" was not the social norm.[12]

I offer this historical backdrop, not to say there was no genuine altruism in the fourth century but to highlight the prevailing cultural assumptions and values that drove the practice of philanthropy. Greco-Roman philanthropy clearly did not always promote true thriving for all people. The vision for Christian philanthropy in *Oration 14* originates from this cultural context, but at the same time radically challenges and reconstitutes what "love of humanity" looks like in light of scriptural truths. Gregory does this not by simply rejecting the cultural ideals of his day. Instead, he filters preexisting Greco-Roman concepts of generosity through a Christian lens that casts a new meaning on *philanthropia*.[13] (This is also true for the other Cappadocians, Basil and his brother, Gregory of Nyssa, who accomplish this to varying degrees in different approaches.) What we recognize in the oration, then, is Gregory's effort to reframe and expand the entrenched, if not socially biased, merit-based philanthropy in light of the scriptural truths about God, truths which restore the inherent dignity and worth of human beings and link person to person in common humanity. Undiscriminating generosity rooted in God's merciful and lavish love to all is the foundation for the kind of philanthropy the Greek Father envisions. Clemency as a quality of impartial generosity was not entirely missing in the classical tradition of philanthropy nor in the writings of earlier Christian authors, but theologians like Gregory of Nazianzus and his Cappadocian colleagues elevated clemency to its position of prominence and made universal almsgiving a distinguishing feature of Christian philanthropy.[14]

---

11. Ferngren, *Medicine and Health Care*, 88–90.

12. Ferngren, *Medicine and Health Care*, 87–88.

13. Susan Holman's contribution stands out with regard to her dialogue with other scholarly works and for her in-depth analysis of the sociohistorical and philosophical factors that flavor the Cappadocian Fathers' understanding and practice of Christian philanthropy. See Holman, *Hungry Are Dying*.

14. See Caner, "Clemency," 229.

PART THREE: THE PRACTICE OF THE PULPIT

Preaching to Human Beings: Theological Anthropology in *Oration 14*

John McGuckin assesses, "What Gregory is offering [in *Oration 14*] . . . is more than a new social policy[:] it is [a] fundamentally renewed anthropology based upon the Christian doctrine of incarnation, [in which] image and archetype [are] reconciled in the hominization of God as a poor man."[15] This analysis sets us up well for this section. For this oration calls the church to care for *all* people on the basis of common kinship of humanity. To make his case, Gregory appeals to the biblical truth that human beings are created according to the image and likeness of God (Gen 1:27).

Common Kinship of Divine Image-Bearers

Drawing on the New Testament, Gregory refers throughout his writings to Christ as the *Eikon*, the image of the invisible God (Col 1:15), the exact representation of the Father's being (Heb 1:3). The Son is the "identical image" of the Father (an expression that appears no less than twenty times in his corpus)[16] because he is consubstantial with the Father (*Oration* 30:20). But to Gregory, Jesus is not just the true *Eikon* of the Father; Christ is the "image of God" in whose image human beings are made. Christ is the eternal Logos who was with God from the beginning as the agent of creation (John 1:1–3) and is the archetype of humanity. In other words, the human person is created in the "*eikon* of Christ" and is thus an "image of the Image."[17] Being created in the image of God by being made in the image of Christ is the essential human nature, the distinctive characteristic that unites the human race in common kinship.

Since being created in the image of the divine *Eikon* constitutes the immutable human identity, Gregory believes that being human is about more than possessing certain attributes or properties. Referring to the lepers, Gregory declares, "They have been made in the image of God in the same way you and I have, and perhaps preserve that image better than we, even if their bodies are corrupted."[18] This is a significant statement about subjects who are disfigured, alienated, and undoubtedly restricted in their capacity, function, and relationality due to their disease. Gregory in no way diminishes the divine image in them. Consistent with his other writings, he weaves throughout this

---

15. McGuckin, *Saint Gregory of Nazianzus*, 151.
16. Thomas, *Image of God*, 40.
17. Thomas, *Image of God*, 82, 25.
18. Gregory of Nazianzus, *Oration* 14.16. Unless otherwise indicated, all translations of *Oration 14* are from Daley, *Gregory of Nazianzus*.

oration a comprehensive and multifaceted view of the divine image that goes beyond the typical categories of human capacity, relationality, and functionality employed in most accounts of the *imago Dei*.[19] Those categories are useful to the extent that they identify important human faculties that allow us to exercise the God-given authority to promote common good. But they are insufficient on their own to capture the totality of what it means to be human. Moreover, they inevitably lead to negative conclusions about certain groups whose expression of human powers and properties are restricted in some way (e.g., people with disabilities). Therefore, rather than locating the *imago* in any one part or aspect of our being, Gregory considers it to be the very essence of the whole human person.[20]

The practical implication for his theological belief is that the poor and suffering have equal worth and are due the same honor by the virtue of their status as God's image-bearer. Every person has intrinsic worth, a worth not dependent on the external factors—background, education, or the ability to reciprocate—that were esteemed in Gregory's culture. Gregory insists that Christians are obliged to show personal concern to all suffering people without partiality. The *imago Dei* is his reason for such inclusiveness. In this, Gregory is calling the church to go beyond the cultural mandate of caring only for members of one's own family and community. The kinship language signals that caring for the sick, homeless, and desperate is not a passionless civic duty for Christians but is a labor of love for a family member. Therefore, the poor, sick, and homeless are not "others," but rather "our own flesh and blood,"[21] "fellow creatures,"[22] and "fellow men and women."[23]

The Created Destiny, Fall, and Redemption of Divine Image-Bearers

Beyond the ontological consideration for the *imago Dei*, Gregory also ties human lived experience and the ultimate human destiny into his theological

---

19. Thomas, *Image of God*, 2.

20. Parts of Gregory's writings that elevate the intellect or soul over the material body have led some readers to conclude that the church father is a Platonist who locates the divine image in human rationality. While it is true that Gregory was a product of his culture and used the concepts available to him (he does link the divine image to the intellect or the soul in a few places), a close reading of his corpus shows that he perceived a dynamic interrelationship of the intellect/soul and the body—a relationship in which the intellect is inseparable from the flesh. See Thomas, "Human Icon," 169.

21. Gregory of Nazianzus, *Oration* 14.5.

22. Gregory of Nazianzus, *Oration* 14.10.

23. Gregory of Nazianzus, *Oration* 14.23, 27.

anthropology.[24] To understand what he says, we need to keep the shape of the biblical narrative in mind. According to Gregory, a key aspect of being in the image of Christ is that by nature, human beings are drawn to an intimate union with the Trinity.[25] The created destiny of human beings is to enjoy God forever by sharing in his nature and life. Thriving for Gregory is, therefore, not a path human beings seek out on our own or something we achieve or merit. The Creator has destined humankind for happiness that can only be attained in union with him. This is the unique gift given to humans, as are also the privilege and mandate to cultivate good by participating in God's creative work.

However, as the biblical story goes, sin broke this sacred communion. Our first parents betrayed their created purpose and turned their backs on God and on each other. Throughout his works, Gregory uses a range of images and expressions to describe sin. In *Oration 14*, he describes the communion-breaking nature of sin, which leads to "otherness." If humanity is a gift from God, the consequence of sin is *inhumanity*. Sin makes us unable to recognize the image of God in each other. His depiction is artistically subtle but poignant, as it makes sin palpable through vivid contrasts between his audience and the lepers:

> They live their wretched lives under the open sky, while we live in splendid houses. . . . These people shiver in thin and tattered rags [while] our clothes are stored away for us in chests. . . . These people are not even supplied with the most basic nourishment, but lie before our doors, faint and starving, not even possessing the bodily power to beg, . . . yet we, by contrast, . . . lie back in splendor on high, raised beds, with coverings so exquisite one scarcely dares handle them, and we are annoyed if we hear so much as the sound of their pleading.[26]

In our fallen condition, we human beings strive to define ourselves by the disparities we create and perpetuate, rather than by our primeval unity and equality.[27] This failure to recognize our shared kinship rather than celebrate it as a divine gift underlies human depravity, which Gregory calls "spiritual sickness, . . . a sickness much more serious than that of the body."[28]

Being the theologian and preacher that he is, Gregory does not leave his listeners in despair. He presents Christ as the one who not only "instantiates

---

24. Thomas, *Image of God*, 2–3.
25. Gregory of Nazianzus, *Oration* 21.1–2.
26. Gregory of Nazianzus, *Oration* 14.16, 17.
27. Gregory of Nazianzus, *Oration* 14.26.
28. Gregory of Nazianzus, *Oration* 14.18.

[the image of God] as the archetype and divine *Eikon*" but also "repairs" it.[29] Christ recapitulates humanity by renewing the original human nature and potential to be united with God. Elsewhere Gregory says, "The Ruler did not leave his created things helpless, and he did not overlook their danger of separation from himself."[30] Rather, God restores "the image which had fallen from sin."[31] Jesus accomplished this by assuming humanity in a hypostatic union of his two distinct natures. Gregory frequently speaks of Christ's sinless life—and in particular, his incarnation—as that which makes it possible for humanity to share in Christ's nature. Because Christ has assumed our full humanity, every aspect of our being is saved. *Oration 14* captures this idea in the proclamation of the good news: "Christ died for [all], taking away the sin of the whole world";[32] he "'bore our weaknesses' (Isa 53.4) and humbled himself so far as to share in the mixture of our nature, [he] 'became poor for our sakes' (2 Cor 8:9), . . . suffered pain and weakness for us, so that we might be rich in divinity."[33]

It should be clear by now that for Gregory, human flourishing originates outside of human effort and is first and foremost a gracious gift of the Father through his Son by the Holy Spirit. That being said, properly recognizing and receiving it as a gift should also lead to the discovery that our created purpose is to fulfill God's intent to bless the world through faithful cultivation of the common good.

The concept of uniting with God, sharing in Christ's nature, or "becoming godlike" may sound strange or dangerous to some who are unfamiliar with this language. However, it helps to bear in mind that "divinization," or *theosis*, is paramount to Gregory's theological contributions as a proponent of Nicene orthodoxy. Moreover, Gregory is not the only one in the patristic tradition to write about deification. Other patristic writers, such as Irenaeus, Clement of Alexandria, and Athanasius take up the concept, as do more recent writers like Jonathan Edwards, C. S. Lewis, Dietrich Bonhoeffer, and Eastern Orthodox scholars. Clearly, the concept is significant. But being foreign to some, it deserves to be clarified.

"Divinization" does not mean that humans are made ontologically the same as Christ, as if human essence and Christ's essence somehow mix or change in the process. Indeed, elsewhere Gregory cautions against such misunderstanding, stressing that creatures cannot be God and that ontological

---

29. Crisp, "Christological Model," 223.

30. Gregory of Nazianzus, *Oration* 45.9. Quoted in Matz, *Gregory of Nazianzus*, 97. Originally from *Patrologia Graeca* 36:636.

31. Gregory of Nazianzus, *Oration* 40.7.

32. Gregory of Nazianzus, *Oration* 14.14.

33. Gregory of Nazianzus, *Oration* 14.15.

distinctions must be maintained.[34] Participation in the divine life is a gift of grace by adoption as God's children.[35] Veli-Matti Kärkkäinen explains *theosis* as "a return to life immortal and the re-shaping of the human being into the image of her creator." It encompasses "the wholeness of new life under God."[36] In this sense, though deification is about participation in the life of the Trinity, it is chiefly about being *truly human* as God originally intended—in a right relationship with him and with each other. Though Gregory's theological language might be foreign and uncomfortable, *theosis* offers a different way of thinking about the nature and purpose of human beings and the nurturing of human potential, one that is distinct from a secular view of thriving centered on the human ability to cause change. In true patristic fashion, Gregory argues that human potential and destiny are inseparably linked to Jesus, the perfect *Eikon* in whose image we have been created, to whose image we have been restored, and to which we are being conformed.

Further adhering to the biblical narrative, Gregory reminds his audience in this oration that the process of *theosis* rooted in creation and restored in salvation will be perfected in the eschaton. Until that final end, the realization of what God has ordained and blessed, the process of "divinization," reinstated in baptism, continues through the Spirit's ongoing work as believers are "transformed into the same image from one degree of glory to another" (2 Cor 3:18 ESV). The work of salvation by Christ is finished (we are justified) but believers must persevere and appropriate that salvation (through sanctification until glorification). Spiritual practices like prayer, contemplation, ascetic endeavors, and acts of mercy are the means by which the Spirit transforms and conforms the believer into the image of Christ. This is why Gregory makes an urgent appeal to love in this oration. He begins *Oration 14* with a long list of virtues that Christians should cultivate, which are "all a good thing" that leads to "dwelling" with God.[37] Then, echoing Paul in 1 Cor 12, he encourages "love of poor, and compassion and sympathy for our own flesh and blood" as the highest virtue.[38] As a skilled rhetorician, Gregory appeals both to the cultural ideal of developing virtues as an honorable way of living and, at a deeper level, to the Christian conscience of his audience that they must prove the genuineness of their faith through its embodiment in life. His sermon is also drenched in eschatological language that prophetically

---

34. Gregory of Nazianzus, *Oration* 23.11; 42.17.
35. Bartos, *Deification*, 7.
36. Kärkkäinen, *One with God*, 23.
37. Gregory of Nazianzus, *Oration* 14.2–5.
38. Gregory of Nazianzus, *Oration* 14.5.

critiques the current state of believers in light of God's coming judgment and also lifts them toward future hope and reward.

Living as Divine Image-Bearers

Gregory instructs us that our eschatological hope is to be made concrete through our lives where glory intermingles with suffering. This is why a person's lived experience, not just her telos and ontology, is integral to Gregory's understanding of the *imago Dei*.[39] In *Oration 14*, Gregory painstakingly sketches the paradox of the universal human experience. Using kinship language again, he describes what it means to be human in our weakness and glory.

On the one hand, humanity is "all wretched alike,"[40] clothed in the same fragile flesh, limited and needy, dependent on the Creator's provision and protection. For this reason, the homeless lepers are "our brothers and sisters before God (even if you prefer not to think so) who share the same nature, . . . have been put together from the same clay from which we first . . . came, . . . are strung together with nerves and bones in the same way we are, . . . have put on flesh and skin like all of us."[41] Again, he is not necessarily referring here to those who belong to the body of Christ, but to the neglected and outcast members of the human family. Yet all humans do share vulnerability to the vagaries of life. Unpredictably, instability, and conditionality is part of the universal human experience in our present condition.

At the same time, there is remarkable beauty and glory in being a human. Humanity is bestowed with "the power to know God and to hope for the Kingdom of Heaven."[42] We possess capacity for extraordinary compassion, courage, integrity, and a sense of justice. We are also alike in that we are sustained by the common grace of God who "lavishes the basic supports of living ungrudgingly on all."[43] Gregory sums up human beings as "both the greatest and the most lowly of creatures, earthly and heavenly, temporal and immortal, heirs of both light and fire. . . . Such is the blend of our nature, and for this reason, . . . whenever we are exalted in spirit because of the image of God, we are humbled because of the earth."[44]

---

39. Thomas, *Image of God*, 3.
40. Gregory of Nazianzus, *Oration* 14.6.
41. Gregory of Nazianzus, *Oration* 14.14.
42. Gregory of Nazianzus, *Oration* 14.23.
43. Gregory of Nazianzus, *Oration* 14.25.
44. Gregory of Nazianzus, *Oration* 14.7.

So, what are we to do about our blended nature? This is the crux of Gregory's theological worldview. That humanity and divinity were inseparably united in Jesus is critical to our salvation. In the incarnation, Christ united himself fully to our humanity and through his cross restored every aspect of our broken nature to bring about a complete humanity. At the same time, Christ not only renewed human nature but also reconciled and unified human relationships. Since this is what Jesus made possible, Gregory believes that the community of the redeemed must mirror our salvation effected by Christ. The world may be motivated by self-glory and self-honor, but the Christian impulse for promoting the thriving of all people without discrimination is God's movement in Christ to undeserving humanity. The fragility of human condition should not make us alienate or turn on each other but should arouse our sympathy and compassion to "care for what is part of our nature and shares in our slavery [to fleshly weaknesses]."[45]

Gregory's use of kinship language further points to the "corporate reality"[46] of personhood, that our existence and flourishing depend on interconnectedness and mutuality. His emphasis on our commonality and unity is not meant to erase individual distinctiveness but instead underscores our fundamental affinity as the prerequisite to respecting individual persons. So, Gregory implores the church: "Think, I beg you, of humanity's original equality, not of its later diversity; think not of the conqueror's law, but of the Creator's!"[47] Beneficence that is commensurate with one's ability is an essential expression of care for our neighbors. Beyond offering material assistance, Gregory also instructs the congregation in a deeper way of loving humanity, which entails *seeing* people for who they truly are in their created nature and destiny as God's image-bearers. Gregory employs long sections in his oration that provide lurid descriptions of the plight of the lepers on the streets to help the congregation take notice of the suffering people in their world. Society has pushed the lepers to the margins and rendered them invisible, but through his sermon, Gregory rehumanizes the people who are called by the name of their disease and makes them seen for the unique persons that they are.

Oration 14 is an earnest pastoral exhortation to the church to enact the love (*philanthropia*) that they have received in abundance from God. Imitating God is key to Gregory. The church is called to imitate God's *philanthropia* in word and in deed. Everything that the triune God has done, is doing, and will do flows out of the abundance of trinitarian love and is for creation. This is evidenced by the gift of God's image in human beings, his self-giving love

---

45. Gregory of Nazianzus, *Oration* 14.8.
46. Young, *God's Presence*, 148.
47. Gregory of Nazianzus, *Oration* 14.26.

demonstrated through his Son for our salvation, and in the faithful presence of the Spirit—the bond of love between the church and God—who guards the saints until the last day. Even the final judgment to which Gregory repeatedly alludes in this oration reminds us of God's holy love expressed in justice: God is a fierce defender of the lowly and will set things right. Philanthropy is, therefore, for Gregory, an outworking of the character of God who is the philanthropist *par excellence*. God drives the process of renewal at both the individual and social levels. God is the preeminent lover of humanity, the first and last philanthropist, the "supreme *Philanthropos*."[48] The church must image this beautiful God through its own *philanthropia* that finds its expression in caring for all people, beginning with the pews and extending to the world.

A Picture of a Philanthropic Pulpit in *Oration 14*

We have covered a lot of ground so far, and we might describe the picture of preaching that emerges from *Oration 14* as follows:

Preaching encapsulates the essential meaning of philanthropy, which is acting out of love for humanity to promote flourishing. The human thriving that Gregory envisages is not simply driven by a desire for "a better society" (whatever that may mean) or the improvement of the quality of life (as important as this is). In appealing to the image of God in human beings, Gregory is not simply trying to alleviate symptoms of injustice: he is concerned with the root issue of how we see and relate to each other. Unless we address the deeper problem, our world—like Gregory's—will focus merely on treating outward symptoms of an underlying spiritual sickness. Sin is the spiritual sickness that breaks our union with God and our solidarity with fellow humans. That breakdown makes us increasingly incapable of recognizing our shared kinship as creatures endowed with the image of the perfect *Eikon*.

Gregory shows through his sermon that through preaching God offers a remedy to our universal sickness in the form of theology. The content of the Christian proclamation is God's self-giving love manifested in the incarnation and cross of Jesus that restores human nature. The sermon is the vehicle by which the Spirit renews and nourishes people's created potential to participate in the life and being of God. In this, the preacher first serves the church, tending to people in the pews by proclaiming, correcting, urging, and exhorting them on their journey of conforming to the image of Christ. Through the Spirit's enabling, the preacher also serves the world by galvanizing the people of God to imitate God's love and care for humanity through tangible actions

---

48. McGuckin, *Saint Gregory of Nazianzus*, 150.

that meet real needs. Central to the work of mirroring God's *philanthropia*, then, is defending and providing for the poor, sick, and forgotten.

Preaching is inherently philanthropic because it is grounded in God's loving purpose and will for human flourishing through Jesus Christ. The one in the pulpit promotes the thriving of all people when that preacher shows them how to be in right relationship with God and, as an outflow of that relationship, how to relate rightly to others. This is what it means to be truly human. The philanthropic pulpit relies on the Spirit to regenerate and revive people to live out their creative purpose of stewarding God's lavish gifts for the common good so that all people can enjoy them equally, to God's glory.

Conclusion

My aim has been to show how preaching encapsulates the essential meaning of philanthropy through the lens of Gregory's *Oration 14*. Gregory's homiletic theology modeled in this sermon shows that preaching is an inherently philanthropic activity in which the pulpit exercises its power to promote true human flourishing as God intended and wills. Though his theological language may seem foreign, it is the vernacular of many patristic pastor theologians and thus, in a sense, it is also our first language. Recovering this language is timely in this cultural moment of a widening gap between "good words" and "good deeds," between preaching and philanthropy. May Gregory's theological framework launch you on a quest to understand how the work and word of the pulpit participates in God's creative work of renewing human nature and vocation in "the image of the Image."

Bibliography

Bartos, Emil. *Deification in Eastern Orthodox Theology: An Evaluation and Critique of the Theology of Dumitru Staniloae*. Eugene, OR: Wipf & Stock, 2007.
Caner, Daniel F. "Clemency, A Neglected Aspect of Early Christian Philanthropy." *Religions* 9 (2018) 229.
Crisp, Oliver. "A Christological Model of the Imago Dei." In *The Ashgate Research Companion to Theological Anthropology*, edited by Joshua R. Farris and Charles Taliaferro, 217–32. London: Routledge, 2015.
Daley, Brian E. *Gregory of Nazianzus*. New York: Routledge, 2006.
Ferngren, Gary B. *Medicine and Health Care in Early Christianity*. Baltimore: Johns Hopkins University Press, 2016.
Gregory of Nazianzus. *Oration 14: On the Love of the Poor*. In *Gregory of Nazianzus*, edited by Brian E. Daley, 75–97. The Early Church Fathers. Edited by Carol Harrison. New York: Routledge, 2006.

Holman, Susan R. *The Hungry Are Dying: Beggars and Bishops in Roman Cappadocia*. Oxford: Oxford University Press, 2001.

Kärkkäinen, Veli-Matti. *One with God: Salvation as Deification and Justification*. Collegeville, MN: Liturgical, 2004.

Matz, Brian. *Gregory of Nazianzus*. Grand Rapids: Baker Academic, 2016.

Merriam-Webster. "Humanitarian." https://www.merriam-webster.com/dictionary/humanitarian.

McGuckin, John A. *Saint Gregory of Nazianzus: An Intellectual Biography*. Crestwood, NY: St. Vladimir's Seminary Press, 2001.

Schultz, Celia E., et al. "Early Roman Society, Religion, and Values." In *A History of the Roman People*, 40–55. 7th ed. New York: Routledge, 2019.

Thomas, Gabrielle. "The Human Icon: Gregory of Nazianzus on Being an *Imago Dei*." *Scottish Journal of Theology* 72 (2019) 166–81.

———. *The Image of God in the Theology of Gregory of Nazianzus*. Cambridge: Cambridge University Press, 2019.

Veyne, Paul. *Bread and Circuses: Historical Sociology and Political Pluralism*. Translated by Brian Pearce. London: Penguin, 1990.

Young, Frances. *God's Presence: A Contemporary Recapitulation of Early Christianity*. Cambridge: Cambridge University Press, 2013.

11

The Purpose and Power of the Pulpit

P. T. Forsyth's Theological Wisdom for Evangelical Preaching

TRYGVE D. JOHNSON

> For "everyone who calls on the name of the Lord shall be saved." But how are they to call on one in whom they have not believed? And how are they to believe in one of whom they have never heard? And how are they to hear without someone to proclaim him? And how are they to proclaim him unless they are sent? As it is written, "How beautiful are the feet of those who bring good news!" But not all have obeyed the good news, for Isaiah says, "Lord, who has believed our message?" So faith comes from what is heard, and what is heard comes through the word of Christ.
>
> —ROMANS 10:13–17 NRSV

INTRODUCTION

LET ME BEGIN WITH two confessions. The first confession is my awareness of the jeopardy of addressing preachers about preaching. To do so puts me at risk of presenting myself as an expert. One thing I have learned in twenty-five years of preaching is that no one is an expert. Each sermon is an event that cannot be mastered; the best any preacher can do is be a witness to a holy exchange, when "what is heard comes through the word of Christ" (Rom 10:17). Each sermon is offered in the innocent hope that God will speak again over the chaotic waters of our lives and make a new creation. That miracle is outside of a preacher's power. This is why preachers are never masters, only apprentices to the Master. As Karl Barth says, neither Christian living nor Christian ministry can "ever be anything but the work of beginners."[1] I assume no expertise, but rather offer some thoughts that will hopefully encourage fellow servants in the King's service.

The sermon—this single event—has had more positive impact on the world than we appreciate. I would argue that the word, faithfully preached, is the oxygen of the church, for it is the sermon that unleashes the word into the wild, allowing the cadence of the Spirit, the breath of God, to echo down the canyons of time. Despite popular opinion, the church is one of the most powerful forces of good in the world.[2] That often begins when the word is proclaimed, loosed into the wild without apology or shame. It is the sermon, when faithfully preached, that teaches the sinner they are a saint and directs them to live a new kind of life. The word is the hope of the world.

My thesis is simple. Christian preaching is in a crisis. My argument is that preaching, and as a consequence the church, has lost its theological nerve. By theology I do not mean a tight system where all knowledge is tidily buttoned up. I mean the way we *think* about *God*.

I make this claim as someone who has spent the past twenty-four years in a preaching ministry. If I am honest, I do not know if I have known a more difficult time to preach. The church is awash with difficult disagreements, confusion over priorities, and has trouble talking about the truth. I wager that there are few who would contest that observation. Coming out of the traumatic triad of a pandemic, racial reckoning, and a contentious political election whose ripple effects still haunt the republic, the church—across denominations, traditions, and perspectives—has struggled to speak with clarity and confidence.

A Homiletical Crisis

Pastors who preach are leaving the church at an alarming pace. One statistic I recently came across suggested that the average length of service for preachers

---

1. Barth, *Christian Life*, 79.

2. For an argument on the outsized positive influence of Christianity on the world, see Holland, *Dominion*.

in Protestant churches in America is down to about four to five years.[3] For that to be a true average, think about how many pastors must serve far less than four years! It takes at least three years just to finish seminary. Why are they leaving?

The Context of Crisis

There are many reasons. It is never about one thing. But I will name a few.

First, preaching is a hard calling. Few understand the difficult demands of preaching. The rhythm of Sunday to Sunday is relentless, let alone the work of preaching at funerals, weddings, and other events. Most are not up for this kind of work; most are utterly unprepared and unformed for the rigors demanded of one's self and one's family.

One has to prepare to be a professional exegete. This is emotionally and intellectually demanding labor. Preaching faithfully requires a constant work of exegesis on at least four levels. First, the preacher has to develop and wield the intellectual skills to exegete scriptural context. Language skills, historical digging, and spiritual sensitivity are necessary to discern the meaning of a text and to put that into our context with a word of conviction.

Second, this requires the preacher to also exegete the cultural context. The preacher must speak into a particular time and place. "What time is it?" This is the constant question of the preacher, which requires the ability to interpret and speak into the culture without being conformed to it. This interpretation requires a capable mind with the ability to discern the seen and unseen. That skill is not easily earned.

Thirdly, the preacher has to exegete people—the human condition. The preacher speaks not merely into a culture but to a people who create and animate the culture. This requires the preacher to have a deep understanding of human nature—a biblical anthropology—that helps one exegete what drives one *away from* or *to* a just and loving God. Human nature is complicated, for as Aleksandr Solzhenitsyn reminds us, echoing the historic Christian tradition of human nature, "the line dividing good and evil cuts through the heart of every human being."[4]

Solzhenitsyn's analysis rings true of the preacher as well, which means that, fourth, preachers must exegete themselves. Constantly. Preaching requires a constant examination of one's desires, conscience, and attitude—in short, one's character. It is easier to speak of the gospel than it is to embody

---

3. Crotts, "Selfish Reason."
4. Solzhenitsyn, *Gulag Archipelago*, 1:28.

a life conformed to the gospel. As one prepares for and approaches the pulpit, one needs to examine one's own life. Failure to do so ruins not only the preacher, but threatens the pulpit itself, and more to the point, the people that pulpit is charged to serve.

Being a professional exegete is simply hard to do faithfully and honestly. Committing to a life of constant exegesis of the word, culture, people, and self is not for the faint of heart. It is especially difficult in a cultural context that increasingly views the preacher and the work of preaching with suspicion at best and, at worst, contempt. It is hard to get up and do this work if one does not feel valued, supported, or even liked, especially by one's own people. The operating assumption that preaching matters is no longer privileged.

This brings us to some of the cultural conditions that contribute to the contemporary crisis in preaching. Anyone who preaches regularly today personally knows these challenges all too well. While they vary depending on the specific cultural context and region, common challenges include:

Technological and media influence: The digital age has transformed the way people access information and engage with content. Many preachers feel they must adapt to new media platforms, social media, and online communication to reach a wider audience and remain relevant in the digital landscape.

Changing moral and ethical norms: Societal attitudes toward issues like gender, sexuality, and social justice have evolved significantly. Christian preachers must navigate these changing norms while upholding traditional teachings and values, which can create tensions and challenges.

Political and social polarization: Many societies are increasingly polarized along political and social lines. Preachers may find it challenging to address sensitive political and social issues without alienating members of their congregation or audience.

Generational differences: Different generations may have varying expectations and preferences when it comes to preaching style and content. Bridging the gap between traditional and contemporary forms of preaching can be a challenge.

Declining church attendance: Across the country, church attendance has been on the decline. A Barna Group study published in 2020 revealed that "one-third fewer Americans attend church weekly now than in 1993."[5] The most significant change the study identified was that "practicing Christians are now a much smaller segment of the entire population. In 2000, 45 percent of all those sampled qualified as practicing Christians. That share has consistently declined over the last nineteen years. Now, just one in four Americans (25 percent) is a practicing Christian. In essence, the share of practicing

---

5. Barna Group, "Signs of Decline."

Christians has nearly halved since 2000."[6] Preachers must find ways to reengage with congregants and attract new members to their communities.

Secularism and skepticism: The cultural atmosphere of Christianity is burning away in the West. This has created a skeptical context in which religious institutions and those who serve them are viewed with distrust. Preachers are asked to address the questions and doubts of a secular audience and demonstrate the relevance of Christianity to a suspicious world. Charles Taylor describes this reality in *A Secular Age*, arguing that "the shift to secularity in this sense consists, among other things, of a move from a society where belief in God is unchallenged and indeed, unproblematic, to one in which it is understood to be one option among others, and frequently not the easiest to embrace."[7] In such a world, we are left with a culture where we are thrown back on ourselves for meaning. The secular age is defined by a cultural assumption that humanity is locked inside an immanent frame, a closed world where there is no hope for a transcendent revelation. This creates, in Taylor's words, the "age of disenchantment."[8]

The Crux of Crisis

Despite these challenges—personal demands, hostile cultural conditions—we still have not named the heart of the crisis in Christian preaching. To this we must focus our attention. The crux of the crisis is a lack of confidence and conviction that God still speaks through preaching. In other words, our problem is a loss of a theological nerve.

The hardest thing about preaching, that which demands the most of preachers and leads to their high attrition rate, is not the emotional grind, the intellectual work, or the hostile cultural pressures and conditions. The hardest part of this work is that it constantly asks us to trust God and not ourselves. It is hard to preach about God if in our hearts we do not trust him!

Why do so many fail to trust God? I wonder if we do not actually think our theology—what we believe and think about God—is real. In many pulpits, the Christian God been reduced to a subject of self-help or a metaphor for progressive social change. But this is not the historic Christian God. I am reminded of what Christian Smith and Melinda Lundquist Denton say in their

---

6. Barna Group, "Signs of Decline."

7. Taylor, *Secular Age*, 3.

8. For some discussions in Taylor's works pertaining to this issue of "disenchantment" see *Secular Age*, 25–89, 97–99, 130–36, 150–52, 232–34, 238–39, 268–71, 280–81, 283–84, 299–321, 322–54, 361–68, 375–76, 378–84, 446–47, 539–48, 550–56, 588–89, 613–14, 714, 773.

book *Soul Searching* when diagnosing the cultural atmosphere shaping young American teenagers:

> We have come with some confidence to believe that a significant part of Christianity in the United States is actually only tenuously Christian in any sense that is seriously connected to the actual historical Christian tradition.... It is not so much that U.S. Christianity is being secularized. Rather, more subtly, Christianity is either degenerating into a pathetic version of itself or, more significantly, Christianity is actively being colonized and displaced by quite a different religious faith.[9]

If this is what young adults are absorbing in church, it suggests that preachers have lost the plot of the story. It suggests a church culture where the triune God of grace—the Father, Son, and Holy Spirit—is no longer preached with conviction and clarity.

Today in the secular age, even for the most earnest, belief in God is deeply felt to be only one possibility among many. Again, Taylor aptly captures the point:

> I may find it inconceivable that I would abandon my faith, but there are others, including possibly some very close to me, ... who have no faith (at least not in God, or the transcendent). Belief in God is no longer axiomatic. There are alternatives. And this will also likely mean that at least in certain milieux, it may be hard to sustain one's faith. There will be people who feel bound to give it up, even though they mourn its loss. This has been a recognizable experience in our societies, at least since the mid-nineteenth century. There will be many others to whom faith never even seems an eligible possibility. There are certainly millions today of whom this is true.[10]

We live in a time and place where God is no longer assumed to be active in our daily life. This new reality means that there is little a preacher can take for granted when preaching Christ other than that the message will not conform to cultural assumptions. In the context of the secular age, the plausibility structure for belief can no longer be assumed in the public square, and as the sociological research from Christian Smith on the National Survey for Youth in Religion indicates, not even in the church itself. Preaching is demanding, existentially so, because it asks the preacher to trust God in a world that no longer assumes there is a God who shows up and, even if there is one, we do

---

9. Smith and Lundquist, *Soul Searching*, 171.
10. Taylor, *Secular Age*, 3.

not have to think about him as a real category in our lives. As Craig Gay writes in *The Way of the Modern World*, "The most insidious temptations to 'worldliness' today do not necessarily come in the form of enticements to sexual dissipation, or even to complicity in sociopolitical oppression, but rather in the form of the suggestion that it is possible—and indeed 'normal' and expedient—to go about our daily business in the world without giving much thought to God."[11] The biggest threat of "worldliness" is not sex, drugs, and rock-n-roll. It is the quiet whisper that suggests that we do not really need God in our daily life and certainly do not need to think about or deal with him.

The assumption that we can live and move and have our being without God is the same assumption that saps the soul of the preacher and rips the heart from sermons. Is our preaching about God, or is it about how God can make us better, more successful, and interesting? Is God an inherent reality of good or a pragmatic idea to help us cope and improve ourselves in difficult situations? This is the heart of the crisis.

Disenchanted Pulpits

Preachers immersed in this culture are not immune from the spirit of disenchantment. I have met many a preacher who has felt this loss of a confidence in God's presence within their own sermons. They go to the pulpit as a job to do, without hope for any change in the lives of people, the community, or themselves. They are on the verge of giving the vocation up. This is the real crisis of preaching; it is not adverse cultural conditions, but a lack of a trust, of faith in a God who speaks through the word. This lack of faith has cut the theological nerve of preaching, leaving the pulpit paralyzed to be pushed around by the cultural powers of our day. And so we turn the focus of the sermon on ourselves. We preach "how-to" homilies; we turn to manipulative gimmicks; we hire consultants who can supposedly make preaching relevant to people; we preach to what people want—inspiring messages that do not mess with their daily life and encourage the pursuit of upward mobility in a market economy—rather than offering them what they need: to be confronted by the God who invites them to surrender their will to him, to hear of the God who is good but not safe.

---

11. Gay, *Way*, 5.

A Guide for the Crisis

The antidote to the preaching crisis is to recover a theology of preaching. Preachers need a theology of proclamation that offers them a steely backbone. But where can this be found? Who can be a guide into the high country where the air is thin but the glory is thick?

One such guide who has reminded me of the importance of preaching when I have felt defeated and discouraged is the Scottish pastor, poet, and theologian Peter Taylor (or P. T.) Forsyth.

P. T. Forsyth (1848–1921) was a Scottish theologian and preacher who left an indelible mark on the landscape of Christian theology in the late nineteenth and early twentieth centuries. While deeply rooted in the Reformed tradition, he also engaged with modern challenges and developments, making his theology a unique and influential contribution to the church. His pen was a pulpit. He wrote over thirty monographs for the church, most notably *The Soul of Prayer*, *The Person and Place of Jesus Christ*, *The Justification of God*, and one of my all-time favorites, *Positive Preaching and the Modern Mind*. One of the most significant aspects of Forsyth's theological work was his approach to preaching, which reflected his broader theological convictions and left a lasting legacy for generations of preachers and theologians to come.

Forsyth was known as "the homiletician's theologian."[12] His work focused on the person and work of Christ, always in relation to a positive conviction that God was reconciling the world to himself. Forsyth understood the church not to be a stone building, but a stone pulpit, whose purpose was to uplift and proclaim the word with clarity and conviction. This purpose opened the world to the power of an encounter with a living God, whose justice is his mercy and whose revelation of Jesus Christ as his deliverance of justice through mercy is the good news that overwhelms the world. For Forsyth, the power of preaching was an "unrepeatable event" where the governing dynamics of God's grace, realized in the cross and resurrection, are located in Jesus Christ, who is God in the flesh, reconciling the world to himself.[13]

Even a hundred years later, Forsyth offers contemporary preachers a homiletic vision for the purpose and power of Christian preaching. He resisted the trendy theological movements of his day, leaving behind a progressive theological agenda that promised progress in favor of a classical Christianity, because in this he found a gospel that was actually practical and transformative in lives of real people. He described preaching as "the Gospel prolonging and declaring itself" and as a "creative sacrament by the medium of a

---

12. See Barr, "P. T. Forsyth," 38.
13. See Goroncy, *Descending on Humanity*, 1.

consecrated personality," and the preacher as a "living oracle of God" that has the power to "make and unmake us."[14] As such he stood against the seduction to make preaching about the charism or skill of the preacher, or worse, to reduce the pulpit to a platform of cultural concerns or the gospel to a reflection of ethical behaviors or a means for political commentary (though he was not afraid to speak into how the gospel shapes culture, ethics, and politics). What Forsyth offered the church instead was a thick theological imagination for why preaching is essential for the church. As such he offers wisdom for us to consider in our current crisis of proclamation. He is a guide who can help us understand what is at stake in preaching by grounding the sermon in the person and cruciform work and witness of Jesus Christ, who is the gospel.

Forsyth's Wisdom for the Present Age

Forsyth's theology of preaching can be understood through several key themes and emphases that he consistently articulated throughout his writings and sermons. These themes not only shed light on his understanding of preaching but also reveal his broader theological framework. Before appropriating these for the present, it is important to note that Forsyth went through his own crisis in the pulpit.

A Preacher's Conversion

Forsyth's homiletic vision is an extension of a theological conversion in his pastoral life. In his early theological career, Forsyth was influenced by liberal theology, which tended to emphasize human progress, moralism, and the idea of God as a benevolent force supporting human efforts for social and moral improvement. This approach often downplayed the divinity of Christ and the atonement. During this early phase, Forsyth wrote, "The theology of progress is our modern faith, and the theology of the atonement is . . . our problem."[15] He was wrestling with the tension between the liberal theology of his time and the traditional Christian doctrines of the cross.

Forsyth's theological conversion is evident in his writings and public addresses as he gradually shifted towards a more conservative theological perspective. In his book, *Positive Preaching and the Modern Mind*, he articulated his growing discontent with liberal theology: "We are drifting to a religion which has no faith in the fall of man, and therefore in Christ as the divine

---

14. Forsyth, *Preaching of Jesus*, 80.
15. Forsyth, *Cruciality of the Cross*, 27.

Savior from it."[16] Forsyth's growing concern was rooted in his belief that liberal theology had become too human-centered, neglecting the core tenets of the Christian faith.

The pivotal moment in Forsyth's conversion can be seen in his book *The Work of Christ* where he writes, "We have not to reconcile God to man, but man to God. . . . God and Christ are at one in the cross, not man and Christ."[17] This marks a significant transformation in Forsyth's theology as he moved from focusing on reconciling a benevolent God to a sinful humanity to recognizing the divine initiative in Christ's work of reconciliation. He wrote of his theological turn in the late 1880s: "From a Christian to a believer, from a lover of love to an object of Grace."[18]

This conversion process culminated in Forsyth's emphasis on the centrality of the atonement as profound reality rather than mere theory. "Atonement is not a theory; it is an event. It is not an idea but a thing. It is not something for me to think of, but something for me to experience."[19] Forsyth's theology had evolved to place Christ's atonement at the core of his faith, highlighting the transformative power of the cross.

Homiletic Vision

This theological conversion from a liberal theology preoccupied with the self to a theological vision that focused on God informed and influenced Forsyth's convictions on preaching as a way to address the crisis of his day. He understood that a pulpit captivated by anthropology rather than Christ's divinity was a crisis of the faith for the church. When the focus of the preacher is human happiness, the gospel is muzzled in a cage and the power of God's healing work is silenced in favor of human self-centeredness. The preacher then merely sees and reflects in the sermon a fragmented self. The pulpit has become a platform to talk about the self rather than God.

> What is the tacit understanding in current religion which leaves it at the mercy of social or other convulsions? . . . In theological language it is anthropocentric religion, which has displaced theocentric. That is to say, it is man's preoccupation with humanity and its spiritual civilization or culture. It is the religious egoism of Humanity, i.e., man's absorption with himself, instead of with God, His

---

16. Forsyth, *Positive Preaching*, 46.
17. Forsyth, *Work of Christ*, 16.
18. Forsyth, *Positive Preaching*, 193.
19. Forsyth, *Positive Preaching*, 22.

> purpose, His service, and His glory. It is a greater anxiety to have God on our side than to be upon His. We are willing to owe many things to God, only not ourselves and our destiny absolutely.[20]

The critical problem, both for Forsyth's conversion and his preaching and theological vision, was the realization that there is nothing we humans as a race can do to save ourselves. There is no personal agency of self-help or improvement, no human wisdom, no best practice, no consultant, no market or communication strategy, no scientific discovery, no technological advance, no title, job, or even spiritual practice that is going to save us. Forsyth understood that the crisis of preaching in his day was that preachers failed to see or confront the crisis that the human race is in moral jeopardy.

> It is not help that either the Church or the world needs most. It is power. It is life. It is moral regeneration. If the greatest boon in the world is Christ's Holy Father, the greatest curse in the world is man's unfilial guilt. Whatever, therefore, undoes the guilt is the solution of the world. Everything will follow upon that peace and power. The righteousness which reconciles and secures everything is the holiness which destroys guilt in its very exposure. It is God's holy and atoning love making a new world in Christ's Cross.[21]

We need power—the power of God—which is his life in us. But we do not have access to this power if we are listening to a lie that says that we can save ourselves. The preacher's task is to expose this lie and make plain the truth facing humanity—that we are lost at sea. Only God can save us. It is then to tell the good news that God has saved us, that he acts for us, diving into the deep water, in the person of Jesus Christ, as one of us, to save us so we can live to be with him forever. This saving act of God is the power that animated his commitment to a primacy of preaching.

The Primacy of Preaching

Forsyth's conviction that preaching should hold a preeminent place in the church is captured in his statement, "Preaching is the first act of the Church."[22] This powerful assertion underscores his belief that preaching is not merely a peripheral function but the foundational activity upon which the life of the church is built. In his view, preaching is the means through which the gospel is proclaimed, faith is kindled, and souls are transformed. There may be no

---

20. Forsyth, *Justification of God*, 24.
21. Forsyth, *Justification of God*, 22.
22. Forsyth, *Positive Preaching*, 41.

better sentiment to capture his commitment to preaching than the opening of his 1907 Lyman Beecher Lectures, which turned into his magnum opus *Positive Preaching and the Modern Mind*: "It is, perhaps, an overbold beginning, but I will venture to say that with its preaching Christianity stands or falls."[23]

This is a bold declaration, especially in a context (much like ours) that had lost confidence in the act of preaching. But Forsyth understood that without preaching the church loses the oxygen it needs to breathe in order to stay alive. Forsyth agrees with Paul who cries out, "And how are they to call on one in whom they have not believed? And how are they to believe in one of whom they have not heard? And how are they hear without someone to proclaim him?" (Rom 10:14). Like Paul, Forsyth privileges preaching as that unique work that is different from all other kinds of speaking, for it is in preaching the word that we hear the revelation of God.

> Preaching (I have said), is the most distinctive institution in Christianity. It is quite different from oratory. The pulpit is another place, and another kind of place, from the platform. Many succeed in the one, and yet are failures on the other. The Christian preacher is not the successor of the Greek orator, but of the Hebrew prophet. The orator comes with but an inspiration, the prophet comes with a revelation.[24]

What the church needs is not charisma or an inspirational word. What the church needs to survive is the revelation of God's self-disclosure that continues to overwhelm the world with grace. It is revelation, who is Jesus, that sustains the church. It is revelation that confronts humanity with the reality of the gospel *as grace*, as the word descends and intrudes and makes alive, rather than that which arises from our own situation and in the end merely throws us back on ourselves. This is why Forsyth argues forcefully, "With preaching Christianity stands or falls because it is the declaration of a Gospel. Nay more—far more—it is the Gospel prolonging and declaring itself."[25]

Forsyth's emphasis on the spoken word as the primary vehicle for conveying the message of Christ is evident in another notable quote: "We need, and the Church is to give, not more Bible, but more Bible power, more living and creating contact with the spiritual world of the Bible."[26] Here he stresses the importance of not merely reciting Scripture but interpreting it in a way that brings it to life, making it relevant and transformative for the congregation.

23. Forsyth, *Positive Preaching*, 3.
24. Forsyth, *Positive Preaching*, 3.
25. Forsyth, *Positive Preaching*, 5.
26. Forsyth, *Positive Preaching*, 89.

This approach is essential for fostering spiritual growth and deepening one's relationship with God.

Of course, Forsyth's commitment to preaching as a primary work of the church was not to say that he put his confidence in preachers. The preacher more than anyone was in need of saving grace. As Forsyth wrote, "The Church does not live by its preachers, but by its Word."[27] Forsyth never put his trust in human agency, but God, through the Holy Spirit, who uses our agency to unleash the word of Christ into the world.

> Preaching is the communication of Christ's word by man to men. It is the chief means by which we can be fed, guided, corrected, comforted, and delivered.[28]

> The sermon is not an essay but a proclamation. It is the instrument of a living Word.[29]

> The preacher is not a chef but a steward. He is not serving a banquet of his own making but a supper which he has received. He is not the author of the message; he is the echo, the reflection, the voice.[30]

> The preacher is not a religious actor or impersonator, but a spiritual man, a man of God, speaking to men of God.[31]

> Preaching is not the performance of an hour. It is the outflow of a life. It takes twenty years to make a sermon because it takes twenty years to make the man.[32]

These quotes reflect his emphasis on the centrality of Christ's message in preaching and the profound responsibility of the preacher as a steward of divine truth, rather than a mere orator.

The Primacy of the Gospel

Central to Forsyth's theology of preaching was the conviction that the gospel message is at the heart of Christian faith and proclamation. He believed that the preacher's primary task was to proclaim the gospel, which he saw as the "good

---

27. Forsyth, *Positive Preaching*, 41.
28. Forsyth, *Positive Preaching*, 28.
29. Forsyth, *Positive Preaching*, 35.
30. Forsyth, *Preaching of Jesus*, 83.
31. Forsyth, *Positive Preaching*, 32.
32. Forsyth, *Soul of Prayer*, 49.

news" of God's reconciliation with humanity through Jesus Christ. Forsyth emphasized the importance of Christ as the focal point of preaching and urged preachers to keep Christ central in their sermons. For him, preaching was not primarily about imparting moral instruction or offering self-help advice; it was about declaring the redemptive work of Christ to save us from sinfulness.

> Behind the tragedy of fate to man's happiness, I have said, is the will's tragedy to God's holiness, the tragedy of guilt. And a God who can deal in mercy with that has fully in hand, at the long last, the misery and mystery of man's fate. The agony in the garden heals all the agony of the race.[33]

What is central for preaching the gospel then is not only Jesus Christ as a person, but his saving work on the cross. For Forsyth, the incarnation of Jesus was for atonement. God came not simply to be with us, he came to save us. He came not simply to show a way, but to be our destiny.

> We believe because He makes us believe—with a moral compulsion, an invasion and capture of us. He becomes our eternal life. To live is Christ. He is our destiny. He is our career. And He is the same yesterday and forever. The soul's goal is always the soul's God. The world's perpetual destiny is the world's Eternal Redeemer. We inherit "a finished work." We receive, in advance, the end of our faith, which is the salvation of our souls in the salvation of a world.[34]

The Primacy of Atonement

Forsyth's theology was deeply centered on the atonement, and this emphasis carried over into his theology of preaching. He saw the cross as the pivotal event in human history, where God's justice and love were fully manifested. Preaching, according to Forsyth, was to expound the meaning and significance of the atonement to the congregation. He believed that the cross should not be reduced to a mere symbol but should be proclaimed as the heart of the Christian message. For Forsyth, atonement is the greatest of all words in the Christian gospel. It is not a Bible word only; it is a gospel word because it is the most expressive word to capture the grace of God. He argues, "We have been encouraged to measure our religion by the sacrifice we make instead of the sacrifice we trust, by the love we feel instead of the love we love."[35] In other

---

33. Forsyth, *Justification of God*, 52–53.
34. Forsyth, *Justification of God*, 47.
35. Forsyth, *Justification of God*, 38.

words, we do not trust our sacrifice for God, we trust that God's sacrifice for us is our redemption from guilt.

Thus, what was central in Forsyth's atonement theology for preaching was an emphasis on the vicarious nature of Christ's atonement, arguing that Jesus Christ acted on behalf of humanity, representing and substituting for humanity in his work on the cross. He believed that Christ's death was not merely an example or moral influence but a true substitutionary sacrifice for humanity's sins. For example, in trying to explain a Christian response to theodicy in the face of World War I, he writes, "The Cross of Christ, with its judgment-grace, its tragic love, its grievous glory, its severe salvation, and its 'finished work,' is God's only self-justification in such a world."[36] It is the only self-justification because through the atonement we are saved, once and for all. Which is why he believed that "the victory in Christ's cross is greater than that in any possible war."[37]

Forsyth is often associated with the doctrine of penal substitution, which teaches that Christ bore the penalty and punishment for human sin on the cross. He believed that Christ's suffering and death satisfied the demands of divine justice and reconciled humanity to God. Forsyth, however, approached this doctrine with a nuanced perspective and emphasized the love and mercy of God in conjunction with divine justice. This put an emphasis on God's holiness and love rather than focusing solely on a legal or forensic aspect of salvation. Forsyth stressed the holiness of God and the seriousness of sin. He saw the atonement as the way in which God's holiness and love met in a profound and reconciling manner. He believed that God's holiness demanded satisfaction for sin, but God's love provided the means for that satisfaction through Christ's sacrifice. In other words, God's justice was satisfied by his mercy on the cross.

The Primacy of Theological Depth

This emphasis on the atoning work of Christ in preaching points to one of Forsyth's most important lessons for preachers today. He preached theologically. Theologians, pastors, and scholars have continued to find inspiration in Forsyth's teachings on homiletics because of its theological rigor, intellectual depth, and spiritual insights. Forsyth argues preachers should be theologians in the pulpit, ensuring that their sermons are firmly rooted in a tested and orthodox theological tradition. He insisted that preachers, on behalf of the

---

36. Forsyth, *Justification of God*, 37.
37. Forsyth, *Justification of God*, 30.

people they serve, need to engage deeply and grapple with complex theological ideas. He believed that theology and preaching have a symbiotic relationship, that they are intimately connected. And he believed that a robust theological framework was necessary to uphold the gravity of the pulpit. This emphasis on a sermon's theological depth meant that Forsyth's sermons were not superficial, rather they invited congregants to wrestle with profound theological truths.

It is instructive here to include a lengthy extract from Forsyth's *Positive Preaching and the Modern Mind* to demonstrate the theological rigor that filled his work.

> It is the wills of men, and not their views, that are the great obstacle to the Gospel, and the things most intractable. The power to deal with those wills is the power of the Gospel as the eternal act of the will and heart of God. And the power of the Gospel as a preached thing is shaped in a message which has had from the first a theological language of its own creation as its most adequate vehicle. To discard that language entirely is to maim the utterance of the Gospel. To substitute a vocabulary of mere humane sympathies or notions for the great phrases and thoughts which are theology compressed into diamonds is like the attempt to improve a great historical language, which is a nation's record, treasure and trust, by reducing it to Saxon monosyllables, and these to phonetics. I cannot conceive a Christianity to hold the future without words like grace, sin, judgment, repentance, incarnation, atonement, redemption, justification, sacrifice, faith and eternal life. No words of less volume than these can do justice to the meaning of God, however easy their access to the minds of modern men. It needs such words to act on the scale of God and of the race. And the preacher who sets to discard them or, what is more common, to eviscerate them, is imperiling the great Church for a passing effect with the small. For a living and modern theology our chief need is a living and positive faith, moving in those great categories, and full of confident power to absorb and organize the sound thought of the time. To rouse and feed this faith is the great work of the preacher. And thus the service the preacher does to theology is at least no less than the service theology does to him. A mere theology may strain and stiffen the preacher. But the preacher who is a true steward of the Christian Word makes a living theology inevitable, which, because it lives, demands new form and fitness for each succeeding time.[38]

---

38. Forsyth, *Positive Preaching*, 197–98.

Forsyth advocated for preaching that was deeply rooted in theology and theological language. He believed preachers should be theologians who engage deeply with the doctrinal content of the Christian faith and bring it to bear on the lives of their listeners in a way they can hear and understand. For Forsyth, theology and preaching were closely connected, and he saw theology as the foundation for effective preaching. For, at its heart, Forsyth understood preaching to be a means to care for souls. And good theology is good pastoral care.

Conclusion

It is this conviction for the care of souls that we need today. We need less focus on how we preach and more concentration on who we preach about and why it matters. Our antidote to the crisis facing the church is a process of retrieval. We need to focus less on ourselves and culture and instead exercise a faithful confidence in the primary work of God in Jesus Christ who has reconciled us, the world, to himself, by the blood of the cross.

Forsyth's legacy continues to influence preachers and theologians, challenging them to proclaim the gospel with depth, conviction, and a deep sense of responsibility to both the church and the world. His call to make Christ central in preaching and to engage with the profound mysteries of the faith remains a timeless and relevant message for those who seek to faithfully proclaim the Christian message.

To those who preach because they still believe, or are still trying to believe, may the wisdom of P. T. Forsyth come as an encouragement that your labor is not in vain. If you are looking for a guide or someone to encourage your weekly preparation, or even if you just need to reflect on the significance of preaching for the life of the church and the world, I have found no better source than P. T. Forsyth. As one of his commentators John Huxtable once wrote, "A few pages of [Forsyth's] work recharges that battery as little else."[39]

In conclusion, Forsyth reminds us that the purpose and power of the pulpit is to speak with conviction and clarity of Christ as a saving reality for all people at all times, to announce the gospel as an invitation to explore God's wide-open country of salvation without bullying, coercion, and manipulation. It asks us simply to trust the truth of the gospel. And truth, like beauty, does not ask for attention. We are charged to simply trust God as the truth. He will do the deep work of salvation as we, like John the Baptist crying out in the wilderness, preach the reality of Christ: This is the Son of God, who takes away the sin of the world (see John 1:29).

---

39. Huxtable, "Forsyth," 77.

Bibliography

Barna Group. "Signs of Decline and Hope Among Key Metrics of Faith." March 4, 2020. https://www.barna.com/research/changing-state-of-the-church/.

Barr, Browne. "P. T. Forsyth: The Preacher's Theologian: A Witness and Confession." In *P. T. Forsyth: The Man, The Preachers' Theologian, Prophet for the 20th Century: A Contemporary Assessment*, edited by Donald G. Miller et al., 31–42. Pittsburg Theological Monograph Series 36. Eugene, OR: Pickwick, 1981.

Barth, Karl. *The Christian Life: Church Dogmatics 4/4, Lecture Fragments*. Translated by Geoffrey W. Bromiley. Grand Rapids: Eerdmans, 1981.

Crotts, John. "The Selfish Reason to Stay at the Same Church for a Long Time." Southern Equip, January 16, 2018. https://equip.sbts.edu/article/selfish-reason-stay-church-long-time/.

Forsyth, P. T. *The Cruciality of the Cross*. London: Forgotten, 2012.

———. *The Justification of God: Lectures on War Time for Christian Theodicy*. Eugene, OR: Wipf & Stock, 1999.

———. *Positive Preaching and the Modern Mind*. London: Hodder & Stoughton, 1907.

———. *The Preaching of Jesus and the Gospel of Christ*. Blackwood, Australia: New Creation, 1987.

———. *The Soul of Prayer*. London: Independent, 1951.

———. *The Work of Christ*. New York: Beloved, 2017.

Gay, Craig M. *The Way of the (Modern) World: Or, Why It's Tempting to Live as If God Doesn't Exist*. Grand Rapids: Eerdmans, 1998.

Goroncy, Jason A., ed. *Descending on Humanity and Intervening in History: Notes from the Pulpit Ministry of P. T. Forsyth*. Eugene, OR: Pickwick, 2013.

Holland, Tom. *Dominion: How the Christian Revolution Remade the World*. New York: Basic, 2019.

Huxtable, W. J. F. "P. T. Forsyth. 1848–1921." *Journal of the United Reformed Church History Society* 4 (1987) 72–78.

Smith, Christian, and Melinda Lundquist Denton. *Soul Searching: The Religious and Spiritual Lives of American Teenagers*. New York: Oxford University Press, 2005.

Solzhenitsyn, Aleksandr I. *The Gulag Archipelago: 1918–1956: An Experiment in Literary Investigation*. Translated by Thomas Whitney. New York: Harper & Row, 1974.

Taylor, Charles. *A Secular Age*. Cambridge: Belknap, 2007.

12

Incarnate, Embodied Power

Bodied Spiritual Practice as a Homiletical Resource

JACLYN P. WILLIAMS

INTRODUCTION

AS PREACHERS, WE ENGAGE deeply with the process and proclamation of God's word. Do we engage holistically with our entire beings? How are preachers empowered along the way? This is an empowerment in the pulpit and throughout the sermon preparation and crafting process. This empowerment is not dependent on the strength of the preacher. This empowerment is inherent to the work of the triune God in creation. This empowerment is the Holy Spirit.

A chasm can form amid our study, exegetical work, contextual and cultural exploration, and placement of the message within local theology. This hollow space is not born of disregard, although that is sometimes a factor. No, there is something more elusive that can take place. A distance can be created by leaning into the mind space and disregarding the space of the body. The connecting point is our spiritual space. The Holy Spirit is the activator of this connecting point. Are we fully allowing the Holy Spirit to invade our sermon process and proclamation? Are we practicing incarnational, embodied preaching through the sermon call, craft, and conveyance?

Incarnational Inheritance and the Holy Spirit

What does the term "incarnational preaching" bring to mind? Perhaps an understanding or definition based on independent study, denominational, or doctrinal influence. Have you ever articulated, in word or deed, what incarnational preaching means for you as a person of faith or a practitioner of faith practices and roles? Your theology of incarnational preaching may be rooted in your experiential and faith knowledge, even if it is not articulated in an explicit theological framework. Even if you have not, perhaps an image comes to mind anyway. What is that image? What does it look like, sound like, feel like? How does this incarnational preaching move and form those in its presence? Do we—preacher and receiver—sense it, even if we cannot define it?

When we break the term down into its parts—"incarnational" and "preaching"—we see a picture forming. We know of the incarnation. God's divine self, wrapped in human flesh, descending into creation to bring and be salvation.[1] Divine relational engagement with humanity. Incarnation is flesh, revelation, word, offering, and Trinity. It is revelation and mystery all at once. This level of integration and paradox necessitates not merely an intellectual understanding but a bodied acceptance. It is a visceral manifestation of being a John 3:8 preacher—one who preaches from the mantle of riding the wind of the Spirit even though we do not know where it is coming from or where it is going. "Sermon performance is an incarnational event, and a more exquisitely appropriate medium for the propagation of the Christian gospel would be difficult to imagine. The preacher is not an imposter or poser or pretender in such an event, but a participant—a player in the ongoing incarnating of the gospel message."[2]

Incarnation philosophy and theology is a vast study and conversation, and we only have time to delve into some corners of this discourse. This chapter focuses on the connection between incarnational preaching and the power of the Holy Spirit. Exploring the incarnation—Jesus of Nazareth—further helps us here. Incarnation is a central theological theme in the Christian narrative. Moreover, it is the hinge point for the Christian understanding of

---

1. "Looking through the lens of incarnation causes us to see God's relation to the world very differently. In Christian tradition, we think of divine incarnation in Jesus of Nazareth as the emblematic expression of God being 'with us.' Once we have seen God in him, we are moved to explore the deeper implications. If this is how God is with us, then surely God's presence must always, already have been profound and pervasive. While we maintain divine transcendence—God is more than the world—through the lens of the Incarnation we now see an immanent transcendence." Case-Winters, *God Will Be All*, 29–30.

2. Childers, "Introduction," 214–15.

divine interaction with creation.³ Jesus Christ was with humanity and all of creation, and preachers must practice preaching holistically—in a manner that cultivates and nurtures "withness." This "withness" includes a reflective and aware presence with self, empowered by the Holy Spirit's clarifying guidance. The holistic nature of a spiritual practice of preaching necessitates engaging, with curiosity, the entirety of the bodied experience of receiving a word from the Lord. Preachers have access to a continual incarnational reality that is not equal to Christ's but is honoring to the witness of Christ. The crux of this honoring is submitting to the Spirit of the Lord resting upon the preacher's person.

Jesus's homiletical method is the beginning for Christian preachers.⁴ What does the flesh of Jesus and how he ministered through embodied word have to say to the flesh of those who minister from the pulpit today? We see that he explicitly acknowledges empowerment by the Holy Spirit. He places his authority in this Spirit-empowered framework.

Preachers are not Jesus Christ, the incarnation. However, we hold this visceral model in our hands, hearts, and spirits. We learn under this visceral tutelage, empowered by the Holy Spirit. This is authority and message embodied. Incarnational preaching can be defined and practiced as the explicit re-presentation—theologically and physically—of Jesus Christ and the reality of incarnational revelation, all in the authority of the Holy Spirit.

EMBODIED PREACHING AND THE HOLY SPIRIT

There is a call from the Holy Spirit and a response from the preacher. There is a cognitive agreement to surrender and a bodied experience of surrender. Preachers needed empowered "enfleshment" to follow the path of the incarnational aspect of preaching. The notion of "deep incarnation" provides a useful theological lens for this pursuit of embodiment. Niels Henrik Gregersen's work supports this exploration. Gregersen argues, "The incarnation is 'deep' in the sense of being deeply embedded in the frail, suffering, and mortal history of the flesh."⁵ This embeddedness of incarnation speaks to the embodied nature

---

3. "Kant begins with the Incarnation as an assumed fact, 'If a human being of such a truly divine disposition had descended, as it were, from heaven to earth at a specific time.' . . . Kant, then, goes on to assume a number of the tenets of theological orthodoxy that Christ 'exhibited in his self, through teaching, conduct and suffering, the example of a human being well-pleasing to God' and also that he instigated 'a revolution in the human race' towards the good." Whistler, "Kant's *imitatio Christi*," 29.

4. Luke 4:21 shows that Jesus is the fulfillment of the Scripture and the model of proclaiming that fulfillment.

5. Gregersen, *Incarnation*, 184.

of incarnational preaching. Embodied preaching resists superficial artifice by going deep into a process and practice of incarnational preaching. This can be realized by offering and allowing the entire bodily experience to be a guide and resource in the preparation and proclamation of incarnate word.

What practical use is this "deep incarnation" connecting to embodiment to the preacher? It is a permission-giving and active theology that allows for the proclamation of ambiguous absolutes, which speak to the surety of the word and truths while advocating for concrete and fluid interpretation and impartation. A deep incarnation-influenced preaching practice of embodiment offers harmony and unity in apparent paradox. There are "hidden transcripts" which are revealed through embracing deep incarnational embodiment within individual and communal stories, beliefs, and values of faith that help frame the preacher and the preacher's homiletical method and manifestation.[6] Therefore, in relationship with the Holy Spirit, preachers can craft an enfleshed practice that guides their exploration and discovery of hidden transcripts that reveal the triune God's message for creation.

Historically, in the Christian narrative, the flesh has been viewed in relationship to sin. Whether through an inheritance from Greek philosophy or cultural and moral interpretations, it has been a complex journey to define the goodness of the flesh for its own sake.[7] The body has been done a disservice. It has been separated and compartmentalized, disconnected from fostering communion with God. This has caused a fracture within the spiritual formation of Christian identity. Philosopher Michel Henry offers a way to reconnect the flesh and spirit. He sees both as being needed aspects of experiencing life in Christ. Henry's work with phenomenology (the philosophical study of experience and consciousness) speaks to a viewpoint that can aid preachers in engaging with God through intentional and pre-intentional means. He writes,

> In being made flesh, however—according to John's Word, which fascinated the Fathers, and tore them from the horizon of thought

---

6. "Maluleke articulates a similar insight when he describes an African Jesus as someone approachable, someone who can be 'taunted' into action, and not least, as someone whom 'Africans are taking . . . by the hand, teaching . . . a few African 'moves' and sensitizing . . . to local issues and conditions.' I find particularly compelling the intentionality with which Maluleke, in his own christologizing, builds upon and gives a mature, prophetic expression to the experiential reality which he finds in African people's attitude towards Jesus. Thanks to his theological work, often done by means of engaging with the 'hidden transcripts' of African Christianity, we have seen the traces and the glimpses of this scandal of reciprocity in African theologies of the cross, the African approach to preaching, traditional choruses, and so on." Urbaniak, "Between the Christ," 198.

7. Wasserman, "Paul Among the Philosophers," 393–402. See Wasserman's discussion of the Platonic influence present in Pauline theology and the topic of sin, specifically in Rom 6–8.

PART THREE: THE PRACTICE OF THE PULPIT

> surrounding the antique world—the Word brings salvation to men. Taking a flesh like theirs, . . . life 'reveals itself' in flesh in a way that no act of thought, philosophical or otherwise, can do, since it is only by being alive that we know, with an invincible certainty, what life is. In the immanence of life in flesh, all of life's modalities are revealed—as what they are . . . Life in the flesh is real life in real flesh, the life that allows each of us at every moment to say, and say with certainty, "I am alive."[8]

For preachers, this offers a perspective that advocates for time spent in reflection to identify their flesh with the flesh of Christ in terms of homiletical formation. The flesh is not deified but is also not denigrated. We do not have to live in a world of extremes. We can live in the world of faith, mystery, and trust empowered by the Holy Spirit.

If these enfleshed, embodied beings are being called to proclaim the jubilee season of the Eternal One's grace, we must holistically process and practice acknowledging the place of the body within this revelation reception reality.

> For You shaped me, inside and out. You knitted me together in my mother's womb long before I took my first breath. I will offer You my grateful heart, for I am Your unique creation, filled with wonder and awe. You have approached even the smallest details with excellence; Your works are wonderful; I carry this knowledge deep within my soul. (Ps 139:13–14, VOICE)

The reality of God-revealing, Christ-professing, Spirit-empowered proclamation calls for the knitted body to be present to the knitted bodies of others as a vessel but also for its own sake. The preacher offers a surrender of self—mind, body, and spirit—to the listeners. And it begins, in a practice, a spiritual practice of incarnational preaching.

Where does this lead us? How do we acknowledge the goodness of God's creative wonder within a spiritual practice of incarnational, embodied preaching? What might this "enfleshment," this embodied practice look like? What is a practice that explores the holistic work of building a ritual that can create space for a practical theology of incarnational preaching? How can we live in our beings as we exegete, study, and consume the word that God is unfolding, the Spirit is empowering, and Jesus is modeling? There is not just one way. The goal is to explore with questioning and curiosity.

---

8. Henry, *Incarnation*, 172, 147.

SPIRITUAL PRACTICE AND HOLY SPIRIT POWER

Practice allows us to holistically say "yes" to the Holy Spirit's movement and empowerment. We seek to explore, understand, and articulate a theology and practice of incarnational, embodied preaching. We seek a pathway that incorporates every moment from inspiration to proclamation and beyond. The body is the vessel of the conception, incubation, labor, and deliverance of the word of God through the power of the Holy Spirit. Rather than ignoring the body or seeking to escape it, why not honor the body as capable of receiving and imparting revelation, knowledge, and the word of God? What if we can sense intuitively God's incarnate word, wrapped in flesh, just as much as we can sense it intellectually?

Participating in this process with the whole of the self by participating with the body, mind, and spirit increases the capacity of the preacher to embody the message. This embodiment makes delivering the sermon a fruitful and mutually beneficial experience, warding off sterility of spirit by fully acknowledging, embracing, and exploring the movement of the Holy Spirit throughout the practice of preaching.[9] This is a distinction rather than a departure. It is the melding of orthodoxy and orthopraxy. Preachers are endeavoring to put their bodies in a spiritual space and the spirit in a body space.[10]

This defining process we are in—what is incarnational preaching—absent a way of implementing the definitions that can guide preachers through their progression, has led to a certain limitation in the process of spiritual formation and the ability to sustain the deep engagement of the preaching life. Theory without practice and meaning-making is hollow. Something has been lost in translation and compartmentalized. The words of Howard Thurman about preaching hint at a way to reconnect what has become disengaged:

> The sermon is the distillation of the thinking, reading, observation, brooding and meditation of the preacher. The assumption is that it is [one's] privilege to withdraw from the traffic of life periodically and regularly in order that [one] may take the kind of long hard look at the world, the society, [one's] fellows, and speak the authentic word which will stimulate the mind, inform even as [one] kindles the emotions, and inspire [one's] fellows to live the good life responsibly.[11]

9. "Through the written word we encounter the revelation of Jesus Christ and his redemptive work, but without an emphasis on the present work of the Spirit in preaching, 'biblical' preaching can become sterile." Samuel, "Spirit in Pentecostal Preaching," 210.

10. "The dichotomy of sight and sound is in any case simplistic, for here is an 'action of body' that makes people listen." Wiles, *Players' Advice*, 70.

11. Thurman, "Worship and Word," 5.

Thurman's words express the need for preachers to have a process of brooding and meditating to wrestle with and receive God's messages, allowing for a formation development that invites experimentation and freedom to enhance what God has placed within the preacher and the community of preachers.

Ritual is practice, and ritual is formation.[12] A practice that engages the body, mind, and spirit is necessary for forming a preacher and an incarnational, embodied preaching method. Through the exercises, we listened first and extrapolated a physical trajectory of Jesus's movements within the text. We listened to his movements and words, the incarnated pathway, allowing a pattern to form. That pattern might hold some importance for the message, and it might hold significance for the formation of the messenger. Expansion of the practice we engaged in may involve taking the text on a walk, inviting a physical consumption of the text, or using this or another text that synthesizes the relationship between incarnational preaching and embodiment that you see as foundational to your theology of preaching as a frame to hold your sermon text. Standing, unrolling, speaking, rolling, and sitting. Empowered by the Spirit.

This participation signals a willingness to receive revelation for the pulpit and the rest of life. Thus, practice is forming skills in oration and spiritual resilience. It is formational for the spirit as well as for the body. This hearkens to Augustine's thought about students of the word opening secrets through practice and sharing those secrets with others.[13]

Conclusion

The moment of preaching is a culmination rather than a commencement. Suppose the preacher can acknowledge, embrace, and practice an incarnational, embodied preaching method. In that case, the possibility is laid for the hearers of the word to do the same, implicitly and explicitly. We place preaching in the authority and power of the Holy Spirit in our practice and our proclamation. Then, the fear and trembling that we encounter, as Paul describes in 1 Cor 2:3–5, can be met not with shame but with surrender to the enabling of the Holy Spirit.

---

12. A discussion about the formative elements of ritual, especially as it is practiced within Christianity, is found within Bell's *Ritual Theory*. Other essential voices within this discourse include Branch's *Rituals of Spontaneity* and Cuneo's *Ritualized Faith*.

13. "There are certain rules for the interpretation of Scripture which I think might with great advantage be taught to earnest students of the word, that they may profit not only from reading the works of others who have laid open the secrets of the sacred writings, but also from themselves opening such secrets to others." Augustine, *On Christian Doctrine*, 11.

When the whole self—as seen through the experience of the preacher with God, the church, Jesus, and the Spirit—is engaged, there is a possibility for a kind of joy that transcends time and space. There is also a joy in the humble reception of the practice in its entirety. Frank Thomas encourages us with his words from *How to Preach a Dangerous Sermon*:

> I once heard someone say that preaching is a terrible joy, and I find that description true of my own experience. Whether I have preached to fifty or to fifty million, it has been nothing but joy to sense a call from the Spirit of God in my soul and train and prepare my mind to be used by God to declare eternal truths within temporal space. It is a humbling joy to have the assignment of communicating a kairos encounter in the midst of this world's kronos.[14]

This joy is embodied by and embedded in the preacher and their process. It is then transferred to the listener-receivers of the incarnate word. It is nurtured, enhanced, and empowered in a lived theological practice of incarnational preaching: standing, unrolling, speaking, rolling, and sitting. May the Spirit continue to guide us with its wind.

Bibliography

Augustine. *On Christian Doctrine*. Translated by D. W. Robertson. Englewood Cliffs, NJ: Prentice Hall, 1958.

Bell, Caterine. *Ritual Theory, Ritual Practice*. Oxford: Oxford University Press, 2009.

Branch, Lori. *Rituals of Spontaneity: Sentiment and Secularism from Free Prayer to Wordsworth*. Waco, TX: Baylor University Press, 2006.

Case-Winters, Anna. *God Will Be All in All: Theology Through the Lens of Incarnation*. Louisville: Westminster John Knox, 2021.

Childers, Jana. "Introduction: The Preacher's Performance." In *The New Interpreters Handbook of Preaching*, edited by Paul Scott Wilson et al., 214–15. Nashville: Abingdon, 2008.

Cuneo, Terrence. *Ritualized Faith: Essays on the Philosophy of Liturgy*. Oxford: Oxford University Press, 2016.

Gregersen, Niels. *Incarnation: On the Scope and Depth of Christology*. Minneapolis: Fortress, 2015.

Henry, Michel. *Incarnation: A Philosophy of Flesh*. Evanston, IL: Northwestern University Press, 2015.

Samuel, Josh. "The Spirit in Pentecostal Preaching: A Constructive Dialogue with Haddon W. Robinson's and Charles T. Crabtree's Theology of Preaching." *Pneuma* 35 (2013) 199–219.

Thayer, Joseph Henry. *Thayer's Greek Lexicon*. Peabody, MA: Hendrickson, 1996.

Thomas, Frank A. *How to Preach a Dangerous Sermon*. Nashville: Abingdon, 2018.

---

14. Thomas, *How to Preach*, 9.

PART THREE: THE PRACTICE OF THE PULPIT

Thurman, Howard "Worship and Word: A View of the Liberal Congregation and Its Sermons." In *The Papers of Howard Washington Thurman, Volume 4: The Soundless Passion of a Single Mind, June 1949–December 1962*, edited by Walter Earl Fluker. Columbia: University of South Carolina Press, 2017.

Urbaniak, Jakub. "Between the Christ of Deep Incarnation and the African Jesus of Tinyiko Maluleke: An Improvised Dialogue." *Modern Theology* 34 (2018) 177–205.

Wasserman, Emma. "Paul Among the Philosophers: The Case of Sin in Romans 6–8." *Journal for the Study of the New Testament* 30 (2008) 387–415.

Whistler, Daniel. "Kant's *imitatio Christi*." *International Journal for Philosophy of Religion* 67 (2010) 17–36.

Wiles, David. *The Players' Advice to Hamlet: The Rhetorical Acting Method from the Renaissance to the Enlightenment*. Cambridge: Cambridge University Press, 2020.

13

Ambrose of Milan and Asia/Trans-Pacific Homiletics and Ecumenics

Reassessment of Mystagogical Preaching with Kapwa *Theology and Their Implications for the Oikoumenē*

NEAL D. PRESA

Introduction

IN 2004, WHEN THE twenty-fourth General Council of the World Alliance of Reformed Churches (WARC)[1] met in Accra, Ghana, for its septennial gathering, delegates vigorously debated and consequently approved the Accra Confession.[2] The adoption of the Accra Confession was historic in that it was the first Christian statement of faith or confessional declaration that framed the gospel as the antidote to global economic systems, principles, and infrastructures that birthed and perpetuated economic injustice and ecological degradation. While the gospel itself, the Lord himself, and Christian worship-

---

1. The predecessor organization to the World Communion of Reformed Churches (WCRC). The WCRC was birthed in 2010 in Grand Rapids, Michigan, with the union of the World Alliance of Reformed Churches and the Reformed Ecumenical Council. The WCRC, whose staff secretariat was based in Geneva and now in Hanover, Germany, is a global fellowship of two hundred and thirty churches/denominations in one hundred and ten countries representing one hundred million Christians in the Reformed, Presbyterian, Uniting, United, Congregational, and Waldensian theological traditions.

2. World Communion of Reformed Churches, "Accra Confession."

ing communities have always sought to challenge the powers, principalities, and values of Pharaohs, Nebuchadnezzars, and Caesars, the Accra Confession indicted economic and political systems of "empire" that commodified people and the earth for financial profit and dominance. While such confessions as the Theological Declaration of Barmen (1934) and the Confession of Belhar with Accompanying Letter (1982) spoke directly to and from the context of Germany under Naziism and South Africa under apartheid, respectively, the Accra Confession was an effort by Global South delegates to interrogate and critique the values and principles of the imperial Global North. The Accra Confession was regarded in the Council's plenary debates as pitting the Global North versus the Global South, wealthy nations/churches versus impoverished nations/churches. The common adage of this existential dilemma was invoked: When the Global North sneezes, the Global South catches a cold. Paragraphs 9 and 10 of the Accra Confession summarized the indictment:

> 9. This crisis is directly related to the development of neoliberal economic globalization, which is based on the following beliefs:
>
> - unrestrained competition, consumerism, and the unlimited economic growth and accumulation of wealth are the best for the whole world;
> - the ownership of private property has no social obligation;
> - capital speculation, liberalization, and deregulation of the market, privatization of public utilities and national resources, unrestricted access for foreign investments and imports, lower taxes and the unrestricted movement of capital will achieve wealth for all;
> - social obligations, protection of the poor and the weak, trade unions, and relationships between people, are subordinate to the processes of economic growth and capital accumulation.
>
> 10. This is an ideology that claims to be without alternative, demanding an endless flow of sacrifices from the poor and creation. It makes the false promise that it can save the world through the creation of wealth and prosperity, claiming sovereignty over life and demanding total allegiance which amounts to idolatry.[3]

In response to this indictment, following the framework of the Belhar Confession, the Accra Confession alternates its response with statements of "We believe"—grounded on trinitarian faith—with expressions of what the

---

3. World Communion of Reformed Churches, "Accra Confession."

fellowship of churches rejected based on that articulated faith. Paragraphs 22 and 23 represented the "We believe" and the corresponding rejection:

> 22. We believe that any economy of the household of life given to us by God's covenant to sustain life is accountable to God. We believe the economy exists to serve the dignity and wellbeing of people in community, within the bounds of the sustainability of creation. We believe that human beings are called to choose God over Mammon and that confessing our faith is an act of obedience.
>
> 23. Therefore we reject the unregulated accumulation of wealth and limitless growth that has already cost the lives of millions and destroyed much of God's creation.[4]

The debate and adoption of the Accra Confession were made more palpable in the fact that delegates visited the notorious Elmina castle and Cape Coast dungeons where millions of enslaved Africans were kidnapped and shipped across the Atlantic. The sickening irony of the setting was that the slave dungeons at the ocean beach level lay beneath the Elmina castle above with its Catholic church built by Portuguese colonizers and successively used by Dutch and British colonizers. Thus, while imperial colonizers were praying and singing to God and enjoying the benefits of their power, literally beneath their feet were millions of people who were commodified, exploited, and whose very humanity was denigrated.

Even though the Accra Confession was adopted, there was much resistance among churches from the Global North as to whether the Confession could be considered a confession of faith in the formal sense. Historically, Christians have been accustomed to confessions of faith like the Apostles' and Nicene Creeds, the Westminster Confession of Faith, and the Heidelberg Catechism, which articulate points of theology such as Christology, pneumatology, ecclesiology, trinitarian theology, hamartiology (sin), and soteriology (salvation). Historic confessions of faith have usually sought to articulate and clarify doctrinal points and settle points of theological dispute. Preaching that is allied with these confessions, likewise, speaks to the cognitive part of our human nature, forming and shaping our thinking through a systematic framing of who we are as Christians and what we believe, with the expectation that "right thinking leads to right living."

While sharing some commonalities with these historic statements, confessions like the Accra Confession or the Belhar Confession are more akin to apocalyptic texts like the book of Revelation or the prophetic works of Jeremiah and Daniel. When the Apocalypse of St. John speaks of the fiery red

---

4. World Communion of Reformed Churches, "Accra Confession."

dragon in Rev 12, New Testament scholar Brian Blount asserts, "John's mythical presentation has a decidedly historical point. The beast is Rome. . . . In making this historical case, John also makes the most of his mythological connection with Daniel. Daniel, too, used the dramatic presentation of mythical beasts from the sea to interpret the struggles of his people against the forces of historical empire."[5] This is what Old Testament scholar Walter Brueggemann calls the "prophetic imagination," a radical discerning of the signs of the times to move God's people to bear witness to God's mighty acts to deliver.[6]

Such prophetic imagination requires a poetic sensibility to go beyond the prose, to peer beneath the veneer of what we see to reality. From the perspective of contemporary pastoral theology, pastoral leadership, and preaching, this is what Craig Barnes calls the "pastor as minor poet"[7] having "gravitas." With respect to discerning this from a pastor to a congregant, Barnes observes,

> No one really cares that much about the worship bulletin, flowers, flag. . . . But they care more than they can express about the daughter who is getting married and moving away, the pending retirement . . . This means that it's the pastor's job to peer beneath the familiar debates about these things that really don't matter to find the spiritual sub-text that is always at work beneath the surface.[8]

He continues, "Our job is to keep an eye out for the strange things the risen and ascended Christ is doing in the congregation, and in the world around it, and then lead the church toward it."[9] Therefore, preachers alike must do what the prophets of old did, which is to mine the riches of the faith led by the Spirit of wisdom and the wisdom of the Spirit and to exercise and embody gravitas. Barnes wrote,

> It is precisely because the clergy have been set apart by the church that they are free to enter into the Holy of Holies in search of visions from God. And this most important quest is what protects them from being reactionary, programmatic, petty or sentimental in their ministry. . . . But their [biblical characters'] delight was in staying in place as part of the biblical drama to which they had surrendered their lives. And that is gravitas.[10]

---

5. Blount, *Revelation*, 246.
6. Brueggemann, *Prophetic Imagination*, 39.
7. Barnes, *Pastor as Minor Poet*, 36.
8. Barnes, "Response," 123.
9. Barnes, "Response," 124.
10. Barnes, "Searching for Gravitas," 276, 278.

Preachers are ordained to the ministry of word and sacrament. In preaching, they are given the holy vocation and sacred task to connect the promises of God in Christ through the fellowship of the Spirit as they seek to connect the Scriptures to people and to the world. To do so, they rely upon the Spirit to discern the subtext of people's lives and the subtext of the reign and presence of God in their lives and in the world, even when the visible evidence seems contrary to that promise. Preaching as an event cannot be seen in isolation; it occurs in the context of worship. And preaching in the context of worship is one of the principal means and venues by which God shapes, forms, informs, and deploys faith to bear witness in the world. My own ecclesial community, the Presbyterian Church (USA), understands Christian worship in this way:

> Christian worship gives all glory and honor, praise and thanksgiving to the holy, triune God. We are gathered in worship to glorify the God who is present and active among us—particularly through the gifts of Word and Sacrament. We are sent out in service to glorify the same God who is present and active in the world.[11]

Preaching in the context of worship is an engagement in the fullness of the gifts of God—word and sacrament—for the people of God. The gift of word and sacrament engages the fullness of the human sensory experiences—oral, auditory, smell, taste, touch. The ministry of word and sacrament, which is a mediated manifestation of power and presence of the divine-human *sui generis*—the enfleshed/embodied Word—dignifies the whole person. This is analogous to Irenaeus's understanding of the relationship of the Son and Spirit in the gospel and how "they work in collaboration—like the two hands of the Father."[12] Preachers and congregants alike, as the people of God redeemed in Christ, are needing to re-engage the faith through its prose and poetic dimensions—the seen and unseen, the text and the sub-text.

What the Accra Confession calls Christians to do is to discern the signs of the times and to do what John did for the worshiping communities in which he served and belonged. Just as the communities in which the Old Testament prophets were given vivid images and apocalyptic language to stir the imagination and the eyes of faith to discern their faith in the context of existential challenges, how do we equip and support the whole people of God to embody and live the faith with the existential challenges we face in our common humanity?

The diaspora of Filipino American communities provides a faith lens that widens the aperture by which preaching in the context of worship can

---

11. *Constitution of Presbyterian Church*, 77.

12. Irenaeus, *Against Heresies* 5.6, cited in Fagerberg, *Liturgical Mysticism*, 54.

help shape and deploy faith in changing landscapes. In a now-concluded, three-year Collaborative Inquiry Team (CIT) research initiative funded by the Louisville Institute, my fellow CIT colleagues of Filipino American religious scholars sought to understand and begin to articulate the latent Filipino American theologies in a time of the COVID-19 pandemic, the endemic of racial injustice, and political polarization. As children of Filipino immigrants, we understood and appreciated the trans-Pacific struggle of grappling with making America home while never being home.[13] Our multilayered identities of being Filipino American and not Filipino meant navigating the existential challenges of being on this side of the Pacific and having to navigate white spaces, all while caring for the flourishing and well-being of our families, friends, and ancestors from and in the Philippines.

Kapwa Theology for the World

What we have tentatively called *kapwa* theology describes a framework of understanding faith as a lived faith that stems from the Philippine reality of *barangay*, or village. One's well-being is related to the well-being of the family, which is related to the village, which is related to the city, which is related to the nation, which is related to the earth. The depth of *kapwa* can be summarized this way:

> *Kapwa* is a Tagalog word used by Filipino psychologist Virgilio Enriquez to help to describe the Filipino mind and heart. *Kapwa* is shared space or shared identity, and with that there is a mutuality and interdependence. My flourishing, to interpolate Jeremiah 29:16, is connected to the flourishing of my family, which is connected to the flourishing of the community, which is connected to the flourishing and well-being of the land, which is connected to the well-being of the nation. And *kapwa* would extend it further to include the *oikoumenē*. In other words, *kapwa* as an articulation and expression of Filipino American experiences of and engagement with faith—faith-in-action and action-in-faith—means that our self-understanding of who we are, whose we are, and why we are cannot be fully understood and appreciated unless and until consideration is given to the interconnectivity we have with neighbors and strangers, and ultimately with God, and therefore the responsibility we have been given to steward the gifts of God for the people of God.[14]

---

13. See Presa, *Ascension Theology and Habakkuk*.
14. Presa, "Sacramentality of Justice," 73.

Our CIT project observed that anyone wanting to understand Filipino Americans, and more broadly, Asian Americans, must account for the religious lives of our communities. In our case, as Filipino Americans, and in my specific case as a Filipino Pacific Islander American, one must pay attention to the influences of Catholic Christianity upon our lives in the diaspora whether one is Roman Catholic, Protestant, or not. Because of the pervasive influence of Catholic Christianity in the Philippines,[15] we must see how Filipino Christians engage the faith and live out the faith. To put it more precisely, because Protestant worshiping communities have often privileged word over sacrament, the cognitive over the mystery, how might the ethos and pathos of what is considered "liturgy" begin to shape and form our preaching in the context of worship? How do we incorporate the whole human being in how we regard preaching in the context of worship? I want to propose what this looks like through the following five elements:

- Re-engage the sacraments (baptism and the Eucharist) as a full partner in the preached word.
- Broaden faith formation that apprentices and orients the whole person towards discerning the sacramentality of all of creation.
- To discern the sacramentality of the world around us enables the people of God to live in the world with faith, hope, and love, and to engage the powers and principalities for God's transformative justice in the world.
- A reassessment and reorientation of mystagogical preaching involves positioning faith initiation and faith formation both within the church and outside the church in the world.
- To be Christian is to be in the world but not of the world, and therefore to be the church is to be fully in the world but not adopting the values of the world. This orientation is modeled after the way of Christ.

Ambrose of Milan and Mystagogical Preaching

In the early church, particularly in the fourth century CE, Ambrose of Milan (c. 374–397 CE) was one of four major mystagogues.[16] Mystagogues engaged in mystagogical preaching, which is preaching that historically prepared catechumens (those who were preparing to be baptized and become initiated

---

15. Only second to Vatican City, the Philippines has the most Roman Catholic adherents *per capita*.

16. The others were Cyril of Jerusalem, John Chrysostom, and Theodore of Mopsuestia.

into the faith) to understand and participate in the sacramental "mysteries." Lutheran liturgy scholar Craig Satterlee summarizes mystagogical preaching as follows:

> Mystagogical preaching is sustained reflection on the Church's rites of initiation. It is *mystagogia*, preaching on the "mysteries" of the Christian faith. It is *preaching* in that it is scripturally based, takes place within a liturgical setting, is addressed exclusively to the Christian community—the baptized and the newly baptized, called "neophytes," and has as its goal the formation of Christians rather than providing religious information to Christians. Mystagogical preaching is distinct from other types of preaching, in that it draws the hearers into the mysteries, moving them to enter spiritually and intellectually into the rites in which they have previously participated but may have understood only in terms of sense perception. Thus the ultimate goal of this sustained reflection is to have a persuasive, enlightening, deepening effect on the hearers' understanding of the Church's rites of initiation that leads them to live in the different, new dimension that is the Christian life.[17]

Catechumens in the Milanese community of Ambrose experienced the fullness of the mysteries that were embedded in the deep dimension of partaking in Christ's own life through the power of the Holy Spirit.[18] The catechumenate involved the following five stages and the elements involved:

- Stage one: enrollment. Those who desired to undertake baptismal preparation would indicate their intention to the bishop. They submitted their names as early as Epiphany (around January 6). They were called *competentes* (as in competition).

- Stage two: Lenten formation. This involved daily moral instruction, fasting, scrutiny (bodily examination of marks of sin or residue of Satan's inhabitation), and learning the Apostles' Creed. This instruction was done in secrecy called the *disciplina arcani*. The *competentes* became anxious and anticipated what would come next.[19]

- Stage three: rites of initiation. This took place at the great Easter Vigil. This included the "*ephphatha* (breathing upon nostrils to open the mind and heart), pre-baptismal anointing, renunciation, exorcism and

17. Satterlee, *Ambrose of Milan's Method*, 2; emphasis original.

18. Satterlee, *Ambrose of Milan's Method*, 148–85. Satterlee examined Ambrose's *De mysteriis* and *De sacramentis*. The former was Ambrose's commentary on the mysteries, or the sacraments of initiation; the latter was his sermons on the mysteries.

19. Satterlee, *Ambrose of Milan's Method*, 149.

consecration of the water, baptism, postbaptismal anointing, footwashing, vesting with white robes, 'spiritual seal,' and procession to the altar."[20]

- Stage Four: Celebration of the Easter Eucharist.
- Stage Five: "Mystagogy or daily instruction on the meaning of the sacraments during the week following Easter."[21]

Each stage was rich with symbolism, designating purification and sanctification in Christ, renouncing the old life and taking up the new in Christ. Notice that the explanation of the mysteries follows the experiencing of the mysteries.

Mystagogy sought the neophytes' (new converts) experience of the mysteries of the faith. Through their reflections upon the experience, the mystagogical preacher (mystagogue) enriched those reflections with reminders of what that means from the Scripture's perspectives. The point of mystagogical preaching was not to arrive at any one particular explanation of baptism and the Eucharist and all the accompanying rites before and after, but rather to pile on meanings. Ambrose explained that baptism was "tomb and womb, death and resurrection, absolution, and new birth. . . . It heals, cleanses, washes away sins, sanctifies, cancels guilt, and makes members of the Church."[22] In so doing, Ambrose drew upon the Scripture's connecting baptism to "creation, the flood, Israel's passing through the Red Sea, the spring of Marah, the cleansing of Naaman the leper, Elisha's floating axe-head, the second tabernacle in the Temple, Jesus's baptism in the Jordan, and his healing of both the paralytic at the pool of Beth-zatha and the man born blind, as well as death and burial, resurrection and birth."[23] Similarly, Ambrose grounds the Eucharist in the prefigured events in Scripture such as "Melchizedek's offering of bread and wine to Abraham, God's raining down manna in the wilderness, and Moses' striking the rock and bring forth water."[24]

Mystagogical preaching engages text, context, and subtext in nuanced ways. For mystagogical preaching, the "text" includes all the mysteries (the rites surrounding initiation of baptism and Eucharist). Mystagogues exegete the mysteries of the faith, which are grounded in Scripture. The context is the lives of the neophytes as they belong, now, to the body of Christ. The subtext is the depth of the neophytes' life in God. Mystagogy shaped the neophytes' faith so that they began to see themselves and the world around them in new

---

20. Satterlee, *Ambrose of Milan's Method*, 156.
21. Satterlee, *Ambrose of Milan's Method*, 148.
22. Satterlee, *Ambrose of Milan's Method*, 255.
23. Satterlee, *Ambrose of Milan's Method*, 256.
24. Satterlee, *Ambrose of Milan's Method*, 199.

ways—through the eyes of faith.[25] Mystagogical preaching intentionally describes and connects the meaning and significance of baptism and the Eucharist/Lord's Table for the whole church and how the triune God employs those sacraments for the church's life in and beyond the gathered community. Mystagogical preaching enriches the faith of new and "veteran" believers by discerning the sacramentality of all of life and faith for the church, and, indeed the whole world.

Liturgical theologian David Fagerberg describes the powerful purposes of the liturgy:

> The twin purposes of liturgy are the sanctification of [humanity] and the glorification of God, and these are exactly the purposes that constitute the mission of Christ.... Liturgy is the perichoresis of the Trinity reaching out to us through the kenosis of the Son in order to invite our synergistic ascent to deification.[26]

To put it simply, the point of liturgy is to enfold us in the life of God so that every aspect of our life reflects Christ and applies Christ's own life upon our own. Mystagogical preaching opens up God's people to both the prose and poetry of the faith—the facts/contents of the faith, and the drama of how that faith is lived out or emerges in the world, often in a subversive manner. Mystagogical preaching enables us to connect physical bread on the table to Christ's claim of being the "Bread of Life." It helps us see the eucharistic table as a foretaste of the heavenly banquet table.

In its broadest sense, *liturgy* means public service for the benefit of the common good. Liturgy, then, is not only that which occurs within the four corners of a church building or the gathering space of a worshiping community. It is not merely the sacerdotal rubrics of what pastors and priests are to do in their words and gestures. It cannot be confined to church activities and events. Liturgy is the entirety of life because all of life, Sunday through Saturday, is lived *coram Deo* (in the face of God), in whose presence we ever live, move, and have our being (Acts 17:28).

---

25. For those of you who belong to ecclesial traditions where the words "liturgy" or "liturgical" connote or denote incense, priestly robes, and formal paraments adorning the chancel area of the worship space, it bears underscoring that all church traditions—whether so-called "high church" (read: super formal) or "low church" (read: informal) and everyone in-between—have liturgy. Your worship bulletins or order of worship, regardless if they are printed on a piece of folded paper or projected on a screen or available online as a PDF, are engaged in liturgy.

26. Fagerberg, *Liturgical Mysticism*, 39.

Enacted Liturgy as Communal Healing

Preaching scholars Matthew Kim and Daniel Wong propose that Asian North American (ANA) preaching should intentionally embody several key elements. They observe that ANA preaching should be "contextual, intercultural, incarnational, Holy Spirit-led, transformational, narratival, and collaborative."[27] An ANA homiletic as Kim and Wong propose offers a preaching framework to address the Filipino, Filipino North American, Filipino/American "experience," described by Lester Ruiz as "polymorphic diasporic multiculturalism." Kim, Wong, and Ruiz basically describe a hermeneutical and homiletical move that engages the world sacramentally. To put it colloquially, there is "more than meets the eye" than what is in front of you in the immediate. Ruiz described that experience as a "way of life marked by diverse and plural worldwide dispersals, displacements, and dislocations of individuals, peoples, and institutions from their traditional moorings or origins."[28] This is the tension of *kasamahan* (organizing and strengthening what it means to be Filipino American among fellow Filipinos) and *bayanihan* (bridging the diaspora with the US majority culture and with the indigenous Philippine homeland).[29] More recently, Daniel Lee of Fuller Seminary's Center for Asian American Theology and Ministry cogently put forward the Asian America Quadrilateral (AAQ) as the sources and methods by which to organize and understand Asian American experiences. Lee's AAQ contextual themes are "Asian heritage, migration experience, American culture, and racialization."[30]

Because Asian American faith is experienced both as the church gathered and the church scattered, the wider and broader perspective of what is regarded as "liturgy" must be recapitulated when we experience preaching. In other words, the aim of preaching in the context of worship must be aimed at the mission of God in the world, which includes the church but does not stop with the church. That Asian Americans live out and experience faith and negotiate faith identities in multiple arenas and contexts both synchronically (at any given time) and diachronically (across time, in union with ancestors—both the living and the dead), preaching in the context of worship must engage and support God's people in their lived experiences to be able to discern the signs of the times and instill the eyes of faith that see the movement of God when external evidence seems contrary. Spatially and figuratively, it is seeing and discerning the sacramentality of the world, as with this eucharistic table at

---

27. Kim and Wong, *Finding Our Voice*, 118.
28. Ruiz, "Filipinos in America," 40–41.
29. Presa, *Ascension Theology and Habakkuk*, 10.
30. Lee, *Doing Asian American Theology*, 67.

PART THREE: THE PRACTICE OF THE PULPIT

the First Presbyterian Church in Wheaton, Illinois, positioned literally outside the church sanctuary:

(Photo courtesy: The Rev. Dr. Kellen A. Smith)

Mystagogical preaching trains our hearts and lives to be attuned to manifestations of God's work in the world and the powerful possibilities of reparation, renewal, reconciliation, and revelation in our midst. This heart attunement and synchronization to God's work in the world is exhibited in the following example.

In his groundbreaking volume *Asian Americans and the Spirit of Racial Capitalism*, Jonathan Tran points us in a direction of where positive engagement of faith in the world discerns the powerful possibilities of the kingdom of God in our midst. Tran wisely and incisively sees that undoing systems of power and privilege must necessarily critique and interrogate political economy which constructed race to support market capitalism and then perpetuated it through a vicious cycle. The construction of race provided social control for "sustained domination and exploitation." Tran summarized it this way:

> The idea of America emerged as racial schemes concretized around local legislative and judicial action that triangulated landed elites relative to temporarily versus permanently bonded labor, landless white versus enslaved black, indigenous peoples versus settler Hispanics, emancipated African Americans versus migrant Asians, immigrant Europeans versus non-white migrants, and so on. The category of race can be counted on to justify each revolution of the arrangement: landed whites own property because they are white; non-whites are property because they are non-white; landless whites position themselves over those disqualified by

race; whites rage whenever entitlements considered theirs by right come to those without standing.... All that matters is race and its circular claims to land, nation, and destiny.[31]

Tran conducts two field studies (limited by the COVID-19 pandemic for in-person engagement) with a Chinese migrant settlement in the Mississippi Delta and with the Redeemer Community Church in the Bayview/Hunters Point (BVHP) neighborhood of San Francisco. For this paper, I will focus on the latter as one who lived in the BVHP of San Francisco for many years.

Tran lifted up what he called Redeemer Community Church's "deep economy." BVHP is on the southeast section of San Francisco where decades ago ghetto neighborhoods were established with low-income housing for mostly African American families, along with rising demographics of Hispanic and Asian American communities. The BVHP was off the beaten path, ridden with crime, graffiti, and frequent police patrols. It lay in a section of the city near a former US Naval shipyard where leftover materials from ships and radioactive soil from the American military industrial complex's development of nuclear weapons were carted off and buried. BVHP was the site of environmental, economic, and racial injustice. What Tran narrates by way of racial capitalism and political economy is accurate when it comes to BVHP.

Redeemer Community Church saw investing in its neighborhood as its calling rather than fleeing from it—as many organizations and businesses did. Understanding its place in the community, Redeemer Community Church developed what they call "neighborhood ecology" and what agroecologists call "cosmicvision," an "orientation toward justice that properly appreciates 'the necessary equilibrium between nature, the cosmos and human beings.'"[32] Redeemer's pastor, Danny Fong, teamed up with Chi-Ming Chien and another church member, Elisa Leberis, together using their computer engineering backgrounds to establish Dayspring Partners, a privately held computer software company that focuses on website design, brand design, software development, and nonprofit consulting. Dayspring Partners then partnered with Redeemer Community Church to establish a Neighbor Fund which offers three thousand to ten thousand dollar low-interest microloans to local businesses based on relationships cultivated in the community.[33] Chi-Ming summarized the vision of Dayspring, which is reminiscent of the Accra Confession:

> The dominant economy that we have shaped—and that shapes us—is Mammon's economy. Mammon's economy has at least

---

31. Tran, *Asian Americans*, 79.
32. Tran, *Asian Americans*, 201.
33. Tran, *Asian Americans*, 217.

three characteristics: it presumes scarcity rather than abundance. It operates out of the law of exchange. That is, every space is transaction; there is no such thing as free gift, only exchange for value. The combination of these two and initial random distributions of power then results in increasing injustice as we see throughout history. But rather than believing that the economy is ultimately governed by the invisible hand of capitalism—that the economy belongs to Mammon—Christians believe in a divine economy of grace—where all is gift and all is grace. Rather than operating as though Mammon reigns, we live out of the reign of God who gives God's self. If that is the case, then our call as Christians is to bear witness to that reality. The powers are powerful—that's why we call them "powers"—and Mammon is no exception. So, we don't actually expect to transform the entire culture. But we do look for opportunities to bear faithful witness, though, and practice a faithful resistance.[34]

Tran depicted the deep economy of the divine economy (*oikoumenē*) versus the market economy with this visual representation:[35]

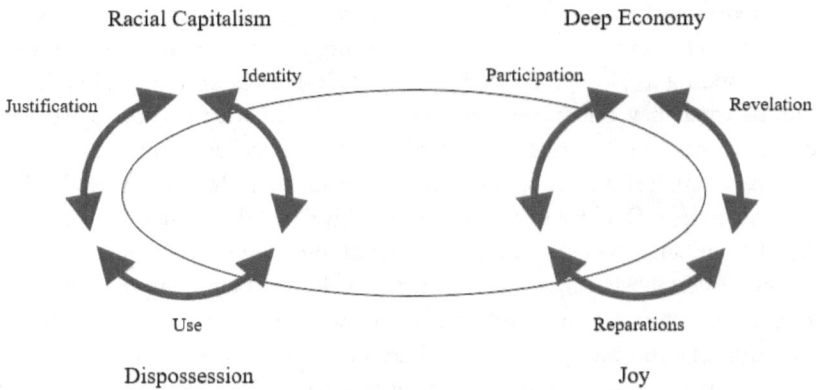

Tran described these twin polarities of racial capitalism's vicious circle of exploitation and domination leading to dispossession, and the deep economy's participation-revelation-reparation. Around these polarities "revolves the life of worship."[36] He goes on to say that "between this world and them (those who

34. Quoted in Tran, *Asian Americans*, 214.
35. Tran, *Asian Americans*, 238.
36. Tran, *Asian Americans*, 238.

fail to take advantage of opportunities), experienced together as an ellipse of dispossession and joy, arrives the world as it is in God, that is, as it really is, as Christ himself shows."[37]

Conclusion

While mystagogical preaching is not what animated Redeemer Community Church, the outcome of what Redeemer Community Church does and what mystagogical preaching aims to do are the same. Mystagogical preaching connects what occurs in the context of the gathered worshiping community to God's work in the world and the call of the church to participate in that divine work. Sacraments become, then, not just rites of initiation for those who will belong to the church community but are extended further, enabling God's people to engage the world sacramentally, to see the world through sacramental eyes of faith, hope, and love.[38] In this way, the waters of baptism are not just invoking the trinitarian name declaring a person to be a son or daughter claimed in Christ; in mystagogical preaching broadly applied, baptism awakens the community of the baptized to the interrelatedness we share in our common humanity with the oceanic waters that connect us all on planet earth, the same waters which are endangered due to pollution, such as the release of toxic radioactive water from the Fukushima nuclear reactor in Japan. The baptismal waters deploy us to work for access to clean water for hundreds of millions of people who are in want, such as the Payatas community near Quezon City, Philippines, who live near the immense garbage landfill. The baptismal waters which name us and claim us as children of God instill in us that many are orphans, childless, estranged from their parents, or have no sense of home.

Likewise, mystagogical preaching broadly applied initiates the church to regard the eucharistic table as not only being united to the very life of the

---

37. Tran, *Asian Americans*, 239.

38. On an ecumenical level, the Fourth Phase of global bilateral dialogue between the World Communion of Reformed Churches (WCRC) and the Pontifical Council for Promoting Christian Unity (now Dicastery for Promoting Christian Unity) of the Roman Catholic Church from 2011 to 2015 focused on the relationship of justification and sacramentality. While the Roman Catholic Church initially desired for the WCRC to join the Lutheran World Federation in signing onto the Joint Declaration on the Doctrine on Justification (JDDJ), the WCRC insisted that bilateral dialogue must first focus on the church's witness with respect to God's transformative justice and not solely on the nature of grace. This was the focus of the JDDJ in that it addressed the sixteenth-century, Protestant Reformation's dispute with the Council of Trent on this question. See World Communion of Reformed Churches, "Justification and Sacramentality."

ascended Christ but also as a call to seek reconciliation and peace at peacemaking tables and negotiating tables. The eucharistic table would call us to seek and pray for peace in Israel-Palestine, Ukraine-Russia, and in many communities around the world. Mystagogical preaching would deploy us to discern concrete ways to address and alleviate hunger, poverty, and areas of economic, racial, gender, and environmental injustices in our workplaces, schools, neighborhoods, board rooms, the marketplace, legislative halls, and, indeed, in every arena of life.[39]

Bibliography

Barnes, M. Craig. *The Pastor as Minor Poet: Texts and Subtexts in the Ministerial Life*. Grand Rapids: Eerdmans, 2009.

———. "Response by Craig Barnes to Bruce Reyes-Chow on Conflict." In *Insights from the Underside: An Intergenerational Conversation of Ministers*, edited by Neal D. Presa, 122-24. Elizabeth, NJ: Broadmind, 2008.

———. "Searching for Gravitas." In *Schools of Faith: Essays on Theology, Ethics, and Education in Honour of Iain R. Torrance*, edited by David Fergusson and Bruce McCormack, 269-78. New York: T&T Clark, 2019.

Blount, Brian K. *Revelation: A Commentary*. Louisville: Westminster John Knox, 2009.

Brueggemann, Walter. *The Prophetic Imagination*. Minneapolis: Fortress, 2001.

Carvalhaes, Cláudio. *Eucharist and Globalization: Redrawing the Borders of Eucharistic Hospitality*. Eugene, OR: Pickwick, 2013.

———. *Liturgies from Below: Praying with People at the End of the World*. Nashville: Abingdon, 2020.

The Constitution of the Presbyterian Church (USA)—Part II: The Book of Order, 2023-2025. Louisville: Office of the General Assembly, 2023.

Fagerberg, David W. *Liturgical Mysticism*. Steubenville, OH: Emmaus Academic, 2019.

Kim, Matthew D., and Daniel L. Wong. *Finding Our Voice: A Vision for Asian North American Preaching*. Bellingham, WA: Lexham, 2020.

Lee, Daniel D. *Doing Asian American Theology: A Contextual Framework for Faith and Practice*. Downers Grove, IL: IVP Academic, 2022.

Presa, Neal D. *Ascension Theology and Habbakuk: A Reformed Ecclesiology in Filipino American Perspective*. New York: Palgrave MacMillan, 2018.

———. "The Sacramentality of Justice." In *Now to God Who Is Able: Vocation, Justice, and Ministry: Essays in Honor of Mark Labberton*, edited by Neal D. Presa and Anne E. Zaki, 64-74. Eugene, OR: Pickwick, 2023.

Ruiz, Lester Edwin J. "Filipinos in America: A Cartography of Diasporic Identities." In *T&T Clark Handbook of Asian American Biblical Hermeneutics*, edited by Uriah Y. Kim and Seung Ai Yang, 40-53. London: T&T Clark, 2019.

Satterlee, Craig Alan. *Ambrose of Milan's Method of Mystagogical Preaching*. Collegeville, MN: Liturgical, 2002.

---

39. For a recent liturgical scholar who demonstrates this, see Carvalhaes, *Eucharist*, and Carvalhaes, *Liturgies*.

Tran, Jonathan. *Asian Americans and the Spirit of Racial Capitalism*. New York: Oxford University Press, 2022.
World Communion of Reformed Churches. "The Accra Confession." 2004. https://wcrc.ch/accra/the-accra-confession.
World Communion of Reformed Churches and Pontifical Council for Promoting Christian Unity. "Justification and Sacramentality: The Christian Community as an Agent for Justice." Report of the Fourth Phase of Catholic-Reformed International Dialogue, 2011–2015. http://www.christianunity.va/content/unitacristiani/en/dialoghi/sezione-occidentale/alleanza-mondiale-delle-chiese-riformate/dialogo-internazionale-cattolico-riformato/documenti-di-dialogo/testo-in-inglese.html.

14

We Are More Than Our Minds

Conforming Heart, Soul, Body, and Will to Love God and Neighbor Through Specific Statements of Application

ERIC REDMOND

INTRODUCTION

ON FEBRUARY 3, 2020, NBC News Channel 5, Chicago, gave the following news update, entitled, "How to Protect Yourself from Coronavirus":[1]

> The Centers for Disease Control and Prevention warned Americans to start preparing for a possible pandemic outbreak of the coronavirus in the United States, noting that it's not a question of "if" the outbreak will happen but "when." While the CDC outlined what level of preparation should look like in US schools and businesses, the warning left Americans wondering how to protect themselves from coronavirus. Here's what the World Health Organization recommends: regular hand washing, cover mouth and nose when coughing and sneezing, thoroughly cooking meat and eggs, [and] avoid close contact with anyone showing symptoms of respiratory illness such as coughing and sneezing. The Illinois Department of Public Health also included: avoid touching your eyes, nose, or mouth with unwashed hands. "There are currently

---

1. NBC News 5 Chicago, "How to Protect Yourself." NBC News 5 updated this link with this title on February 26, 2020, and February 27, 2020, with different information.

no vaccines to protect against human coronavirus infection," the IDPH wrote online.

A second news story on NBC5 added that wearing masks in public and using hand sanitizer could limit the spread of the virus. The anchor ended the segment by responding to the reporting journalist with these words: "Such good information. Thank you. While we all need to know more about the coronavirus, you can find out more by going to our website. Log onto nbcchicago.com or download the free NBC-Chicago app."

Later in the pandemic, the CDC would post the following recommendations for protecting oneself from coronavirus:

To help prevent the spread of COVID-19:

- Wear a mask to protect yourself and others and stop the spread of COVID-19.
- Stay at least six feet (about two arm lengths) from others who don't live with you.
- Avoid crowds and poorly ventilated spaces. The more people you are in contact with, the more likely you are to be exposed to COVID-19.
- Get a COVID-19 vaccine when it's available to you.
- Clean your hands often, either with soap and water for 20 seconds or a hand sanitizer that contains at least 60 percent alcohol.
- Avoid close contact with people who are sick.
- Cover your cough or sneeze with a tissue, then throw the tissue in the trash.
- Clean frequently touched objects and surfaces daily. If someone is sick or has tested positive for COVID-19, disinfect frequently touched surfaces.
- Monitor your health daily.[2]

Even with scores of news reports like this almost daily for much of the last two years, the US still suffered over eighty million COVID-19 cases and over nine hundred eighty thousand deaths from the coronavirus. Can you imagine the toll if we had not had news reports like the ones from NBC Chicago or directives from the CDC? What would that have meant for the US and people we love? What would that have meant for you and me?

---

2. The CDC has updated the guidelines numerous times since 2020. The original post containing these guidelines has been removed. The CDC's dynamic COVID-19 archive maintains searchable records only as far back as July 30, 2021, at the time of this writing.

PART THREE: THE PRACTICE OF THE PULPIT

What if the news reports had told us all the facts about the coronavirus and ended the story there? What if the news told us about the origin in Wuhan, China, the first known case in the US and the first known deaths in California and Washington state, of it being an airborne illness, and of it being spread by close proximity to those infected for fifteen minutes, but never told us what to do in response, leaving that for us to figure out on our own? Rather than ending with the directives from the World Health Organization and the IDPH, how would we have felt if the reporting journalist instead had said, "This is such good information," and then not said anything about the news website or app? How would we have felt if she had said something like, "May the universe or some divine being apply this news story to our hearts"? Would that have been sufficient to address a pandemic virus?

News journalists do not leave behavioral change to chance. They do not leave us with only right thinking about tornado preparations, cancer screenings, cyber-attacks, strong undertow or drowning warnings, vehicle, baby product, toy, or food recalls, or about improving physical, mental, emotional, financial, or relational health. They tell us exactly what to do to: *Go to a windowless room in the basement; share with the family your plan for locating one another if you are separated; stay out of the water; take your vehicle to your dealer for an adjustment; update your software; throw out food with this UPC code; apply fifty SPF sunscreen to your skin every four hours; get a colonoscopy if you are over fifty.* These directives take the guesswork out of having the appropriate responses to the given news stories so that you and I can be safe from danger and enjoy all this life has to offer.

As people of the greatest news story ever known to humankind, we need to take a lesson from local and national news journalists. Rather than leaving responses to sermons to chance, like news journalists, we tell people exactly what to do to prepare to meet God. That is, to be obedient to God in all things. To do so, I think we should look to Jesus, who gives us help by telling us the goal of both the Old and New Testaments.

The Greatest Two Commandments as the Goal of Obedience

Three times in the Gospels we are told about the two greatest commandments (Matt 22:37–39; Mark 12:30–31; Luke 10:27). We know some things about these commandments: *First, the entirety of the goal of the Old Testament is summed up by these two commandments.* "On these two commandments depend all the Law and the Prophets," says Jesus (Matt 22:40 ESV). Or, to clarify, to be obedient to all that is written in the Hebrew Bible, one should follow the greatest and second greatest commandments.[3]

For Jesus, Moses writes about Jacob's dream of the ladder to get the readers to love God with all their heart, soul, mind, and strength, and to love their neighbor as they love themselves. The editor of the historical books writes Judg 5 about the details of Deborah leading the victory narrated in Judg 4 so that the readers might love the Lord God with all their heart, soul, mind, and strength, and love their neighbors as themselves, not to fuel debates over the role of women in the church.

David's three-year famine (2 Sam 21:1–14), Hezekiah's turning to the wall (2 Kgs 20:1–11; Isa 38:1–22), Job's naming of his second generation of daughters "Dove," "Sweet-Scented Spice," and "Horn of Eye Paint" (Job 42:14–15), Jeremiah's burial of his loincloth (Jer 13:1–11), the resounding chorus of praise in Ps 150, the full contents of Micah, and Malachi's pronouncement of the return of Elijah (Mal 3:1–4; 4:5–6)—to name a few—all are written so that upon reading these passages and books and hearing them preached and taught we will increase in loving God with heart, soul, mind, and strength, and in loving neighbor. The entire Old Testament exists with this goal in mind.

Second, they represent the two tables of the law, and thus intend to shape us as worshipers and as ethical people. The greatest commandment corresponds to the first table, or the first four of the Ten Commandments: (1) "You shall have no other gods before me"; (2) "You shall not make for yourself a carved image, or any likeness of anything that is in heaven above, or that is in the earth beneath, or that is in the water under the earth"; (3) "You shall not take the name of the Lord your God in vain"; (4) "Remember the Sabbath day, to keep it holy." The second greatest commandment corresponds to the second table, or commandments five through ten: (5) "Honor your father and your mother"; (6) "You shall not murder"; (7) "You shall not commit adultery"; (8) "You shall not steal"; (9) "You shall not bear false witness against your neighbor"; (10) "You shall not covet your neighbor's house . . . or anything that is your neighbor's."[4]

---

3. "There is no question here of the priority of love over law—i.e., one system over another—but of the priority of love within the law. These two commandments are the greatest because all Scripture 'hangs' on them; i.e., nothing in Scripture can cohere or be truly obeyed unless these two are observed. The entire biblical revelation demands heart religion marked by total allegiance to God, loving him and loving one's neighbor. Without these two commandments the Bible is sterile." Carson, "Matthew," 465.

4. David Baker argues that the two tablets of the law separate at the fifth commandment rather than the fourth commandment: "The honouring of parents forms the conclusion to the first division rather than the introduction to the second. However, whether two distinct groups of commandments were deliberately written on separate tablets, or whether the material was spread over two tablets on the basis of how much text fitted on one tablet, is

The two greatest commandments are designed to shape us into deeper worshipers of our great Savior—people with no other gods before God, who do not make idols or misuse God's name, and who take Sabbath celebrations seriously. They are designed to make us people with solid moral convictions— with the kind of convictions that keep one from lying about election results, bullying fellow church staff members,[5] attacking a sitting judge,[6] or slapping a fellow comedian for joking about your wife's haircut.[7]

Third, the two commandments are inseparable, providing one way to fully obey God, not an either/or option.[8] The two commandments do not allow one to love God but not neighbor or to love neighbor but not love God. One could not honor one's parents while worshiping another god. One was not pleasing the Lord by refraining from bringing false testimony in court if he was racing to find manna on the seventh day of the week. It made little difference to use the Lord's name in holy ways if one was sneaking out of her marriage. The goal is to be a person who follows both tablets of the Law at all times. We are to love the Lord with heart, soul, mind, and strength, and love our neighbor.

Fourth, the repetition of the commandments in the New Testament is intended for those with faith in Jesus. The Gospels were written after the ascension of Christ and the Day of Pentecost. They were intended to instruct the earliest members of the church in God's requirements. Those believers would have read that the *greatest* thing they could do to please God is love him in this four-fold way. They would have been confronted with the *second greatest* thing to do: namely, please the Lord by loving one's neighbor as oneself. Paul says to the believers in Rome, "For the commandments, 'You shall not commit adultery, You shall not murder, You shall not steal, You shall not covet,' and

---

difficult to ascertain. The scarcity of writing materials in the ancient world, and the fact that the first few commandments are much longer than the later ones, may point towards the latter as being more likely." Baker, "Ten Commandments, Two Tablets," 11.

5. On abuses amounting to bullying by former Mars Hill pastor Mark Driscoll, see Bailey, "Mark Driscoll Charged"; Paulson, "Brash Style"; Shellnutt, "Former Mars Hill Elders"; Shellnutt and Lee, "Mark Driscoll Resigns"; Welch, "Rise and Fall." See also Cosper, "Who Killed Mars Hill?"

6. See Hurtado et al., "Donald Trump"; Wolf, "Trump's Attacks"; Wolf, "Read This."

7. Stevens, "Will Smith Hits."

8. Carson notes, "The two commandments, Jesus says, stand together. The first without the second is intrinsically impossible (cf. 1 John 4:20), and the second cannot stand without the first—even theoretically—because disciplined altruism is not love. Love in the truest sense demands abandonment of self to God, and God alone is the adequate incentive for such abandonment." Carson, "Matthew," 464. Similarly, Leon Morris comments on Matt 22:40, "Anyone who loves God and people wholeheartedly is not going to come short in religious observances, nor in doing what is proper to other people." Morris, *Gospel According to Matthew*, 564.

any other commandment, are summed up in this word: 'You shall love your neighbor as yourself'" (Rom 13:9–10). To the Galatians Paul writes, "For the whole law is fulfilled in one word: 'You shall love your neighbor as yourself'" (Gal 5:14). Similarly, James says to the Jewish believers in the diaspora, "If you really fulfill the royal law according to the Scripture, 'You shall love your neighbor as yourself,' you are doing well" (Jas 2:8). Therefore, the greatest and second greatest commandments offer a rubric for what we are seeking to do in application of the Scriptures, for the application of the Scriptures intend love for God and neighbor. I want to obey Jesus's greatest and second greatest commandments, you do too, and so do those with whom you fellowship and serve.

Heart, Soul, Mind, and Strength

What is involved in each of these elements of loving God, and what does it mean to love one's neighbor as oneself?

In both the Old and New Testaments, "heart" is the seat of the emotions, the place of one's character (like "pride of heart"), the formation of dispositions, motives, intents, and goals.[9] The "soul," refers to your person as the immaterial or spiritual part of one's being.[10] "Mind" refers to a place of reasoning cognitively or intellectually.[11] "Strength" concerns the power one has and how one chooses to use such power.[12] Putting all four together involves the entirety of a person in loving God.[13]

---

9. John Nolland writes, "In the Gospel pericope, 'Your heart' denotes a response to God from the innermost personal center of one's being.'" Nolland, *Gospel of Matthew*, 911. I also recognize the overlapping of "heart" with similar terms, as Carson notes, "From the viewpoint of biblical anthropology, 'heart,' 'soul,' and 'mind' (Matt 22:37) are not mutually exclusive but overlapping categories, together demanding our love for God to come from our whole person, our every faculty and capacity." Carson, "Matthew," 464.

10. "The ψυχή is thus the 'seat and center of life that transcends the earthly.'" BDAG, s.v. "ψυχή." Cited in EDNT, s.v. "ψυχή, ῆς, ἡ." However, I recognize that there are difficulties in defining "soul" in this way vis-à-vis "spirit." Per Edward Schweitzer, "Although ψυχή can never be sundered from the purely physical life, it is not identical with it. . . . The difficulty with πνεῦμα is not to let God's Spirit working in man become an inner spiritual life that is given to man. . . . With ψυχή, however, the difficulty is the opposite one of not restricting the God-given life to the purely physical sphere which is threatened by death, but also embracing therein the gift of God which transcends death." TDNT, s.v. "Ψυχή, Ψυχικός, Ἀνάψυξις, Ἀναψύχω, Δίψυχος, Ὀλιγόψυχος."

11. The noun διάνοια means "the psychological faculty of understanding, reasoning, thinking, and deciding—'mind.'" LN s.v. "διάνοια."

12. Mark uses ἰσχύς instead of the LXX use of δύναμις in Deut 6:5. It refers to exceptional capability, with the probable implication of personal potential—"capability, strength." LN s.v. "ἰσχύς."

13. "The challenge is to a comprehensive engagement with God with the total capacity

PART THREE: THE PRACTICE OF THE PULPIT

"Neighbor," as discerned from the Parable of the Good Samaritan, includes anyone needing to be served. But this is not an exclusive concept, for the neighbors of Rom 13:9 and Gal 5:14 are believing members of their churches. Moreover, believers are called to love their enemies and to be wise toward those outside of the church (Matt 5:4; Col 4:5). So "neighbor" covers everyone.

To "love"—or rather, to *cherish* God and neighbor (for "cherish" is the concept encompassed by desire and corresponding actions toward both God and others)—involves cherishing God with one's emotions, spiritual being, intellect, body, and will, and to cherish neighbor involves directing our cherishing toward both believer and unbeliever alike.

If this is so, in seeking to make Scripture applicable, our task as news anchors of the greatest unchanging News Story in the history of the world is to tell people specifically how to practice the News emotionally, formatively-spiritually (or with our spiritual discipline to form the soul), bodily, volitionally, intellectually, missionally (to unbelievers), and communally (or in community toward fellow believers). We are to take the guesswork out of the development of the full character of the hearer so that we do not leave sanctification to chance.

We must do more than explain how not to make provision for the flesh to obey its desires (cf. Rom 13:14); we must explain how not to make provision for the flesh so church members will know exactly what to do to stop provision for the flesh. We need to say, "Do not walk into a convenience store; take the apps of your favorite stores off your phone; turn off the TV by nine o'clock; go to bed when your wife goes to bed and do not stay in your den alone; confess your flesh struggle in your small group and allow them to ask you about it daily."

Or, to help our people love God and neighbor with respect to praying without ceasing (cf. 1 Thess 5:17), we need to tell them to begin and end each day with the Lord's Prayer, to keep a prayer journal of requests and answers, to review it after you pray in the morning, at lunchtime as you can, and before going to bed so that you might even be aware of things for which you should be praying, to take three minutes of your lunch hour to pray, to read a different book on prayer annually, and to remember in prayer the name of one unbeliever in the sphere of each person on the ministry team of which you serve. Then you can reply, "Oh, that's how I can pray without ceasing!"

When I was pastor of a church plant, I used to say after sermons, "On Monday share with someone the message you heard today." But one Sunday, I added these words: "When someone asks you about your weekend, say, 'I heard a great message on Sunday about [the topic]. It taught me how to [blank]. I

---

of all of one's faculties." Nolland, *Gospel of Matthew*, 911.

would love to share more about it with you later.'" The membership responded to me by saying, "Pastor, we always wanted to do what you said and share on Mondays. But we didn't know how. Now you have told us how to do it."

Four Potential Objections

Before proceeding to applications, I must dispense with four potential objections.

Moralism

First, telling people exactly what to do could lead to moralism or legalism—the simple practices of moral behavior for behavior's sake or for the sake of earning God's favor. While this is true, that does not mean we should not tell them to cherish God and neighbor. That cherishing must start with the one who died for us and rose from the dead. Telling others what to do is not an attempt to do good apart from reliance on Christ's death and resurrection.

Predictability

Second, if we do this weekly, it could lead to predictability in sermons and lessons, leading hearers to tune us out. This, too, is true, so we must be creative. Avoid listing "do's and don'ts" every week. Cloak applications in an illustration, analogy, or personal testimony. Instead of saying, "Step 1: read Pss 93–100 daily," say, "I have been reading Pss 93–100 daily to increase my personal worship of Christ," or "I remember reading that John Leroy Doe had the habit of reading Pss 93–100 daily."

Usurping the Spirit

A third objection could be that we are taking on the role of the Holy Spirit. But it is the Spirit who gives shepherds, teachers, teaching gifts, and biblical community. This objection assumes a privatized, individualistic sanctification. But that misses the very nature of the Christian life as communal. It is to suggest that one always gains wisdom from the Spirit apart from the wisdom imparted to other saints. It is also a nice way of saying we do not want pastors and teachers telling us how to live our Christian lives and we do not want fellow church members involved in our stuff. But the Spirit can speak both through the mechanic and beyond the mechanics. We are simply giving something with which the Spirit can work.

PART THREE: THE PRACTICE OF THE PULPIT

Minimizing the Ability of the Hearer

Fourth, why not trust others to be intelligent enough to figure out applications. To this objection I start by saying, "Oh?" Does the believing teenager figure out on her own that bad mouthing her mom to her friends at school is not honoring her mom? Does the Christian husband figure out that not giving his wife access to his texts and emails when she is insecure about the women working with him on a project is not loving his wife as Christ loved the church? Did Christians in the majority culture figure out on their own that a paralyzed response to the George Floyd incident might compound the repetitive stings of racism for African Americans when a simple phone call to ask how they were doing would have communicated love? Do churches headed toward deep infighting know to call in denominational or other parachurch mediators before their implosions? Do congregations understand that if you do not put a multi-week evangelism training series in the new membership process that only about 10 percent of their members will even try to share their faith with others and evangelizing the neighborhoods around their churches won't happen? Unless we tell our people *how* to put their faith into practice, they will not figure it out on their own. Telling people *that* we should honor, love, call, listen, use mediation, and prioritize evangelism is different from telling them *how* to do these things. Sin will eat figuring it out on our own for breakfast.

APPLICATION

Our goals as believers include making a safe society safer, making a lost society hear and see Jesus the risen Savior, and to mature a church called to proclaim the excellencies of him who called us out of darkness. Knowing this, here are some ways to apply the contents of this chapter, following a paradigm that loves the Lord emotionally, formatively-spiritually, bodily, volitionally, intellectually, missionally, and in community.

Love God with heart/emotions/dispositions. What emotional and dispositional (like humility and patience) response in you most dishonors the Lord or fails at dependency on him. Patience? Anxiety? Laziness? Critical spirit? Envy? Rudeness? Within the next twenty-four hours, find two trusted believers—not including your spouse—and share with them your struggle and desire to please the Lord in this area, asking them to pray for you faithfully the next sixty days and to be intentional about asking you weekly about your progress.

1. *Soul/spiritual formation.* With that emotional/dispositional concern with which you want to love the Lord more, find one Scripture to memorize related to that concern and read it every day for the next sixty days.

Each evening (or morning if you work at night), write in a journal what reading the Scripture that day has done to help you submit your emotion or disposition to the Lord. Write down anything else you see the Lord doing with that emotion over the sixty days.

2. *Strength/Body.* Before you go to bed in the evening, reduce your TV or social media intake by thirty minutes each of the next thirty days. Turn off the phone, laptop, tablet, and TV, and use that additional thirty minutes to go to sleep early. As you retire, ask the Lord to use the additional sleep to give you physical strength and self-control over your poor emotional responses. You may have to reduce your caffeine intake to accomplish this application.

3. *Strength/Volition.* Set a time once per week to take five to ten minutes to review all the application points above and notes from this article. Share the main idea and application points with one mature believing friend this week.

4. *Mind/Intelligence.* Read *The Spirit of the Disciplines*,[14] *Renovation of the Heart*,[15] *Spiritual Disciplines for the Christian Life*,[16] *Habits of Grace*,[17] or *An Infinite Journey*[18] over the next sixty days, reading as far as you can in each. Read a little each day, even if only one page a day.

5. *Neighbor-Believer/Member.* In your smallest community (small group/Bible study/Sunday School/leadership team in your ministry), invite your fellow members to do the same with one of their own emotions/dispositions. Invite the group to pray for all the other members of the group by name through the sixty day period. Invite them to journal and bring their journals to share testimonies of what the Lord is doing in their lives. Hold each other accountable to go to bed early. Read the same book on spiritual disciplines together. On Sundays in which the Lord's Supper is served during those sixty days, sit together in the same service and plan to share a meal together afterward.

6. *Neighbor-Unbeliever.* Over the sixty days, daily ask the Lord for opportunities to share with an unbeliever—kindly and graciously—the work Jesus is doing through you with respect to your emotion/discipline. Be specific to say that the power of the death of Jesus and his resurrection

---

14. Willard, *Spirit of the Disciplines*.
15. Willard, *Renovation of the Heart*.
16. Whitney, *Spiritual Disciplines*.
17. Mathis, *Habits of Grace*.
18. Davis, *Infinite Journey*.

from the dead is changing you. Be bold and courageous and leave the outcomes to Jesus. Pray daily for the persons with whom you get to share your story.

Hopefully your sixty days will lead to you loving the Lord our God with heart, soul, mind, and strength, and loving your neighbors as yourself with new habits and renewed spirits. Moreover, the specific statements of application should change several friends and members with you. May Jesus be glorified by more than our minds.

BIBLIOGRAPHY

Bailey, Sarah Pulliam. "Mark Driscoll Charged with Abusive Behavior by 21 Former Mars Hill Pastors." *Religion News Service*, August 22, 2014. https://religionnews.com/2014/08/22/mark-driscoll-charged-allegations-21-former-mars-hill-pastors/.

Baker, David L. "Ten Commandments, Two Tablets: The Shape of the Decalogue." *Themelios* 30 (2005) 6–22.

Balz, Horst Robert Gerhard Schneider. *Exegetical Dictionary of the New Testament* (*EDNT*). Grand Rapids: Eerdmans, 1990–993.

Bauer, Walter, et al. (BDAG). Greek-English Lexicon of the New Testament and Other Early Christian Literature. 3rd ed. Chicago: University of Chicago Press, 2000.

Carson, D. A. "Matthew." In *The Expositor's Bible Commentary: Matthew, Mark, Luke*, edited by Frank E. Gaebelein, 3–599. Grand Rapids: Zondervan, 1984.

Cosper, Mike, host. "Who Killed Mars Hill?" *The Rise and Fall of Mars Hill*. Podcast audio. June 21, 2021. https://www.christianitytoday.com/ct/podcasts/rise-and-fall-of-mars-hill/who-killed-mars-hill-church-mark-driscoll-rise-fall.html.

Davis, Andrew M. *An Infinite Journey: Growing Toward Christlikeness*. Greenville, SC: Emerald House, 2014.

Hurtado, Patricia, et al. "Donald Trump Is Already Attacking the Judge Handling His Hush Money Case and Spelling His Name Incorrectly." *Fortune*, March 31, 2023. https://fortune.com/2023/03/31/donald-trump-judge-new-york-trial/.

Kittel, George, et al. *Theological Dictionary of the New Testament* (*TDNT*). 10 vols. Grand Rapids: Eerdmans, 1964.

Louw, Johannes P., and Eugene Albert Nida (LN). *Greek-English Lexicon of the New Testament: Based on Semantic Domains*. New York: United Bible Societies, 1996.

Mathis, David. *Habits of Grace: Enjoying Jesus Through the Spiritual Disciplines*. Wheaton, IL: Crossway, 2016.

Morris, Leon. *The Gospel According to Matthew*. Downers Grove, IL: InterVarsity, 1992.

NBC News 5 Chicago. "How to Protect Yourself from the Coronavirus." February 26, 2020. https://www.nbcchicago.com/news/health/how-to-protect-yourself-from-coronavirus/2226754/.

Nolland, John. *The Gospel of Matthew: A Commentary on the Greek Text*. Grand Rapids: Eerdmans, 2005.

Paulson, Michael. "A Brash Style That Filled Pews, Until Followers Had Their Fill." *New York Times*, August 22, 2014. https://www.nytimes.com/2014/08/23/us/mark-driscoll-is-being-urged-to-leave-mars-hill-church.html.

Shellnutt, Kate. "Former Mars Hill Elders: Mark Driscoll Is Still 'Unrepentant,' Unfit to Pastor." *Christianity Today*, July 26, 2021. https://www.christianitytoday.com/news/2021/july/mars-hill-elders-letter-mark-driscoll-pastor-resign-trinity.html.

Shellnutt, Kate, and Morgan Lee. "Mark Driscoll Resigns from Mars Hill." *Christianity Today*, October 15, 2014. https://www.christianitytoday.com/ct/2014/october-web-only/mark-driscoll-resigns-from-mars-hill.html.

Stevens, Matt. "Will Smith Hits Chris Rock After Joke About His Wife, Jada." *New York Times*, March 27, 2022. https://www.nytimes.com/2022/03/27/movies/will-smith-chris-rock-oscars.html.

Welch, Craig. "The Rise and Fall of Mars Hill Church." *Seattle Times*, February 4, 2016. https://www.seattletimes.com/seattle-news/the-rise-and-fall-of-mars-hill-church/.

Whitney, Donald S. *Spiritual Disciplines for the Christian Life*. Colorado Springs: Navpress, 1991.

Willard, Dallas. *Renovation of the Heart: Putting on the Character of Christ*. Colorado Springs: Navpress, 2002.

———. *The Spirit of the Disciplines: Understanding How God Changes Lives*. New York: HarperOne, 1999.

Wolf, Z. Byron. "Read This: How Trump Defended Criticism of Judge for Being 'Mexican.'" CNN, April 20, 2017. https://www.cnn.com/2017/04/20/politics/donald-trump-gonzalo-curiel-jake-tapper-transcript/index.html.

———. "Trump's Attacks on Judge Curiel Are Still Jarring to Read." CNN, February 27, 2018. https://www.cnn.com/2018/02/27/politics/judge-curiel-trump-border-wall/index.html.

Subject Index

Accra Confession, 187–89, 191, 199
Ambrose of Milan, 193–96
anthropology, 83, 137–38, 147, 150–57, 162, 169, 209
Apostles Creed, 189, 194
Athanasius, 153
atonement, 48, 168–69, 173–75
Augustine of Hippo, 13, 94–95, 97, 119, 184

Baltahasar, Hans Urs von, 54
Basil the Great, 146–47, 149
Barth, Karl, 98, 100, 102–3, 161
Bible church(es), 46, 50
Bonhoeffer, Dietrich, 81, 119, 153
Bullinger, Heinrich, 94, 98–99, 101, 103–5

Calvin, John, 55–56, 99–100, 102, 105–7
Chrysostom, John, 117, 120, 122–23, 125, 193
Clement of Alexandria, 153
Confession of Belhar with Accompanying Letter, 188

disenchantment, age of, 164

divinization, 153–54
Donne, John, 130

Edwards, Jonathan, 153
eikon, 150, 153–54, 157
Eucharist, 132, 193, 195–97, 201–2
evangelicalism, ix, 112, 145
evangelism, 18, 145, 212

Ferguson, Sinclair, 56
Forsyth, P. T., 167–76

Gregory of Nazianzus, 120, 125–26, 146–59
Gregory of Nyssa, 146, 149
Gregory the Great, 119–20, 126

hamartiology, 81, 189
Heidelberg Catechism, 189
Herbert, George, 41, 44, 129–42

imago Dei, 146, 151, 155

kapwa theology, 192
Keller, Timothy, 4, 6

SUBJECT INDEX

Lewis, C. S., 153
liberal theology, 168–69
liturgical, 102, 138, 194, 196
liturgy, 193–94, 196–97
Lloyd-Jones, Martin, 19
Luther, Martin, 64–65, 99
Lyman Beecher Lectures, 171

mystagogical preaching, 193–96, 198, 201–2

Newbigin, Lesslie, 66–67
Nicene Creed, 146, 189
Noce, Augusto del, 113, 118

Oden, Thomas, 52
ordo salutis, 54

Payne, Daniel A., 60
penal substitution, 174
philanthropia, 145–46, 149, 156–58
philodoxia, 149
philotimia, 149
pneumatology, 146

reconciliation, 55, 65, 169, 173, 198, 202

Second Ecumenical Council, 146
Sibbes, Richard, 67
social hierarchy, 148
social justice, 145, 163
Solzhenitsyn, Alexander, 162
Spurgeon, Charles, 31, 43, 48, 65, 94
Still, Willam, 62

Taylor, Charles, 164–65
theological anthropology, 147, 150–57
Theological Declaration of Barmen, 188
theosis, 153–54
Thirty-Nine Articles, 131, 138
Thomas à Kempis, 61
threefold office, 53, 104
Trinity, 53, 83, 146, 152, 154, 179, 196

union with Christ, 52–68

Westminster Confession of Faith, 189
Webster, John, 106
Whitefield, George, 62, 94
World Alliance of Reformed Churches, 187

Scripture Index

Genesis
1	7
1:1	83
1:3	8
1:26–28	83
1:27	50
3	84
3:1	8
3:15	8
16	118

Exodus
12	73
12:1–28	48
19:19	32
20:18	32
29	73
35:1	8

Leviticus
4	73

Numbers
28	73

Judges
Book of	25

Ruth
Book of	7

1 Samuel
3:11–14	58
8	117

1 Kings
18:38–40	58
19:3–4	58

2 Chronicles
Book of	7

SCRIPTURE INDEX

Nehemiah
8:8	8

Job
3	43
26:14	32
37:2	32
40:6	32
40:9	32

Psalms
139:13–14	182
145:4	9

Proverbs
4:23	130

Ecclesiastes
2:1–11	43

Isaiah
6:8–10	58
6:9–10	59
44:6–8	8
49:3–4	59
49:4	66
52:7	98
53	37, 48
53:4	153
53:10–12	66
55:11	7
58:6	46
61:1–2	46

Jeremiah
1:17–19	58
14:14	58
14:17–18	58
15:1	58
20:1–20	58
20:14–18	58
23	116
38:6	58

Ezekiel
34	116

Lamentations
1–5	58

Joel
2	36

Jonah
Book of	7

Matthew
3:11	36
4	85
4:2	86
4:3	85
4:4	86, 104
4:6	85
4:7	86
4:10	86
5–7	124
5:10–12	124
5:11–12	45
5:17	45
5:21–22	45
7:21–27	45
7:28–29	35, 45
8:20	86
9:8	35
9:35	8
10:5–7	8
10:16	34, 39
10:19–20	39
10:20	39
10:40	34
12:18	35
12:28	35
13:3–8	93
13:13–15	59
13:18–23	93
13:54	33
14:2	33
14:23	41

SCRIPTURE INDEX

15:24	34	4:36	33, 34
17:5	100	4:43	34
21:37	34	5:16	41
22:29	47	5:17	33, 34, 35
24:9	45	5:24	34
26:2	47	6:12–13	41
26:64	33	6:19	33, 34
27:46	48	8:46	34
27:50	48	9:48	34
27:51–53	49	9:53–54	32
28:5	48	10:1–2	42
28:18–20	15, 34	10:16	34
28:19	21	11:47–51	59
28:20	91	11:49	58
		21:15	39
		21:36	42

Mark

		22:15	48
1:8	36	22:19	48
1:14–15	41	22:40	42
1:14	104	22:41	41
1:27	35	22:46	42
1:35–39	41	22:69	33
3:17	32	23:34	124
5:30	33	23:46	66
6:34	13	24:26–27	46, 59
6:46	41	24:32	35
9:1–2	34	24:44–49	35–36
9:1	33	24:46–47	46
9:37	34	24:47	98
10:45	47		
11:24	42		
11:25	42		

John

12:6	34	Book of	7
13:11	39	1:1–3	150
16:6	48	1:29	47, 176
		1:33	36
		1:36	47

Luke

		3:5	39, 65
1:35	36	3:6	39
3:16	36	3:8	179
3:21–22	35	3:14–15	47
4:1	35	3:30	82
4:14–15	46	5:37	33
4:14	34, 35, 36	5:39	7
4:16	46	6:63	39
4:18–21	8	7:16	34, 100
4:18	34	7:39	39
4:21	46	8:29	34
4:32	34		

John (cont.)

10:11	47
10:14	116
10:15	47
10:17–18	47
10:36	34
11:1	40
11:9–13	40
12:27	47
14:26	38
15:5	40, 90
15:26–27	39
16:13–14	39
16:23–24	42
17:1	47
18:1	42
20:21–22	35
21:17	104, 116

Acts

Book of	12, 79
1:4–8	36
1:8	34, 35
2	37
2:1–4	63
2:4	36
2:14–36	47
2:18	36
2:23	48, 96
2:33	36
2:35	48
2:42	42
2:43	34
3:6	34
3:13–15	48
3:17–26	47
3:18	48
4:7–8	37
4:7	34
4:8–12	47
4:12	37, 55
4:29	41
4:31	37, 42
4:33	37
5:12	34
5:29–32	47
5:30–31	48
6:2	8
6:3	35, 37
6:4	37
6:5	37
6:6	42
6:7	8, 37, 108
6:10	37
7	59
7:2–53	47
7:52–53	59
7:52	48
7:55	37
8:5	37
8:26–40	37
8:32–35	48
9	57
9:16	59
10:34–43	47
10:38	34, 35
10:39–40	48
10:44–45	40
10:47	48
11	40
11:1	40
11:15–18	40
11:18	40
12:5	42
12:12	42
12:24	108
13:3	35, 42
13:4	34, 38
13:5	38
13:7	38
13:8	38
13:9	38
13:10	38
13:11	38
13:12	38
13:16–41	47
13:27–31	48
13:49	9
15	21
15:3	35
15:22	35
16:6–10	38
16:7	34, 38
16:9	38
16:10	38

SCRIPTURE INDEX

16:12	38
16:14	38
17:2–3	46
17:6	107
17:28	196
19:20	108
19:21	38
20:7–12	79–80
20:22	38
20:23	38
20:24	38
23:11	38
26:3	48

Romans

1:1–7	6
1:4	63
1:16	9, 30, 50
5	56
6	56
8:11	63
8:17	57
10:13–17	160
10:14	8, 171
10:15	98, 99
10:17	161
15:13	41
15:19	36, 41
16:25	96

1 Corinthians

1:10–11	26
1:12	26
1:13	26, 55
1:14–16	26
1:17	26, 87
1:18	9, 30
1:23–24	48
1:23	87
1:24	50
1:27	87
2:1–5	25, 27, 28, 33
2:1	48
2:3–5	66, 184
2:3	28, 30
2:4–5	xii
2:5	28
4:11	59
4:13	59
4:16	107
5:7	48
9:16	87
9:26	93
11:24–25	48
11:26	48
12	154
12:3	65
14:9	93
15:1–7	46
15:3	48, 96
15:31	57

2 Corinthians

Book of	7
1:3–4	89
1:5	60
1:8–9	66
1:23—2:1	121
2:4	121
3	11
3:18	154
4:6	119
4:7	66, 140
4:10	57
4:11	61
4:15	61
5:17	55
6:4–10	59
7:8–12	121
8:9	153
10:3–4	123
11:7	118
11:20	118
11:23–27	59
11:30	87
12:9	66, 87–88

Galatians

2	21, 65
2:20	62
3:13	55

SCRIPTURE INDEX

Ephesians

1	105
1:3	55
1:18	107
3:7	36, 40
3:14	42
3:16	36, 40, 42
3:20–21	91
3:20	40
4:11	104
4:12	104

Philippians

1:29	62
2	56
2:6–8	118
3	56, 57
3:8	57
3:9	55
3:10–11	55
3:10	60, 63
3:20—4:1	67

Colossians

1:15	150
1:17	75
1:24	60
2	56
2:8	96
3	56
3:12–14	123
3:16	9

1 Thessalonians

1:4–5	29
1:5	28, 36
2:4	97
2:13	6, 29
2:19–20	67
5:14	11

1 Timothy

1:11	97
3	12
3:1–6	14
3:6	81
4:16	123
6:20	97

2 Timothy

1:14	97
2:8–9	57
2:15	6
2:24–26	123–24
3:12	60
3:15	7
3:16	7
4	5, 11, 22
4:1–5	4–5
4:1–2	5, 90
4:2	5, 7, 11, 15, 98
4:3–4	16
4:3	96
4:8	67

Titus

1:3	97

Hebrews

1:1	98
1:3	150
3–4	12
3:13	9
3:15	101
10:25	9
12	12
13:7	117

James

Book of	30
2:26	31
3:14	123
5:16	42

1 Peter

1:11	59
1:12	36
1:19	48
2:9	107
4:13	57
5:1–4	116–17
5:4	67

1 John

2:2	48

Revelation

Book of	7
4:11	84
5	71
5:2	71
5:5	72
5:6	48, 73–74
5:9	20
5:12	48, 75
5:13	75
7:14	48
12	190
12:11	48
13:8	48
19:9	48

www.ingramcontent.com/pod-product-compliance
Lightning Source LLC
Chambersburg PA
CBHW020407230426
43664CB00009B/1225